How To Pick a Lover

How To Pick a Lover

For Women Who Want to Win at Love

WESLEY L. FORD

To order additional copies of this book, contact:
Xlibris Corporation
1-888-795-4274
www.Xlibris.com
Orders@Xlibris.com
49212

CONTENTS

Chapter 7
MÉSALLIANCES: SELECTING EXOTIC LOVERS....................185

Chapter 8
THE WANTON FACTOR: ON LUST AND WOMANHOOD 217

Chapter 9
"PLEASE, SIR, I WANT MORE!" 247

This book is dedicated to my lifelong friend, mentor and colleague, Jean E. Veevers. Without her, this book would not have been possible.

INTRODUCTION

The first great step is to like yourself enough to pick someone who likes you, too.
— Jane O'Reilly, "View from the Bed," *Ms.*

This is not exactly a how-to book. There are none of the usual strategies about where to find a lover, what to say when you do find him, and where and when to say it. You've already read all those books: the one with the surefire "rules" you can follow to land a big diamond ring, the one about how someone is "just not that into you," the one about how *you're* from one planet and *he's* from another and other such themes.

What this book *will* do is demystify the process of how to pick a lover by exploring the psychosocial nature of love relationships. As my editor, Sylvia Moscovitz, said to me during the course of putting this book together, "Where the hell was this book when I needed it?" It will outline certain personality and character traits of different types of men and challenge many of your attitudes and beliefs about courting and being courted. It's a kind of toolkit, which offers the profiles, potentials, and pitfalls of different types of lovers and different types of relationships *with* those lovers.

The issues here are not about how to meet men, they are not about how to make love, and they are not about how to choose a husband, but rather how to pick a lover. How you go about choosing a lover is a complex and important process that needs to be understood if your choices are to result in enjoyable and rewarding experiences. While there are no guarantees, there are some helpful guidelines that can minimize your likelihood of making bad mistakes and maximize your likelihood of making choices that are right for you. What is needed is a different pattern of courtship. And with that in mind, this book focuses on a relatively new issue: how to pick the most perfect man available for the most perfect love affair possible.

In short, this book has been written to help you navigate the minefields you are likely to encounter when picking a lover and to make it easier for you to more readily recognize those male attributes and behaviors—negative and positive—that should be paid attention to when choosing a lover. And if you are already in a relationship with a lover, it may do one of two things: make you look more closely at your relationship or appreciate it for what it is. So happy reading! And then . . . happy hunting!

CHAPTER 1

A LOVER IS A LOVING, LOVABLE MAN

*The great differences between people in this
world is not between the rich and poor
or between the good and the evil. The big
difference between people are the ones who
have pleasure in love and those who haven't.*
—Richard Brooks, *Sweet Bird of Youth*

When a woman thinks about a lover, it is very likely that her first response is to smile. Before reading further, take a moment to think about what the word "lover" means to you. What's *your* first response?

Did your face light up with anticipation or reflect a quiet happiness? Did you feel tender or wistful? Did you gaze into the middle distance or focus on your rings? Whatever your reaction, it's a given that you certainly thought about something . . . and someone.

Your second response is most likely an audible sigh. It may be a little sigh of repressed excitement or, perhaps, a deep sigh of sadness. However you feel, it's another given that when you think about a lover, you think with emotion. The lover of your fantasies and the lover in real life, the man of today and the man of the past, the man you married and the man you did not are all conjured up until, often, they are fused into one composite man who becomes your general image of a lover.

In your mind's eye, you see the men you have loved, some from a hopeless distance and some from personal experience. You see the men who have loved you but who were bashful, shuffling their feet and looking at their hands. You see the men who loved you and who were daring and bold, holding you tight in elevators while whispering shocking things in your ear or pressing their thighs tightly against yours while moving across the dance floor.

The more you think about what the word "lover" means to you, the more these images blend until you are left with one image in sharp focus. And you sigh.

It is likely that for you, as for most women, the actual act of picking a lover is more complex and thought provoking than is the act of thinking about it in the abstract, as there is always the very real possibility that you will make a bad choice with very real consequences. Throughout the pages of this book, we will explore how to minimize your likelihood of making bad choices and increase your likelihood of choosing only lovers who will bring you joy. In so doing, we will be focusing on two themes. First, how do you go about deciding what you want in a lover? And second, once you have decided, how do you go about having the most meaningful and enjoyable love affair possible?

Remembrance of Loves Past

What lips my lips have kissed, and where, and why
I have forgotten, and what arms have lain under
My head till morning.

—Edna St. Vincent Millay

Usually, as a man, a sociologist, and a writer, I try to live in the present or, if necessary, in the future. But late one night, I found myself steeped in nostalgia. It was after a dinner party. All the dinner guests had left with the exception of a lifelong woman friend of mine, and we sat, talking as old friends do. Cozy in the glow of the dying embers of the fire and light-headed from having finished the last of the champagne, we drifted into reminiscences of past loves.

Counting on her fingers and toes, my friend realized that over the years, she had had many lovers, many with whom she had carnal knowledge of the very best kind. How many? It doesn't matter. Many. More than she could count on her fingers and toes. More than we could count on both our fingers and toes. Needless to say, the number was a long way from a "one and only," but not all that many, given her thirty-five years of experience. As you may gather, she started young—sixteen to be exact—when sixteen was very young. In those days, the belief was that a "sweet sixteen" had never been kissed, much less initiated.

Looking back on her experiences, my friend believed that she had been very lucky. Men worth being loved by had loved her, and she had shared with them more magic moments than many people ever get to experience. She was lucky enough to have had two wonderful affairs that led to marriage and four other wonderful affairs that did not. For many years, she was happily monogamous. Yet, for one reason or another, the promised happily ever after did not pan out for her. She had had some loving friendships that she cherished and some brief encounters. There were even some one-night stands, which were almost always a mistake.

In the now classic musical *My Fair Lady*, Professor Higgins discusses the nature of men and immodestly concludes, "By and large, we *are* a marvelous sex!" He is right: by and large, men are marvelous . . . at least in my friend's experience. They have been good to her, most of the time; and the elusive butterfly of love has, for the most part, lived up to its elusive promises of love. And yet, there were times when . . .

Erotic Errors

---

*Good judgment comes from experience, and
experience—well, that comes from poor judgment.*
—Anonymous

As a seasoned woman, my friend had seen much of life and her mind was full of memories while her eyes saw clearly with hindsight. Of her lovers, she remembered six who were wonderful and made her heart sing and seven others who were charming and considerate and who remained intimate friends for many years. So what about the rest of her lovers whose number shall remain discreetly vague? The rest were mistakes. They were the error part in trial and error. They involved consent followed by regret. She did say yes but then realized she should have said maybe or even a resounding "no! never!"

Like many women before her, she had often met with disillusionment, realizing too late that what she had anticipated would be a good encounter and a worthwhile experience had turned out to be distressing or embarrassing or degrading or just plain boring. She would come home thinking about what happens "when lovely women stoop to folly" and would then resolve, "never again."

Ah, too soon old and too late smart. Had she known then what she knows now, she would never have become involved with many of those lovers. She would have noticed that they were wearing large labels saying Mistake, and she would have taken a cab home. Or better yet, she would never have gone out with them in the first place. A lot of grief—or, at the very least, wasted time—could have been avoided by saying, "I'm sorry, Harry, I can't go to the movies with you next Tuesday night, I have to wash my hair. In fact, I will be washing my hair every night from here on till eternity."

If she had known then what she knows now, she would have said, "No, John, I can't go to the premiere with you, I have to watch this week's episode of *Desperate Housewives*. Maybe some other year."

If she had known then what she knows now, she would have had only encounters ranging from nice to wonderful and would have skipped all the ones that had left an unpleasant aftertaste. So with the benefit of hindsight and maturity, she now consoles herself with Oscar Wilde's observation: "Experience is the name so many people give to their mistakes."

The Need for Love

To live without loving is not really living.

—Molière

If so many of the delicious, delectable enticements of taking a lover and having an affair turn out to be tasteless or leave a bitter aftertaste, why do so many women continue to embark on so many adventures year after year? Probably for the same reason people buy lottery tickets. Because when the affair does live up to your hopes and expectations, or when you win the lottery, it is, in fact, well worth the gamble. It is every bit as wonderful as you imagined it would be.

To love and be loved in return may not solve all life's problems, but it does make them easier to bear. Loving and being loved puts a bloom on your cheek and a spring in your step and hope in your heart. It makes ordinary, everyday events seem like fun, and it transforms extraordinary ones into truly joyous experiences. You feel more confident, more energetic, and more optimistic. You take more delight in the pleasures of the world and are more tolerant of its trials and hardships.

Love is not a panacea. It does not cure cancer or stop inflation or prevent war. It does not stop you from growing older. It is, however, the world's best palliative; and by lessening the pain of living, it increases enjoyment of life. No wonder poets have, for centuries, been waxing eloquence on these themes. No wonder so much of your time and attention and energy is taken up, one way or another, in the quest for the kind of lover who can open up this cornucopia of feeling and delight.

THE IMPORTANCE OF LOVE

Man's love is of man's life a thing apart,
'Tis woman's whole existence.
—George Noel Gordon, Lord Byron, *Don Juan*

Byron's aphorism is widely quoted, usually by men who find themselves unable or unwilling to express the emotional intensity expected by their girlfriends or wives. It is important to remember, however, that Byron was writing in the nineteenth century, not the twenty-first, and that the men and women of his time were different in many ways from the men and women of today.

There are some people who do place love and love relationships so centrally in their lives that romance constitutes practically their whole existence. To them, this aspect of life is *the* most important thing. Some of the people who do this are women, but some men also feel this way. Philosophers are never quite sure what to do with such individuals. People for whom love is the raison d'etre of their lives may be either very wise or very foolish, but they are very different from ordinary people. Their emotional lives have more depth, which increases their potential for both greater pleasure and greater pain.

For most men and most women, love relationships are important, but they are not necessarily *the* most important thing in life. These people value love and eroticism, but they are also concerned with more pragmatic issues: developing a career, being creative, carving a place for themselves in public life, earning a living, or having and caring for children.

Let's suppose that you do not think that a love affair is the be-all and end-all of existence. You may still feel that you want to have a good love affair . . . that you would enjoy it, that you are entitled to it, that you will be sad if you never get to experience it.

And you will wonder: *What is it that I would want in a lover? How will I know him?*

What Does "Lover" Mean?

"When I use a word," Humpty Dumpty said,
in a rather scornful tone, "it means just
what I choose it to mean—neither more nor less."
—Lewis Carroll, *Alice's Adventures in Wonderland*

Relationships with men involve a complex assortment of possibilities. As a little girl, you start out with boys as playmates and friends; and if you are lucky, you continue to have men as playmates and friends all your life. Toward adolescence, you acquire boyfriends who are something other than friends who happen to be boys. Your grandmother called them beaux.

From among these boyfriends, you eventually come to have a steady boyfriend (as opposed to the unsteady kind). A steady may turn into someone who wants to marry you, and if you agree, you get a fiancé and then a husband.

Think of your own romantic attachments with men. Where in this progression is there room for a lover or for lovers? What has the word "lover" come to mean to you?

Love means many things to many people—being a lover does as well. For our purposes, the concept of a lover can be summarized succinctly. *A lover is a person of the opposite sex with whom one has an intense relationship, based on romantic affection or sexuality or both, which has no purpose other than the expression of that romantic affection and/or sexuality.* A lover is like a friend, except that friendship is usually less intense and is usually asexual. A lover is like a husband, except that the husband-wife relationship has many purposes other than the fostering and expression of love and lovemaking.

Friends and Lovers

The feeling of friendship is like that of being
comfortably filled with roast beef; love, like
being enlivened with champagne.

—Samuel Johnson

A "lover," as I am using the word, is a friend, but a special kind of friend. The difference between a friend and a lover is the difference in intensity between loving platonically and loving romantically. The lover has the important extra component of physical love as well as the cerebral kind. That addition of sexual intimacy increases the romantic intensity of the relationship and moves it to another level. While the difference may be only a matter of degree, such a difference can be very important indeed: compare the state of being "in the pink" with that of being "in the red."

In *My Fair Lady*, Professor Henry Higgins is beleaguered by the romantic expectations of Eliza Doolittle and finally exclaims in exasperation, "Why can't a woman be more like a man?" The answer, at least in this context, is very simple. A woman cannot be more like a man because the male-female relationship between lovers or would-be lovers is charged with passionate intensity. What Henry Higgins really meant was "why can't a lover be more like a chum?" Now, that is a very different question. When men and women are friends, and that is quite possible under many circumstances, they act quite differently and do not expect as much from each other in emotional terms. A woman *can* be more like a man, but only in relation to men whom she considers to be acquaintances or friends, not in relation to men she loves or whom she wishes would love her.

The tragedy in *My Fair Lady* is that Henry Higgins wanted, or thought he wanted, a friend and he created Eliza Doolittle to his own specifications for his own purposes. Were Eliza to be a chum, she would not need flowers

28

and the centrality of her emotional life would be elsewhere, with the man who loved her and vice versa.

Henry Higgins certainly liked her, but he did not love her. That difference in the degree of affection makes all the difference.

HUSBANDS AND LOVERS

To be a lover is easier than to be a husband, for
it is more difficult to show intelligence every day
than it is to make pretty speeches from time to time.
—Honorè de Balzac

In our culture, we have constantly been told that love and marriage go together "like a horse and carriage" and that one cannot have one without the other. Nonsense.

Love and marriage are, in fact, two quite different phenomena, although sometimes being in love leads to marriage and, conversely, sometimes being married leads to love. Love involves a relationship between two lovers who share an affectionate and/or erotic attraction for each other. Marriage involves a relationship between a husband and a wife. Sometimes, they also love each other, but their interaction always involves much more than that; the decisions about getting married, staying married, or getting unmarried always involve many more factors than mere attraction or lack of it.

Everyone has strong opinions about the familiar, traditional roles of husband and wife. When you ask what a good husband should be like, there is a predictable response and quite a lot of agreement. He should be stable, reliable, kind, a good provider, and a good father. He cuts the grass. He clears the table without being asked. He suffers through your mother's conversation and your brother's silence and is a model of manhood for your sons.

The role of husband ideally complements the role of wife to make an effective partnership. The roles are diverse, and they evolve as the marriage evolves. Husband and wife engage in a whole series of joint enterprises. They raise children together, buy real estate together, paper the bathroom together, and worry about growing old together. A good husband is realistic about life insurance and makes sure the mortgage is paid. When you have to bury your dead, he helps you plan the funeral. When you break your leg, he teaches you to walk on crutches and brings you chicken soup.

Husbands and wives may love each other and may be lovers, but they are much more than lovers. The husband is judged not only by who he is but also by what he does. A husband can fulfill his part of the marital bargain in an exemplary way even if he does not love his wife, as long as he likes and respects her. Similarly, a wife may behave in an exemplary way although she is not in love with her husband. They have undertaken many duties to each other, and they trust each other to perform these duties. Judging by our high divorce rate, which involves about one in two of all couples, these roles do not always work out as planned. Then again, one might as readily note that in one out of two marriages, the commitment *is* a lifelong one, the roles of husband and wife *are* defined and fulfilled, with at least minimum satisfaction, for both the man and woman.

The role of lover is a much simpler and more straightforward one. A lover is valuable to you if you find him lovable. You like to look at him; his company pleases you, his body appeals to you. He is valued for his own unique charisma, and all that is required of him is that he loves you back. The quality of your interaction with him is what draws you to him. There is no reason to be with a lover other than for the pleasure he brings you. When he ceases to bring you pleasure or when you cease to please him, then the interaction stops. The first duty of a lover—perhaps the only duty—is to give you pleasure in love. A lover who is not lovable, or who does not give you emotional and sexual pleasure, is redundant.

LOVERS SHOULD BE EQUALS

Male domination has had some very unfortunate
effects. It made the most intimate of human relations,
that of marriage, one of master and slave, instead of
between equal partners.

—Bertrand Russell

Woodrow Wilson contends that "you cannot be friends on any other terms than upon the terms of equality." Friendship between people who are not equals may be possible, but it is very difficult to sustain. The high-status person is always in a position to do things, which will help the low-status person in important ways. The motivation of the low-status person is always tinged with awareness of this possibility.

There is love between master and slave sometimes, but it is tenuous as is their friendship. There is love between a mentor and his protégée, but it is contingent upon the mentor continuing to be wise and the protégée continuing to be obedient or show gratitude. There is love between a patron of the arts and artists he sponsors, but the artists can never forget that patronage can be withdrawn at any time. The patron often feels he or she has a right to act patronizing, and the beneficiary is not free to protest. These relationships may be worthwhile and rewarding, but they are something other than friendship or love.

The best friendships are between peers who consider themselves to be more or less equal. The love relationship between a man and woman, in its essence, should involve a situation of equals in which neither has control over the other and neither has a motive for being there other than the relationship itself.

The French author and philosopher Albert Camus summarized this idea very well when he said, "Don't walk in front of me, I may not follow. Don't walk behind me, I many not lead. Walk beside me and be my friend."

Love for Its Own Sake

If you choose rich friends, expect to be bought;
If you choose expert friends, expect to be patronized;
If you choose useful friends, expect to be used.
— Jayson VanVerten

There are many platitudes and homilies written about friends and the value of friends and how friendships ought to be. A great deal of the descriptions and advice come down to variations on two essential themes: friends should value friendship for its own sake and should treat each other as equals.

When you choose someone to be a friend of either gender, you look for a number of intrinsic qualities. You look for someone you can like and admire, someone who is fun and supportive, someone who is pleasant to be with, and someone who enriches your sense of self-worth. A friendship is supposed to be an end in itself, not a means to an end. You may learn from your friends, but you do not select them in order to be taught. You might get advice from them, but you do not select them because of their potential as counselors.

We disparage people who seek out only those friends who will come in handy or provide useful contacts. Such people exploit the affectionate feelings aroused by friendship and are, in effect, playing a kind of low-level confidence game. You may have friends who are, in fact, useful to you; but you are not supposed to have selected them for that purpose and are not supposed to drop them when they are no longer useful. The value of the friendship is ideally supposed to be intrinsic rather than extrinsic—valued for itself alone, not for what it can do for you.

A relationship with a lover is like a friendship in that it is also supposed to be an end in itself. You take a lover for no other reason than for the enjoyment of the person's affection and companionship, which, for most people, includes lovemaking. As with friends, some lovers also provide some benefits, but this is not the purpose of your association with them. A lover may buy you exquisite dinners. You may appreciate the opportunity to fly first class instead of coach. You may receive a number of gifts and tokens of affection. But—and it is an all-important but—these benefits are incidental.

The lover is not merely a friendly bill-paying animal as are some escorts. You do not get involved with him in order to get a ticket to the South Seas or to have a contact to facilitate your career or to get the rent paid. There is a big difference between having love and having money and making love in order to have money. The lover relationship, like friendship, is valued for what it is, not for what it does for you.

It is not hard to sort out how you feel on these issues. Ask yourself: if a particular man stopped the material benefits I get from our relationship, would I still want to see him?

In a love relationship, the answer is an unambiguous yes.

ON CHOOSING A LOVER

Freedom simply means the power to carry out your own emotions.
—Clarence Darrow, *Freedom in the Modern World*

Love is important to most women. With increasing sexual freedom, the importance of love has come to mean granting importance to erotic relationships as well as to affectionate ones. Not all women want a lover, but a large number of them do consider taking a lover as an option; and once they have considered it, they eventually go ahead and do it. But how does it all happen? And more importantly, how can it be made to happen with the most happiness for everyone concerned?

As already noted, choosing a lover is an important and complex process; and while there are no guarantees, there are some guidelines that can decrease your risk of making bad choices and increase your likelihood of joy. These guidelines involve a new pattern of courtship in which you must start to take an active as well as a passive role. That is what much of this book is all about.

Perhaps the overall focus of the book will be made clearer by first having a brief discussion about what we are not concerned with. We are not concerned with subject matter related to how to meet men, how to make love, or how to choose a husband. All these themes have been explored elsewhere. What we are concerned with is a relatively new issue: how to find the most perfect man available for the most perfect love affair possible.

Not About How to Meet Men

Before you meet a handsome prince, you have to kiss a lot of toads.

—American folk saying

One topic of perennial interest to most unmarried women and to quite a few married ones is how to meet new men. There have been lots of books on this subject, and they offer essentially the same advice over and over again. Be friendly. Let your friends know that you are interested. Go where the men are.

Many women hit the ski slopes or become sailing aficionados. At any age, going back to school opens a whole new world of possibilities. Some women who can afford it try dating agencies or marriage bureaus while others seek out Internet dating sites such as eHarmony, Salon.com, or JDate.

The Internet has made it relatively simple for women to meet all types of men for all types of occasions. Web sites exist for men and women wanting one-night stands, individuals looking to date or marry, sadists seeking masochists or married people seeking married people, or individuals in search of specific fetishes or physical attributes. It's an endless smorgasbord.

William Novak's book, *The Great American Man Shortage*, written more than twenty-five years ago, contains a lot of such commonsense advice on how to meet men that is still applicable today. Felicia Rose Adler's book, *Master Dating: How to Meet and Attract Quality Men*, offers some helpful strategies for how to meet men of quality.

Meeting men is not very difficult. The woods are full of them. So are the subways and theaters and parks. Men are, after all, nearly half of the population. More and more women meet a wide range of men in the course of their work, or at work-related functions. One woman ran into the man she remembers as her most adorable lover when her Chevrolet mangled his

Mercedes—not the most auspicious beginning. Men are everywhere. They fix your teeth and change the oil in your car and try to sell you shoes. They stand around theater lobbies and volunteer as big brothers for your son and offer you advice on your stock portfolio.

The issue of how to meet men is really not worth the ink used to discuss it. Unless you are housebound or handicapped or very shy, meeting men is not a serious problem. Even if you get fussy and restrict yourself to those over eighteen and under sixty-five, there are still many left. There is a veritable supermarket, an entire entrepôt, a great emporium of possible men. Even women who are older or less attractive than most can have an amazingly large number of men from which to choose. If you are young, and especially if you are young and attractive, you stumble over them everywhere.

Meeting men is easy. Meeting men who are pleasing to you is harder. How you meet prospective lovers does not matter: what does matter is what you do with them after you meet them. For a woman who wants to pick a lover, the best advice is very simple: meet as many men as possible and, from among those men you meet, be as selective and as persnickety as possible.

The wider you cast your net, the more possibilities you have for catching fish. Remember, however, that most of the fish you catch are neither regulation size nor good to eat; and since the fisher's quota is strictly enforced, you are wise to toss most of them back immediately.

NOT ABOUT HOW TO MAKE LOVE

Sexual pleasure, wisely used and not abused, may
prove the stimulus and liberation of our finest and
most exalted activities.

—Havelock Ellis

The sexual revolution in the sixties and seventies was, in part, a revolution of sexologists who emerged as a newly recognized and lionized kind of social scientist. They did not only believe in personal corrective therapy but also produced many useful how-to books, which told and showed you how to have a good sexual relationship. The pictures began to be more informative and graphic, the value judgments few and far between, and the advice explicit and practical. The whole approach was aided and developed by the Sensitivity Training movement and the growth of encounter groups, offering couples real guidelines on how to improve their communication skills, sexual or otherwise.

In 1972, Alex Comfort published the runaway best seller, *The Joy of Sex: A Gourmet Guide to Lovemaking*, followed a couple of years later by *More Joy of Sex*. More than eight million copies of Comfort's *The Joy of Sex* have been sold since it was first published in 1972, and in 2002, he published *The Joy of Sex: Revised and Completely Updated for the 21st Century*. Bookshelves now abound with books of this nature. *The Sex Bible: The Complete Guide to Sexual Love*, published in 2006, and *The Good Girl's Guide to Bad Girl Sex*, published in 2007, represent just a few of the myriad of books of this genre. These manuals have come a long way since classics like van der Velde's *Ideal Marriage*. With a little practice on your part, they provide sound guidelines for how to make love. But for all the expertise they offer, they do not cover all the questions.

Sexual manuals and guidebooks to erotica can teach you a lot about what to do to, with, and for a lover once you are part of a loving couple. However, you still have the problem of finding the right person to do it with. All the techniques and picture books in the world are not going to help you if you are with the wrong person—or at least the wrong person for you. What good does it do you to know about sensitivity exercises and erotic techniques if the man you are with is too insensitive, impatient, or set in his ways to try them?

One way to evaluate lovers is simply to go to bed with them and see what happens, if anything. However, if the encounter is unpleasant, or even if it is simply unsatisfactory and unrewarding, the experience is not enriching for either person and may turn out to be degrading, alienating, or even dangerous.

It would be wonderful to be able to know *before* getting involved with someone, *before* taking him into your bed, that the prospective encounter was going to be a positive one. *How to Pick a Lover* is an attempt to prevent mistakes of this kind, which can be so costly to one's ego and so damaging to one's self-esteem.

Experience is a good teacher, but she sends very hefty bills.

Not About How to Pick

a Husband

"Will you marry me?" is not only a proposition,
it is also a job offer.

—Jayson VanVerten

On the one hand, you want to pick a lover who will seem desirable for more than one night. On the other hand, it is not necessary to pick each lover as if you were picking a husband.

Selecting a husband is a serious business with real and long-lasting consequences. To marry is to select, for the foreseeable future, a particular lifestyle, not to mention a standard of living, place of residence, social status, and perhaps, even religion and citizenship. The decision of who to marry may be a reversible decision; but the divorce process is often difficult, traumatic, and costly.

There are as many books about how to pick a husband as there are books about how to meet men. What do you want in a husband? How do you recognize in advance a man who will be a good husband for you versus the not-so-good kind?

The traditional view of love and marriage involved a double standard for men and women. A man might sow his wild oats before marriage or even after marriage, but he still wanted his wife and the mother of his children to be a "good" girl. A "good" girl was one who was a virgin until she married. Thus, if a woman wanted to make a respectable marriage, it was important that she not take a lover. At the very least, it was important that she not surrender her virginity to anyone other than the man she expected or hoped would marry her.

In contrast, men have always known that there were two kinds of girls: the kind of girl you marry and the other kind. Fathers gave their sons good advice: "Never confuse 'I love you' with 'I want to marry you.'" The fact that a man did not intend to marry every woman he was involved with did not prevent him from having significant or rewarding relationships with his mistresses. Some affairs were strictly sexual relationships, some were romantic liaisons, and some were full-blown love affairs.

Let's, for a moment, consider traditional marriage from the woman's perspective. If she wanted to find someone suitable whom she would eventually marry, then she had to screen even her casual dates with that in mind. She instantly recognized many men as not the kind of men she would want to marry; and she eliminated them so as to concentrate on the bachelors who were, in her books, eligible. She was likely to want the men she dated to have the right religion, the right social class, and the right prospects.

Nowadays, however, it is no longer axiomatic that women remain virgins until they marry or, at least, until they meet their future husband. If you are marriageable, whether or not you are a virgin, then you too can enjoy worthwhile lovers who appeal to you but who are not potential mates. You may decide that you do not want to marry, or you may decide only that you do not want to marry *yet*. You are, in fact, free to pick a lover.

The relationship we will be discussing here, the relationship of a woman and her lover, is not at all like marriage. It is not for the alliance of extended families or for the raising of children or for the buying of houses and social security. The sole purpose of the love affair is to give pleasure. Since it is a less serious decision, with fewer implications, you do not need to be guided by the same restrictions that would apply to the selection of a husband. If what you want is a good love affair, you are free to enjoy many different kinds of men for many different kinds of reasons. In order to select the right one, all you need to find is someone who pleases you now and for the foreseeable future.

Sparkling eyes, a dazzling smile, and the ability to party up a storm may not be an adequate basis for a marriage, but they can be more than an adequate basis for a frivolous weekend of impassioned sex.

ALL ABOUT THE NEW COURTSHIP

*Most marriages are brought about by the following
simple, yet fateful consideration: the man marries
the woman he wants; the woman marries the man
who wants her.*

—Arnold Haultain, *Hints for Lovers*

In the Middle Ages, the pious expressed the fatalism of the time with the aphorism: "Man proposes but God disposes." In less religious times, some irreverent person offered the modification: "Man proposes but woman disposes." This phrase conveys the essence of traditional courtship: a man selected the woman he wanted to marry, and then he proposed to her, perhaps on bended knee. Once he had asked, she had the option to say yea or nay. Since interaction is seldom really that one-sided, punsters went on to have more fun with the phrase. One punster offered: "Man supposes he proposes." Another suggested: "Man proposes and woman imposes."

However it was phrased, traditional courtship was problematic for a woman, for her role in it had to be either completely passive or at best oblique. A man had a much better chance of getting what he wanted in a mistress or wife. He could actively pursue his choice. The woman, in contrast, could only hope that she would be pursued by the right kind of man. In addition, the man was more or less free in most instances to proposition any woman whom he desired or to propose to any woman he wanted to marry. She might not accede to his wishes, but whether she did or did not, he did not usually have to select her for any reason other than his attraction to her.

A woman, on the other hand, was not free to have lovers who were not, at least, potential husbands. And the selection of a husband involved many variables other than attraction. Her choice of a husband would affect almost all aspects of her entire future, and it had to take into account money, property, social position, children, respectability, and so on. First of all, she had to be concerned with what her husband had, and second, with what he did or would do. Only after that could she focus on the kind of man that he was. In this sense, although women are supposed to be more romantic than men, men could be more romantic than women. He could have an affair for love, and he could marry for love: she could not—or at least could not—without great personal cost.

So much for the bad old days. Now think about the other options that are available to you in today's world. If you are not looking for a breadwinner and if you are not securely locked into a chastity belt, you can start to think about taking a lover for no other reason than that he strikes you as lovable! You can choose him for the warmth of his laughter or the gleam in his eye or the desirability of his body—in short, for any of the ephemeral and idiosyncratic kinds of reasons that men have traditionally used to evaluate a woman's beauty and charm. You can be drawn to him for his conversation and wit or his brawny body or both. You are free to experience love for love's sake. Once you realize this, you begin to look at men and at love affairs with a new perspective. Rather than waiting to be chosen, you can do the choosing. Rather than choosing for pragmatic reasons, you can choose for romantic ones.

Back in 1925, Anita Loos suggested that "gentlemen prefer blondes." That attitude sold a lot of peroxide and left women wondering if, perhaps, blondes do have more fun. It wasn't until several decades later that the sexy actress, Mamie Van Doren, pointed out, "It is possible that blondes also prefer gentlemen!"

Isn't it time we started to wonder what *women* prefer?

CHAPTER 2

MASCULINE MAGNETISM

More and more women are coming to use men as "mere sex objects,"
which is a welcome switch for both sexes.

—Brendan Francis

When you look at a man as a sex object or as a love object, you look at him in terms of the kind of person he is. You don't think about what he is or what he has accomplished or how much money he has, but rather about his unique essential self.

Is he lovable? Do you want to reach out and brush his hair back off his forehead? Is he sexy? Do you fantasize about how his arms would feel around your waist? Does he make you feel sexy? Do you start to wonder if somehow it would be possible for all the other people in the room to miraculously vanish so that the two of you could snuggle down by the fire and see what happens next? Does he make you feel loving? Can you suddenly see yourself walking hand in hand on a beach at dawn, looking into each other's eyes? Do you imagine the two of you speaking the sentimental clichés found in Hallmark valentines or posing in the romantic scenes depicted in perfume advertisements?

Does he have sex appeal, that much-desired special something that makes heads turn and hearts throb? Does he give off that certain aura that's so strong that you get weak-kneed and forget all your prior commitments? Would you have fun together sharing a mutual interest such as rock climbing, scuba diving, or exploring a new exhibit at the museum? If women are, or can be, sexual creatures with sexual appetites, what more logical choice for a sex object than a delectable man?

If a woman has enough resources that she does not need a man to support her financially and if she is not immediately concerned with finding a suitable man to marry, she can begin to look around for someone to love and to make love with. She can judge men in much the same way as men have usually judged women.

The idea of men as sex objects rather than as providers and protectors is still a somewhat new idea. It places men in an unfamiliar role, and many of them still don't play it well.

ON PHYSICAL APPEAL

Wine comes in at the mouth
And love comes in at the eye;
That's all we shall know for truth
Before we grow old and die.
　　　　—William Butler Yeats, "A Drinking Song"

If you pick up any anthology of sayings or jokes and look up the topic of sex appeal, you will find lots of references to physical traits: perky breasts, long shapely legs, full lips, and round buttocks. There are laudatory comments about long blond hair, or long hair of any color, and effusive praise for peaches-and-cream complexions and big blue eyes with long black eyelashes.

What you will *not* find, interestingly, are many direct references to what makes a man physically attractive. What gives a man sex appeal?

If women have had opinions about a man's sex appeal, they seem to have made it secondary to their opinions about his material standing. More often than not, a man's appeal seems to be based on his pocketbook. Traditionally, as many women have recognized, and rightly so, her fortune is often dependent on his. If his bank balance is large enough, he is attractive; if he is poor, he is not. As the saying goes, "There ain't no such thing as an ugly millionaire."

Maybe not. But what happens when women begin to focus on the attributes that constitute masculine appeal rather than on an assessment of wealth or achievements? The idea that women should do so at all is somewhat revolutionary for many people. The standards for what is or is not sexy or appealing in a man vary widely from one woman to the next, just as they do when men are judging women. There's an inexplicable alchemy that is enhanced by a combination of basic physical equipment, clothes and sense of style, and a certain kind of personality and manner.

Let us begin by considering masculine magnetism in terms of its most obvious component—that of physical appeal—because, in truth, love really does "come in at the eye."

THE BODY BEAUTIFUL

The beauty of the male has not yet been portrayed by the only one who can do so—the female.

—G. C. Lichtenberg

When men think about the ideal woman, they have a lot of models to choose from. From the beginning, the Roman goddess Venus, also known as Aphrodite by the Greeks, was the goddess of love and beauty, and these two traits were intrinsically connected in the Roman mind. Representing fertility, the mound of Venus was and is the focal point of most art that symbolizes her, clearly linking fertility with love and beauty. Poetry anthologies are filled with men writing about the women they love and why. They are like catalogues of virtues and enticements, many of which focus on the physical appeal of a beautiful young woman and the desire to bear children with her. In Greek mythology, the fabled beauty of Helen of Troy was celebrated for having launched a thousand ships.

Women, however, seem to have had little to say about the comparable attributes that define masculine appeal, something that would seem to be a fundamental subject.

In discussing masculine beauty, there is not even an adequate vocabulary to express appreciation. An attractive woman is easy to describe. She is "pretty," or perhaps "beautiful"; or she is said to be "charming," "vivacious," "cute," "gorgeous," "comely," "fair," "dainty," "radiant," "blooming," "glowing," "ravishing." She is a "blonde" or a "brunette" or a "redhead."

How do we then describe a male equivalent? We cannot exactly call him "pretty," although some men certainly are. A man is not exactly beautiful even if his features are very regular. "Good-looking" might do although it is rather faint praise. "Handsome" or some variation such as "hot," "gorgeous," "or sexy" are really the only appropriate terms of approbation as opposed to the dozens of different ways in which female beauty can be described.

Whatever the term, there are without question some men of extraordinary physical appeal. Since beauty is less universally valued in men than in women, many men cultivate it less seriously and attend to it less meticulously. Nevertheless, there are some men who are so fit and broad-shouldered, so even of feature, with such piercing blue or sparkling brown eyes and muscular bodies that you must stop and stare at their perfection.

If you are an artist, you want to paint them; if you are a photographer, you want to photograph them; and if you are a dancer, you want to dance with them. Whoever you are, it is a joy just to look at them. They can be found in *Gentleman's Quarterly* and *Esquire* magazines, perfectly groomed and immaculately dressed.

The cliché is that such exotic creatures are like Greek gods although few women know much about Greek gods and fewer still have seen one. A wife, reminiscing about her honeymoon, sighed, "When I married him, he was a Greek god. Now he's just a Greek."

The Adonis Complex

Let us leave pretty women to men
devoid of imagination.

—Marcel Proust

We may well add, let us also leave pretty men to women without imagination. The trouble with beautiful men is not that their beauty does not last. The real trouble is that, like many beautiful women, they are prone to manifest the Adonis complex.

From an early age, in many circumstances, beautiful men and beautiful women find that being beautiful is enough. While people of ordinary looks bring presents to the party, all beautiful people need to bring is presence—their own beautiful presence to be admired. They bring to conversations their beautiful eyes for others to drown in. They bring to arguments their winning smile. And it works.

The beautiful lover often seems to feel that being beautiful is all that needs to be expected of him. He expects you to be grateful for even minor attentions. He expects either to be made love to or, at his pleasure, to take his pleasure from you. He does not concern himself with your response since just looking at him is supposed to guarantee it. He does not make love with you but allows you to love him.

People accustomed to being on a pedestal are often reluctant to climb down. And in any event, for a man or a woman, a pedestal is a poor place to lie down—and there is never really enough room for two.

Don't Be a Body Freak

The price of perfection is prohibitive.
—Jayson VanVerten

In the past, women complained that the image of the ideal woman was the *Playboy* model: eighteen or nineteen years old with gargantuan breasts; a vacuous, cocotte smile; and smooth, unblemished skin. She was young enough to give the illusion of virginal innocence but old enough to give consent. She was epitomized in the sort of showgirl made famous by Vargas in his provocative cartoons for *Esquire* magazine years ago.

Today's ideal image is that of the Barbie doll with huge, surgically augmented breasts, legs that go on forever, and an anatomically impossible tiny waist. Whatever the ideal image, such women are quite unlike the girl next door and, in fact, are quite unlike even very beautiful women seen in real life. All of their imperfections and flaws have been airbrushed away by an army of photographers and technicians using the latest photographic equipment and digital software. As the noted sexologist Simon Van Velikoff observed, "The Playboy bunny discreetly has no pubic hair. She also has no moles or stretch marks or vaccinations. In the heat, she does not sweat. In the cold, she does not shiver; and probably, she never has a period."

In real life, real women—like real men—are a walking collection of imperfections. Do you have fillings in your teeth? Do you have crooked teeth or braces to correct them? Do you wear glasses, or have you settled instead for contact lenses and tears? Do you have bags and dark circles under your eyes from insomnia? Do you have worry lines on your forehead? Do your feet sometimes swell? Can you pass the pencil test for sagging breasts and buttocks, or does the pencil you place there nestle in snuggly. Do you have scars from a trauma, appendectomy, or C-section? Do you sometimes feel like the "before" part of an *Oprah* glamour makeover?

And even if you are cursed with all the above, do men still love you? Of course they do.

A man cannot go to bed with the idealized Playboy bunny unless you are willing to count the imagined couplings of his juvenile fantasies. That paragon of airbrushed perfection does not exist. And even if she did exist and even if he could find such a paragon of female beauty, he would not necessarily want her.

Too much perfection is intimidating and is in itself a barrier to intimacy. It is more than possible for a lover to flinch slightly at some of your imperfections (without making it apparent, of course) while still accepting you as a whole and desirable woman and loving you both erotically and tenderly.

"Love me, love my nose," says Barbra Streisand, and so we do. It is important for all women to learn to do the same.

No one denies that a beautiful body is a wonderful thing. Yes, a man with a flat stomach and washboard abs is nicer to look at, and nicer to touch, than a man with an abundant jelly gut so common among middle-aged men. Yes, strong arms that can sweep you off your feet, literally and figuratively, are nicer than the undefined and soft arms of a desk jockey. But neither wonderful arms nor a full head of hair are essential. In fact, some women even prefer a little extra flesh on their men. Many women even refer to that extra weight affectionately as "love handles."

If you want a loving lover who provides fulfillment on many levels, you cannot afford to be a committed body freak. Your lover does not have to have the body beautiful; he only has to have some features you consider exactly right. One teenager, proudly showing her boyfriend's picture, mooned, "Doesn't he have the most divine earlobes?"

Your lover does not have to be physically perfect: he only has to have enough attractive characteristics that make him physically appealing to *you*. He does not have to have the whole package and certainly not the whole package as judged by the standard of the beautiful boys that adorn the pages of *Playgirl* magazine. In fact, it is rumored that many male models are gay, but since it is all fantasy anyway, perhaps that does not matter from a purely aesthetic standpoint. What you need in a lover is warmth, tenderness, passion, versatility, and sensitivity. A great body is merely icing on the cake.

IF YOU MUST BE A BODY FREAK,

BE BROAD-MINDED

There's one thing about baldness—it's neat.
—Don Herold

If you are so programmed that you can only love beautiful men and if the nonbeautiful are simply not appealing, then you have to think very carefully about what constitutes beauty. You have to contrast what would be ideal with what would be good enough.

Here is your exercise: think in your mind of whoever you consider to be physically the perfect man. There is any number of celebrity sex symbols you could choose from. George Clooney? Brad Pitt? Antonio Banderas? Warren Beatty when he was younger? Denzel Washington? Adam Levine? Any of the Backstreet Boys? Leonardo DiCaprio?

To keep him generalized, let us call him the all-star man. Think about the all-star man and ask yourself: if he were only five feet six, would he still do? The list of men whom many women would dismiss as too short includes such luminaries as Burt Reynolds, Dustin Hoffman, Richard Dreyfuss, and even the great Humphrey Bogart.

A lot of people who loved Clark Gable would have had trouble coming to terms with his false teeth. Sometimes, he would shock recalcitrant fans by taking them out in public. And the story goes that Bogey always licked his lips in his movies because he had a very irritable stomach and had to take Maalox all day, which left a white coating in his mouth.

How would you feel about your all-star man if he happened to be bald, or balding? According to Vidal Sassoon, who perhaps speaks from a biased position, "Hair is just another name for sex." Many bald men, however, report that having a baldpate is an unfailing sex magnet. Perhaps women who find Andre Agassi magnetic and sexy are responding to something other than the absence of hair, but even if this is the case, they apparently are able to consider hair expendable. Indeed, many men are now shaving their hair completely off because a number of movie stars and athletes have once again redefined being bald as being sexy as Yule Brenner did in the 1960s.

There are many kinds of beauty. If you insist on using beauty as a criterion because that is how you are programmed, then at least try to include as many men as possible within the definition of "attractive enough." If you have only one type—if to be attractive to you a man must be tall, blond, strong, athletic, with blue eyes, a movie-star smile, and no moles—then perhaps you should consider as your next holiday a bicycle trip around Sweden. If you can love tall or short, dark or blond, blue eyes or black eyes, you can go to Italy as well, not to mention Argentina or Israel.

To this, as to every rule, there is an exception. If you are so imprinted on one particular body type and so conditioned to respond to it that you cannot have an orgasm unless you are holding on to muscular arms that are seventeen inches in circumference, well . . . then you are going to be stuck with bodybuilders and weight lifters. You will have the same limited range of erotic relationships as does the man who can only be turned on by a blonde with long legs and big breasts.

In all likelihood, you will find yourself turning down real men only to end up mooning over your favorite movie star or sports figure or over *Playgirl* magazine pictures of beautiful young men who, dressed or undressed, are equally unavailable except as fantasy playmates.

Proviso: Love and the
Elephant Man

Beauty is only skin deep, but ugliness goes to the bone.
—Evan Esar

There is a play, and subsequent movie, based on the story of the Elephant Man, an unfortunate in Victorian England who was afflicted with a grotesque deformity of head and body. You may feel many things for the Elephant Man, from sympathy to respect to affection, but you may legitimately shrink from the prospect of making love with him.

For each person, there are some attributes which are so offensive, so intolerable, that a person with such deficiencies is disqualified as a lover no matter what his other attractive features may be. If your early conditioning or your present sense of the aesthetic leads you to a definite judgment, then you must follow your instincts. Apart from the obvious fact that there is no need to martyr yourself by doing some kind of erotic social work in an intimate situation, it is almost impossible to conceal a sense of distaste if that is what you feel. Letting someone see, or even suspect, that you view them with revulsion is not so much insulting as it is wounding. If you can't anticipate having sex with, at minimum, a sense of mildly pleasant anticipation, then it is better for everyone not to have sex at all.

Before you designate someone as an "elephant man," however, you might pause and think about what features are absolutely essential and what features are merely preferable. Before eliminating all handicapped persons, remember that many persons are handicapped in some way, if you compare them to the perfect health and physique manifested by an eighteen year old. You are entitled to some prejudices, but you should remember that to be prejudiced means to *prejudge*.

Some things that, in the abstract, sound rather distasteful turn out, in fact, to be not so bad or even irrelevant. One woman married a man who had lost one arm at the shoulder in a boyhood accident. They had a turbulent relationship, but she reported that his having only one arm was not a relevant factor and that, whatever his other limitations, he was a great lover.

Could you love a blind man? A deaf one? How about one with a limp? With an artificial leg?

Let's start with some easier questions. How about a man with a glass eye? a toupee? false teeth? Many physical problems are not exactly appealing but are within the realm of tolerable. Except in extreme cases, they are easier to live with than the less apparent psychological problems.

If you find a potential lover who has the other, more important, positive psychological traits, you might at least try to reconsider your need for physical perfection.

GILDING THE TIGER LILY

Clothes are still the most telling signature:
The banker's pin-stripe, the cowboy's hat, the
hippie's poncho, or the sweet-man's cape—
they all tell you how he sees himself, and
how he wants to be seen.

—Jayson Van Verten

The man who is self-consciously concerned about his appearance has generally been frowned upon. In the past, we called him a dandy—someone excessively concerned about clothes and appearance—like a "fop," an expressive term thankfully now out of fashion. He used to be known as a dude although this, nowadays, refers to almost any young man. Today, we call men with a healthy concern about their appearance metrosexuals. What is wrong with the metrosexual, from a pejorative male point of view, is that he is trying to make himself attractive, which is exactly why he appeals to women.

What makes one man's look more appealing to women than another's goes far beyond how he chooses to dress. It's also a matter of attitude: he genuinely cares about his attractiveness and appearance and how others perceive him. We laugh, or at least smile, at the teenage boy who spends hours in front of the bathroom mirror combing and recombing his hair with no visible improvement in either his hair, which looked fine anyway, or in his acne, which did not. The attitude that he has, however, is to try to make himself look good. That is the attitude that a person who aspires to be a sex object, male and female, is *supposed* to have.

Among the stereotypical jokes about women, a perennial theme is that they are overly concerned with how they look. They spend too much money on building unnecessarily large wardrobes. They invest too much effort in beauty props such as hairstyles, makeup, or Botox treatments and are, in general, preoccupied with their appearance. They also take too much time to get themselves together, thereby always making themselves and their escorts late.

In spite of the jokes and jibes, however, the final results are usually appreciated. The woman who dresses up for a man not only makes herself more attractive but also signals that she cares that men find her attractive. It is no accident that one of the most telling symbols of the feminist revolt was the refusal to continue with established beauty rituals such as wearing makeup and shaving one's legs. It was not just that. By refusing to indulge in these traditionally feminine rituals, women looked less attractive au naturel. It was also that their attitude was infuriating to many men. These women did not seem to care about the male response or lack of it, which was in and of itself a revolutionary thing.

One route to equality would be to have everyone equally asexual so that no one would be a sex object for anyone else. Another route that is just as egalitarian, but a lot more enticing, would be to have everyone equally sexual and equally concerned with being a sex object. Why is it that sex appeal is not considered to be something men have or do not have in the same way that women have *it* or don't have *it*? And why is it assumed that if women can do something about their natural level of appeal, men cannot do so as well? They would not only look better and smell better, but they would convey a more appealing attitude, conveying a desire to please and a desire to be admired.

In the 1950s and '60s, young men from rich families were sometimes referred to as gilded youth. These fortunate sons were concerned mainly with the pursuit of their own pleasures, and they had the time and resources to devote to fashion and the good life. The French called them jeunesse dorée. Nowadays, one need not be rich or young to express the same attitudes.

Metrosexuals are today's gilded youth, and they are promising potential lovers. Unlike their more traditional counterparts, they are concerned about their appearance and have developed an aptitude for pleasure.

THE WELL-GROOMED LOOK

My old man figures that if he has shaved,
tucked in his shirt and done up his fly,
he's ready to go anywhere.

—Farm wife in the Midwest

Helena Rubinstein, who was in the business of beauty, maintained that "there are no ugly women, just lazy ones." Christian Dior backs her up with the contention that "there are only those who do not know how to make themselves attractive." The range of beauty aids is wider for women than it is for men, but there remain a number of things that men can do to increase their appeal.

The first and most basic beauty ritual of all is so obvious it should not need saying, and yet it does. For sex appeal, for most women's taste at least, men should be clean. Making love is more appealing with clean bodies, freshly scented with perhaps a trace of soap. Squeaky-clean-all-over, kissable bodies, carefully groomed to be touched and admired. Women are schooled at an early age to consider complex cleansings and beauty rituals as part of their daily routine. Men, who are less dependent upon their appearance, often skimp in this area.

One sign of a good lover is that he considers himself to be a sex object and he wants to be attractive to you. That consciousness is reflected in many ways, but grooming is one important one. His nails are clean, his hair is well styled and frequently washed.

Shaving once a day, or even twice if necessary, tells a woman that a man wants to be kissable, wants to kiss, and wants to give pleasure. There was a young bride married to an Italian construction worker with a very heavy beard. Her delicate skin would become scraped and sore from his beard, so he shaved after work instead of in the morning. Looking back on her marriage years later, she laughed and said, "One day, I went into the bathroom, and he was shaving himself before breakfast, and I knew that the honeymoon was over!"

For ex-flower children, growing a beard can be another route to attractiveness, but it too must be shaped and shown some care and attention. It does not matter what standards and taste you and your man have about how to be groomed . . . only that you have some standards.

What counts is both his attitude that pleasing you by being fastidious is important and your positive response to his being bathed, shaved, and clean.

THE EYES HAVE IT

Oh dreamy eyes,
They tell sweet lies of Paradise,
And in those eyes the love-light lies
And lies—and lies—and lies.
—Anita Owen (with apologies to Thomas Moore)

Part of a man's appeal lies in the way he looks at you. It is no accident that the language of love is often depicted as being the language of glances. Cervantes called the eyes "those silent tongues of love." Presumably, all facial expressions play a role when people glance at one another; but when men and women exchange glances, the eyes are the most pivotal. It is apparent to everyone when a man is giving a woman "the eye."

The most appealing kind of man is willing to meet your eyes and to hold that eye contact especially when you are talking with him.

On the other hand, he does not stare. The hard, bold stare is an aggressive act and often signals an intention or a wish to dominate. When men are about to fight, they stare each other down. You don't want a man who stares you down, but you do want one who will look at you. The man who does not meet your gaze may be too shy, but more likely, he is using the avoidance of eye contact as a conscious or unconscious means of maintaining the social distance necessary for authority and control.

But then again, Ring Lardner, an American journalist and screenwriter, once said of one of his friends, "He gave her a look you could have poured on a waffle." Such a look is very hard to resist.

SOMETHING IN THE AIR

Many a woman who has a dozen perfumes that
smell differently is married to a man who
has a dozen pipes that smell the same.

—Evan Esar

For centuries, women have been scenting themselves with perfume. They do it not for their own pleasure, because perfume is soon lost to the wearer, but for the pleasure of the men around them. The trace of something in the air, the heady sensation of bending down to a neck or a neckline and suddenly inhaling a higher intensity of scent, like a bee entering a flower, is an undisputed turn-on.

Your taste in such things, or your nose for such scents, may range from floral to earthy to musk, which is surely the most suggestive of all scents. Whatever scent you choose, being perfumed, assuming it is not overdone, is a potent attraction.

The woman who wears perfume is performing a provocative come-hither act by deliberately smelling good. She is inviting men to enjoy her scent and to come closer in order to enjoy it more. Any sex object worthy of her Chanel knows the manifold return to be expected on her investment in an exquisite perfume. It is only a small step from here to wonder why it is that only women should smell good. Don't women also have noses? Don't they also experience *cathexis* (in psychoanalytic terms, the libidinal energy invested in some person, object, or idea) from the association of scents and experience?

There are few emotional triggers with as much power as scent to bring to mind, in almost total recall, memories of a particular time or place or person. A whiff of a remembered smell for a particular place, a familiar bed, or your mother's kitchen, and you are transported. Many real estate agents, when "staging" a house to show it at its best, will light cinnamon sticks or bake cookies because the smells evoke those wonderful memories of simpler times.

I know a woman who went through her divorce dry-eyed, facing the judge and the jury with equanimity. When she went back to her formerly shared apartment, however, she walked into the bathroom and caught the scent of her now ex-husband's all-too-familiar aftershave. Undone, she finally burst into the uncontrollable tears of final loss.

A man who wants to be a sex object—that is, a man who is serious about wanting to attract you to his person—understands that scent can be an important part of this process. He not only keeps himself very clean, but he adds to his natural scent something else, a certain something in the air. It might be Unforgivable, Obsession, Corduroy, or simply Homme. Remember those men in the 1980s who wore English Leather or Nothing at All?

Not that many years ago, perfume for males had to be disguised as aftershave. Now, in the prospective lover, it is nice—and possible—to find a man who selects a pleasing and distinctive cologne and routinely wears it for your pleasure.

Sexones: Body Chemistry

Pheromones may be the "body chemistry" that attracts people to each other . . . they do not have to be consciously perceived to have an effect.

—Janet Hyde, *Understanding Human Sexuality*

Among animals, sexual arousal is very dependent upon pheromones, which are sexually attractive odors that facilitate communication. A single lady moth of amorous intent can draw hundreds of gentlemen moths from a radius of many miles. She exudes the original something in the air, and they are irresistibly attracted. Similar effects are known for such mammals as dogs and primates.

While there has been considerable debate about the existence of comparable odors called sexones in humans and what their possible effects might be, researchers at the University of California-Berkeley recently found the first direct evidence that people secrete a scent that influences the hormones of the opposite sex. According to the Berkeley researchers, women who sniffed a chemical called androstadienone, present in male sweat, experienced elevated levels of an important hormone, along with heightened sexual arousal, a faster heart rate, and other effects. Compared with other animals, humans may not be as attuned to the sense of smell and we may not rely on it nearly as much as we do on other senses like sight or sound; but apparently, for women, there is nothing like the smell of a man's sweat.

A young friend of mine came back from a Caribbean vacation, proud of her all over tan and bubbling with enthusiasm about her adventures. She reported, "I was just sitting on the beach one day, next to this almost-naked man whose skin glistened lightly in the sun from having been washed by the sea; and I knew, I just knew, that his toes would taste delicious. And so they did!"

Whether or not the debate about the existence of sexones has finally been settled and whether or not we understand what role they play in human sexuality, the fact remains that every person has a distinctive body scent. You don't have to be a German shepherd to recognize the scent of people you know well. You remember, although you will find it difficult to express, the scent of your mother, your father, your brother, or any person you have lived in close contact with for a long time.

There are almost no words to describe such very real perceptions. Some people do smell wonderful. Some don't smell at all, and some smell bad. There is really no debating such judgments. Everyone who is unwashed for many days smells, although if you are unwashed as well, your sensitivity may be reduced. Even squeaky-clean bodies have a scent or develop one if they work up a good, clean sweat. One man's good, clean sweat is heady; another man's good, clean sweat is just sweaty.

Napoleon Bonaparte once wrote to the Empress Josephine, "I will be home in five days, six days at the latest. Pray do not bathe until I arrive."

You cannot defend a taste you cannot even describe because there are no words. The test, however, is simple: do you want more or less? Do you want to come closer, or do you want to pull away?

Despite what the deodorant commercials say, body odor may play an important role in physical attraction. Some body odors are enticing, and in that case, Napoleon was not so far off base after all. However, some body odors are not, and there is no defense against that judgment or any polite way to explain to a potential lover, "Yes, but . . . I don't like how you smell."

In any case, if the sexones are heady enough, all of the rational decision-making process may become irrelevant!

Clothes That Make the Man

Almost every man looks more so in a belted trench coat.
—Sydney J. Harris

The importance of clothes varies a lot, depending upon the occupations and social level of the men involved. For blue-collar workers, clothes on the job make little difference; and apart from being practical, all they need to be is reasonably clean.

Clothes off the job are something else. Regardless of how expensive they are, it is important that they fit and that they be suitable. When you first see a man, you almost always take what he is wearing into account. A man who dresses badly by most standards becomes invisible unless he has an exceptional physique. In higher social circles, clothes do make the man to a large extent because that man is in a milieu where other men are well dressed. The man who looks as if he reads magazines such as *Esquire* or *Gentleman's Quarterly*, and takes their advice seriously, does have an edge over men who do not as do men who take the time to cultivate other fashionable looks such as the preppy, sporty, or edgy look. They are demonstrating that they too take their wardrobe and being well dressed seriously.

Women are taught that their intimate apparel, be it bras and slips or nightgowns and negligees, is an important component of their attractiveness. In the same way that they dress carefully for work or for socializing, they are expected to dress carefully and attractively at home even when there is only their husband or their lover to see them.

An amazing number of men have yet to learn such a basic rule. An elegant executive who wears a thousand-dollar custom suit and whose tie is always pure silk and always correct may be quite capable of sitting around for breakfast on a Sunday morning in his white cotton shorts or in an ancient, spotted and badly fitting bathrobe that nobody, not even Brad Pitt, could get away with and still seem appealing.

A man who takes his obligation to be attractive seriously will also make a point of dressing attractively when it's just the two of you. The older he is or the less perfect his body, the more important this becomes.

Your willingness as a woman to accept with pleasure a wide variety of bodies, in shape or not, might well be contingent upon the expectation that men with less-than-perfect physiques, at least, present themselves as well-groomed and as well dressed as possible.

THE IMPORTANCE OF PRESENCE

*A manly appearance, faultless boots and
clothes, and a happy fierceness of manner,
will often help a man as much as a great
balance at the banker's.*
　　　—William Makepeace Thackeray, *Vanity Fair*

When you have considered the things that make up a man's outward appeal—all things that would, for instance, be apparent in a photograph of him—you are still left with the paradox that the men who are objectively the most attractive are not necessarily the men who are the most appealing. Beautiful men doubtlessly find this unfair and interpret such judgments in terms of feminine perversity.

What is involved, however, is more than a casual whim. Masculine appeal depends a great deal on presence, which unfortunately is very difficult to define. In the theater, one might call it star quality. In politics, it is known as charisma. Among public speakers, it would be called poise. For salesmen, it is a question of having a knack; for singers, it is a matter of soul.

Presence is the quality that makes one man get noticed where others, equally handsome and presentable, are ignored. It makes one man memorable while another is quickly forgotten.

Thackeray's oxymoron "happy fierceness" may seem to be a contradiction in terms, but it is an apt description of one component of presence. One popular song from a number of years ago proclaimed, "It all depends on the way you let your shoulders ride back." Presence may, indeed, be somehow related to carriage and movement, but perhaps only to the extent that such kinetic variations convey a sense of confidence in oneself. None of these descriptions really help to define presence, but you will recognize it when you encounter it.

You will be able to sing the Beatles' lyrics along with Barbra Streisand: "Something in the ways he moves attracts me like no other lover."

A Stranger Across
a Crowded Room

Some enchanted evening ...
You may see a stranger across a crowded room.
And somehow you know, you know even then,
That somehow you'll see him again and again.
—Oscar Hammerstein II, *South Pacific*

A man viewed as a sex object is viewed in terms of his potential as a leading character in your own private erotic and/or romantic fantasy world. This is what is meant when someone is described as being a dream. If you were free to dream up anyone at all, with any characteristics at all, for your own movie with your own script starring You and Him, then He would look and act, walk and talk, just like the made-to-measure dreamboat.

Alas, dreams are by nature ephemeral. It is difficult to analyze why one man seems so sexy and another one, equally good-looking, seems dull. It is hard to know why one man evokes an immediately sympathetic response while another one evokes only apathy. Worse, what makes a man seem lovable one day may not make him seem so lovable the next.

It is difficult, rationally, to believe in love at first sight. Even falling in love in the more precipitous way needs a little time for the feeling to develop and be recognized. Love takes time. And yet ...

Some people you remember, in graphic detail, from the first moment you see them. Of the hundreds of brief encounters you may have in a month, one stands out as if you had taken a colored snapshot in your mind. A man who grabs your attention in this riveting way may hold more promise for you than others you meet but do not find immediately memorable.

A professor friend of mine was giving a lecture, and just as she began, a young man came into the back of the lecture hall. Most latecomers generally huddled in the back of the room where they could be inconspicuous. This one, however, walked directly down the center aisle to sit in the front row, smiled at her, and then kept looking at her throughout the lecture.

My friend found it rather disconcerting. She began to wonder if she had anything to say that was worth that kind of attention. She can still visualize him as he walked down the steps to the front of the lecture hall before any kind of interaction had begun. She can still recall that he was wearing a green Lacosta T-shirt with the little alligator on the chest and an enormous black onyx ring which was too big for his slender fingers. His blue jeans were deliberately faded, and he carried a small plastic bag from Kmart. In that context and in an entirely ordinary outfit, why did she remember that the T-shirt was green or even what kind of shirt it was? Or that he carried a bag at all, let alone where it was from?

He approached her after the lecture, and they talked, and of course, they eventually went for coffee and then eventually . . .

CHAPTER 3

THE SENSUOUS LOVER

*All sensuality is one, though it takes
many forms . . . It is the same whether a
man eat, or drink, or cohabit or sleep
sensually. They are but one appetite,
and we need only to see a person do any
one of these to know how great a
sensualist he is.*

—Henry David Thoreau

Making love and having sex are sensate acts: they depend on the sensations of the body for their value and satisfaction. However obvious that may seem, many people appear to forget that physical love is just that: physical. It is touch and sensation: the experience of touching and being touched, the sensation of arousal and climax and satiation.

If you want to find a lover who will take you far into the realm of the senses, who will explore the erotic possibilities all around us, then you must, first of all, find a truly sensate man. No Calvinists need apply.

You need a man who fundamentally believes that sensation is important, a man who is aware of his body's messages and who takes the care and feeding of his body seriously. Only if he has reached this stage can you trust that he will also take *your* body, and *your* care and feeding, equally seriously. You need a man who is sensuous, someone who attends to that which can be experienced. You also need a man who is sensual, someone who is concerned with the feeding of appetites, with the gratification of the senses. A voluptuous man.

The average man on the street, if asked by an interviewer doing a Gallup survey, would affirm that yes, indeed, he does like to get laid. Remember, however, that getting laid is a far cry from having someone make love to you, which is a far cry from your making love with someone. The traditional cowboy wanted *it*, but *it* to him was on the order of "wham, bam, thank you, ma'am!" The sensuous man is concerned with something more than the simple tension reduction that accompanies orgasm. To him, the process of making love will be as important as the final goal of physical release. The sensuous man, even when he is an inexperienced and somewhat inept boy-child, wants to make love with style.

Masculinity, Femininity, and Androgyny

Men's men: they gentle or simple, they're
a much of a muchness.

—George Eliot

What exactly is it that is seen as attractive in men? Although there is some lip service given to being tall, dark, and handsome, definitions of an attractive man usually focus on how he should behave, not on how he looks.

Basically, folk wisdom reiterates that he should be "all man," that is to say, not at all womanly. He should be full-blooded, preferably red-blooded as well, virile or potent (which tells you exactly where he should be full-blooded!). He should be vigorous or powerful or strong and is expected to be two-fisted—a rather strange appellation since it's usually taken for granted that two hands are standard-issue and unremarkable human equipment. He should have hair on his chest, which traditionally shows maturity and is supposedly associated with virility. He should be a he-man, which is redundant. (Can there be a she-man, other than a transsexual?) In short, an attractive man should be a full-blooded, two-fisted, virile, he-man with hair on his chest and blood in his eye.

Descriptions of a macho man can end up sounding Neanderthal. A macho man is definitely not a quiche eater. And by implication, he is not quite a gentleman, at least, not in the European sense of the word. He is also perhaps not quite the kind of man you want for yourself, nor the kind you would want your daughter to marry.

Zsa Zsa Gabor had a definite and concise opinion: "Macho does not prove mucho."

THE ANDROGYNOUS MALE

What is most beautiful in virile men is
something feminine; what is most beautiful
in feminine women is something masculine.
—Susan Sontag

Coleridge maintained that "the great mind must be androgynous." To that, we must add that great lovers must be androgynous as well. The man who is most desirable as a lover must have some of the traits which are usually thought of as belonging to women; the woman who is most desirable as a mistress must have some of the traits which are usually thought of as belonging to men.

Androgyny is a complicated concept. From its roots, you can tell it refers to a combination of the sexes: "andro" meaning male (as in "androgen," the male sex hormone) and "gyn" meaning female (as in "gynecology," the branch of medicine devoted to women). Androgyny refers to a kind of personality which combines both male and female traits. The combination can result in a person with a wide range of these kinds of behaviors with which they feel comfortable. The androgynous person is flexible and versatile and, more than most people, is able to escape the limitations of rigid sex roles.

The man who is androgynous is not someone who is effeminate or womanlike. However, he may have some of women's better features, such as a capacity to feel and to express tenderness. The woman who is androgynous is not someone who is masculinized or manlike. However, she may have some of men's better features, such as a healthy acceptance of heightened sexuality. In either case, androgyny does not necessarily have anything to do with being homophylic (being of the same race or having common ancestry), or with having homosexual tendencies. Some homosexuals may also be androgynous, but most are not.

Why seek an androgynous lover? In the first place, such a man is quite secure in his own masculinity: secure enough to ignore the exaggerated demands of macho culture and to create his own style. He can admit to a wide range of emotions—wider than the typically macho emotions of lust and rage—and he can express them in a variety of ways. In the second place, the androgynous man, who is in some ways like a woman, can understand women better than his macho brother ever will. He is therefore more sympathetic to women in general and to you in particular. He can be assertive without being aggressive; he can be dominant, in some circumstances, without being a bully; and he can follow, in other circumstances, without being a wimp.

The androgynous man is as handy with a mix master as he is with a chain saw, as concerned with table settings as with the Dow Jones; he is as interested in poetry as he is in the World Series. He is, truly, a man for all seasons.

The Lady's Man as Lover

What lasting joys the man attend
Who has a polished female friend.
—Cornelius Whurr, *The Female Friend*

Often, a man who is androgynous is a man who has a number of women friends. The best lovers are usually those who are the most bonded to women. A man with women friends, obviously, can relate to women on a number of levels in addition to the erotic one. If he seeks out women friends and if he is successful in maintaining friendships with them, you know that he must enjoy their conversation and be sympathetic to their concerns. He is what is often called a lady's man. It is important to note that the lady's man, unlike the macho "man's man," actually likes women.

The special term for the love of or liking of women is "philogyny." Why is it that the kinds of men who are philogynous have such a negative image? Referring to someone as a "lady's man" usually has a negative connotation, but in the literal sense, it only means a man who strives especially to please women and to attract their attention and admiration. Doesn't that sound like someone who might make a good lover?

A "womanizer" is defined as a man who chases women. What else should he chase? gold? goats? other men? The man who is called a womanizer is almost as bad as one who is called a philanderer. The dictionary defines a "philanderer" as a man who makes love without serious intent. How serious did you want him to be? As serious as mortgages? As serious as vacuum cleaners? As serious as crabgrass or the crabs?

The dictionary also notes that a philanderer is one who carries on flirtations or one who loves. His intentions may not be honorable, but his bed may still be an honorable place. The philanderer is likely, at least, to be a man who likes women, who likes sex, and who appreciates sensual delights.

You might not want to marry one, but you might well enjoy having one as a lover.

The man who likes women, call him what you will, is one who enjoys flirtation and who understands dalliance.

The Libido Factor: The Gift of Passion

A passionate nature always loves women, but one who loves women is not necessarily a passionate nature.
—Chang Ch'ao, *Sweet Dream Shadows*

You can find a man who looks wonderful. He can be tall and lean or muscular and come gift wrapped in exquisite clothes. He can be articulate and affectionate, perceptive and polite, sybaritic and sensuous. And yet . . . if a man is not also passionate, he will still have to be considered as more suitable for the role of friend, escort, or surrogate brother than for the role of lover.

Not all men have the gift of passion. Some are just apathetic in general. They care about women as much as they care about other things, but in their lives, their emotions run the gamut from *A* to *B*. These men are calm, unruffled, and placid. This kind of emotional cool is a great asset in many situations where others are getting hysterical, but it is not a desirable trait in a lover.

Other men are quite capable of passion, but their passions are something other than erotic. They may be passionate politicians, for example; but when you start to consider them as lovers, you find they are still prone to making speeches. Their emotional energy, such as it is, is dissipated into other concerns, leaving little energy for love relationships.

BEWARE THE COURTLY
GENTLEMAN

It's hard for a girl to know sometimes if a man is a perfect gentleman or just not interested.

—Evan Esar

A typical complaint from women who are dating is that their escorts come on too strong too fast. While you, as a woman, are still considering whether or not you even like him, much less whether or not you want to sleep with him, he may be all over you. His hand "accidentally" wanders from your waist up to your breast and down to your inner thigh and beyond. He makes suggestive comments and puts his tongue in your ear and holds you down in a hammerlock embrace, while all the time you're feeling as though you're being loved to death by an amorous Saint Bernard: "Down, boy! Down! Bad dog!"

After a number of evenings, which usually end in a tussle and leave you breathless and with torn clothing, it is a refreshing change, finally, to go out with a man who acts like a gentleman instead of an incipient rapist. A gentleman who kisses your hand or your cheek. A gentleman who manages to hold your coat for you without breathing down your neck and who can help you out of a car without putting his hand under your skirt. A gentleman who manages to have an ordinary conversation, which is not constantly salted with double entendres. Under these circumstances, a woman can relax and watch the show without feeling that, at the slightest sign of reduced vigilance, the wolf is going to pounce on the lamb, resulting in yet another tussle and lots of heavy breathing.

However, a courtly gentleman who is too polite can also be a sign of impending trouble albeit of another kind. One young wife reported her sad tale. "John was so respectful of me when we were going out. It was a delight after all those men on the make all the time. I thought it meant he loved me—but he was still respecting me three months after our wedding!"

The man who is not sexually aggressive may be behaving politely, or he may just be apathetic. Sometimes, the two very different patterns can seem much the same.

Restrained Impatience

A gentleman is a patient wolf.
—Henrietta Tiarks, British socialite

There is a lot of talk about the difficulty of playing the woman's role to everyone's satisfaction, and so there should be. It is difficult. But the male role can also be a difficult one.

Consider the dilemma of the man who wants to make love to you and is interested and turned on and has all those other desirable responsive traits. He wants you to know that he is interested, but he is wary about coming on too strong and seeming like a boor, thereby scaring you away and turning you off. If he is too respectful, you are insulted because he does not seem to want you. If he is not respectful enough, you are again insulted because he is acting as if you are easy and he is not concerned with your responses. He has to show his arousal, but in a subtle way. He has to indicate interest, but not exert pressure. What you are really looking for is a demonstration of interest that is, at once, genuine but also patient and restrained. You want to be sure that he is not sexually apathetic and not impotent and not gay, but you don't want him to come on like a john or a rapist.

Men with wide experience and a sense of delicacy can talk themselves out of this dilemma by verbalizing their desires in an inoffensive way, leaving it up to you to move closer or to back away. A woman friend was dining in an elegant restaurant, wearing a suitably formal evening dress, complete with jacket. Partway through dinner, the room felt warm; and she casually slipped the jacket off, revealing a considerable expanse of warm skin. Her escort looked at her with new appreciation and then leaned over to request formally, "Would you please pass the saltpeter?" She did not know whether or not saltpeter actually works to depress the libido, but she thought he had made his point in a suitably subtle and witty—but still very flattering—manner.

Although words and wordplay can partly resolve some dating dilemmas, the preliminary drama of courtship is usually played out without words and is therefore fraught with ambiguous nonverbal clues. To make the situation still more complex, strangers, who are not yet adept at interpreting each other's actions, often act out sexual scripts that involve nonverbal gestures. These nonverbal gestures represent social and interpersonal norms that are used to guide sexual interactions between men and women. For the most part, sexual scripts are initiated by men and responded to by women. The most desirable kind of man, under these difficult circumstances, is one who expresses his erotic appreciation but who is quick to notice a hesitant or negative response on your part and backs off accordingly. He is one who offers but does not demand.

One young man, who had unusual success with otherwise unpredictable teenage girls, confided to me his secret: "I don't ever grab a girl like most guys do. Being grabbed would make anybody nervous. I just smile and open my arms and wait for her to walk into them. If she doesn't want to, she can't be offended, but you'd be surprised how many of them do."

Even though this young Lothario was only sixteen, I was not at all surprised by his success.

The ideal prospective lover is one who has solved the paradoxical dilemma of being able to express impatience patiently. Some men discover it for themselves at sixteen; some men never learn it.

"Not Tonight, I Have a Headache"

Several excuses are always less convincing than one.
—Aldous Huxley, *Point Counter Point*

Another version of the need for patient impatience occurs with more established couples. It was not so long ago that both professional and lay commentators on the social scene remarked on a very common marital dilemma: the husband's desire for sexual intercourse exceeded his wife's desire. As a consequence, she showed considerable ingenuity in creating circumstances in which she could tactfully avoid his advances. Wives who were not sexually inclined had a lot of headaches. They had to finish the ironing. They were concerned about the possibility of waking the baby or of being overheard by older children. When all else failed, they were simply too tired.

That was then.

Today, with a new and heightened sexuality being a characteristic of many young wives, it may happen that the husband must protest that he is too tired. Or that he has a headache.

The truth is that when and if the feeling is there, desire conquers the tiredness. In fact, being tired—or fevered or ill or anxious or worried—can add its own sensuality. Lovemaking under such adverse psychological conditions may not be as focused or as intense, but it can be consoling. It can provide, at least, a temporary distraction from real problems.

When sex is working well between a couple, then having sex is not just one more damn task to be done before the day's work is over but a reward and consolation. If you do have a headache, at least, perhaps the rest of your body can feel well or, if not well, at least better. This, of course, does not apply to real illness or to very serious distress. Headaches, maybe, but not migraines. Fevers, maybe, but not fevers of 104 degrees.

One kind of man to regard with some skepticism is the lover who can make love or who wants to make love only under the most ideal conditions. He must not be too busy, but not too bored; not too tired, but not too manic. It must not be too warm and not too cold; not too bright, but not too dark. There must be some wine, but not too much; some serious conversation, but nothing too heavy. And so on.

Such ideal conditions are, of course, desirable, but all possible combinations of what is ideal do not come along very often. If a man really savors your body, he will do so in spite of other distractions rather than using the distractions as an excuse.

A man with a headache one night is unfortunate; a man with a headache seven nights in a row is trying to tell you something. He is transmitting the same message of indifference and/or rejection as is the proverbial housewife who covers herself with cold cream and goes on ironing relentlessly until two in the morning when she feels it is safe to go to bed because she can hear her husband snoring.

In Search of a Sybarite

Puritanism—the haunting fear that someone,
somewhere may be happy.
—H. L. Mencken, *A Mencken Chrestomathy*

If the purpose of a lover is to give you pleasure and to take pleasure from you, then you must find a man who takes his pleasures seriously. Amazingly, not all men do. There is a Calvinist streak, a Puritan attitude that we in the Western world have not yet entirely escaped . . . a sort of view that life is grim and serious and something to be endured bravely and that pleasure is not only mostly impossible but probably immoral.

The proper Puritan can feel vaguely guilty because he is having a good time. Pleasure is viewed as a kind of sin in and of itself, not to mention that the indulgences, which often yield pleasure, are often viewed as sins as well. The very term "indulgences" is a clue to such an attitude.

Fortunately, there are also men in the world who are stoic only when stoicism is truly needed. The rest of the time, they freely indulge in whatever pleasures come their way. They are not necessarily ne'er-do-wells who live only for wine, women, and song. They do know, however, that wine, women, and song, or their equivalents, are key to living happily. A true sybarite is a joy to be around since in taking his own pleasure seriously, he takes yours seriously as well. A true sybarite has a genuine love of sensual pleasure, and usually, that includes a genuine desire to share. If he is also rich, then he can perhaps add a number of luxuries to increase his pleasure . . . and yours. Even if he is relatively poor, but has the right attitudes, many pleasures are available to be shared.

It is not necessarily true that the best things in life are free, but many of them are indeed freely available, if you take the time to enjoy them.

GOURMET, GOURMAND, GLUTTON

'Tis not the meat, but 'tis the appetite
Makes eating a delight.
—Sir John Suckling, *Fragmenta Aurea*

The first appetite a baby knows, the last appetite an old man still enjoys, is the love of food. Whatever one's taste in food, there is a genuine joy in being hungry and then in being fed. The French have much to teach us when they aspire to live to eat rather than merely eating to live.

What does a man feel about his daily bread? A good sign is the man who is a gourmand, who loves to eat, who is, as the English would say, a trencherman. The Yiddish term "nosher" is even more expressive. The sybarite is a man who enjoys food for the pleasure it gives him.

The man who delights in feeding you, who likes to watch you eat, who feeds you with his hand and off his plate is giving an expressive clue to his appetite for feeding you in other ways.

The association of food with other appetites is well established in our language. Sexual urges are called sexual hunger. To be "lickerish" means both to be fond of and eager for choice food and to be lustful and lecherous. Eating is the most basic kind of fun with the mouth—and fun with the mouth is basic to making love. We did not need Freud's discussions of orality to make that association. It is not accidental that a fundamental part of many courtship practices is to eat together. Remember the famous scene in *When Harry Met Sally* in which a woman diner and her waiter watch with astonishment as Sally (Meg Ryan), sitting at another table, demonstrates to Harry (Billy Crystal) a fake orgasm? When Sally is finished, the women diner, wide-eyed and mouth ajar, turns to her waiter and gasps, "I'll have what she's having." Or the lascivious finger-licking eating scene in *Tom Jones*?

A man to consider seriously as a lover is a man who takes you out to dinner or cooks dinner for you and makes that dinner an erotic event in itself.

Love of food, yes, but not too much love of food. The glutton is seldom a good lover. His sensual drives, whatever they may have been in the past, have been misdirected into what amounts to food lust. He ends up crapulent, half sick from overeating, and probably obese as well, which will limit his ability to move freely and engage in many sexual positions.

Perhaps there is one exception here, and that is if you are obese as well. If you have finally found someone who loves you and finds you attractive even though you are overweight, or who is at least willing to tolerate your weight, then you can sit down together to relish the wonderful joy of eating and renounce other pleasures. For the gourmand, the combination of food and sex is the most sensate act of all.

For everyone else—well, it is useful to remember that for a dinner date, there can be no one better than a man who is a gourmand. He will take food seriously and arrange for you to dine extensively and well, with three desserts if you want them.

But beyond the dinner date, the after-dinner cordials are unlikely to be cordial. Rather, he is likely to loosen his belt, open his fly a few inches to let his belly bulge, and doze off in a happy stupor.

The uncharitable term for such indulgence is "to pig out." The sensualist who pigs out occasionally, consuming two large lobsters and a pound of butter, is one thing; the fat man who does it all the time is something else.

LOVE OF WINE

I often wonder what the Vintners buy
One half so precious as the stuff they sell.
—Omar Khayyám, *The Rubáiyát*

The folk wisdom maintains, "Who loves not wine and woman and song remains a fool his whole life long." The woman who loves not wine, men, and song is likewise a fool. The love of wine and other intoxicating elixirs is another sybarite delight.

Poets down through the centuries, starting with Omar Khayyám, have sung the praises of wine very eloquently. Omar wanted for his paradise not only a loaf of bread and his ladylove but also a jug of wine underneath the bough. For many people, a day without wine is like a day without sunshine. You can have many such days of course. And some cloudy-rainy days do have their own dark, damp charm, but such days are not as fully savored as the sunny ones.

The oenophile, who is a connoisseur of wines, conveys some of the same erotic potential, as does the gourmet who is connoisseur of food. He understands the concept of an acquired taste and has developed a palate sensitive enough for full appreciation of sensuous delights. He may have a connoisseur's taste in women as well.

A little wine is a blessing, not only for your stomach's sake and, according to the latest research for your heart's, but also for the gentle relaxation and sense of well-being it brings. Modern and experienced lovers may not be suffering too much from the need to lessen inhibitions in order to make love, but they may well be suffering from many kinds of tension and anxiety that go with a fast-paced modern life. Men and women come together, still breathless, from the last-minute memo or an eleventh-hour meeting at the office, and having to find a cab in the rain at rush hour. Before they can focus on themselves and on each other, they need to become calm, relaxed, and centered.

It is, of course, quite true that one does not need to have alcohol to accomplish all of this. You can do it with deep breathing or yoga or a pot of tea. But there is little doubt that for most people, a little champagne or a chilled martini enhances the process and accomplishes it all more smoothly.

Ogden Nash said it all in his famous quip, "Candy is dandy, but liquor is quicker."

It is not accidental that so many of life's special occasions are celebrated with a bottle of wine or champagne: weddings, births, promotions, homecomings. The lover who brings with him a bottle of wine is not only making a gesture to set a romantic mood and create an ambience for a sensuous interlude. He is also suggesting that the two of you together is something to celebrate. Advertisers of various liquors and wines constantly show them being consumed in intimate groups: two people on a beach or in front of a fire. The images they portray are very evocative, and many of life's most serious and memorable encounters do occur under such circumstances. The true sybarite is likely to be a man who appreciates his drinks and thinks it both proper and delightful that you drink with him.

To drink, of course, is not the same as to be drunk. The true sybarite also knows that drunkenness is not conducive to lovemaking. When he has had too much, the alcohol singing in his veins may increase his desire, but it usually decreases his performance.

The man who is too frequently drunk or who has a drinking problem is not a very desirable lover. When you bring him home, you have to decant him into bed where he most often goes directly into a snoring sleep. With too much drinking, the erotic tone is spoiled. As with food, the love of wine must be tempered by sufficient restraint.

There is a vast difference, however, between someone who tempers his drinking for maximum enjoyment and someone who concurs with the philosophies expressed in turn-of-the-century temperance leaflets that ranted against the evils of the Demon Rum. The moderate drinker is likely to be much more fun and a better, more permissive, and more accepting companion than the zealot who views alcohol use as yet another kind of wickedness.

DANCE, DANCE, DANCE

Dancing is a perpendicular expression of a horizontal desire.

—George Bernard Shaw, *New Statesman*

Think about an act in which bodies move, more or less in unison, for the purpose of pleasure. Think about him moving rhythmically with you for the purpose of joy. Think about all that, and you will immediately see that the early Puritans and others of their ilk who banned dancing (especially ballroom dancing) as lewd were not being paranoid. They were, indeed, quite perceptive.

According to *Webster's Unafraid Dictionary*, one definition of sex is simply "the most intimate form of dancing." Dancing is erotic; or rather, it can be erotic if done correctly, as anyone who has watched the popular TV show *Dancing with the Stars* well knows. The way a man dances is often a graphic and revealing metaphor for the way he will make love. It is not a matter of formal steps or of technique, although these certainly help, but of the feeling of physical response to music and to another person. It's more a rhythm of the bones, a natural give-and-take, advance and retreat, which is not unlike the rhythm and the give-and-take of making love.

Watch and feel how he dances. Does he hold you so tightly that you cannot breathe while he relentlessly pushes you in a straight line? Don't be surprised if he is not a gentleman later and that you may be forced to try to breathe while holding his full weight. Or is he so tentative and hesitant that nothing ever happens? He is not likely to learn after midnight, in bed, the sense of naturalness and confidence he did not have beforehand on the dance floor.

It is, of course, not nearly this simple. There are men who can dance very well, thanks to childhood dance lessons their mothers made them take, but who do not enjoy it. Dancing, to them, is a useful social skill, like being able to play bridge and tennis. Stewards on cruise ships must have such a skill, and their smooth rhythms—and smoother lines—mean nothing. It is merely a requirement of the job. There are men who cannot dance well, in the sense of not being trained, but who feel the music and move to it anyway. Certainly, anyone can do slow dancin', swayin' with the music.

If you find a man who dances by himself, as so many women do, then that tells you a lot. Wanting to dance is an affirmation of the life force and shows an ability to derive pleasure from one's body.

Watching a man on the dance floor is one clue, albeit one among many, of how he will be in bed.

Moderation and Mediocrity:

On Letting Go

I have not been afraid of excess: excess on occasion is exhilarating. It prevents moderation from acquiring the deadening effect of a habit.

—W. Somerset Maugham

Having sex, even having quite nice orgasms, can be a relative cerebral experience. The sensations are nice, but not astounding; the emotions are interesting, but not profound. The act may be sort of interesting, but not fascinating, and certainly not awesome or wonderful.

On the other hand, sometimes the earth does move.

One condition necessary for profound sexual experiences is the ability to let go—to follow a feeling or a thought as far as it takes you—and thereby lose your sense of self and (sometimes) your sense of time and space. Psychologists talk about the "oceanic feeling." Druggies talk about "blowing your mind." Songwriters talk about "flying to the moon." All mean the same sensation of being on a roller coaster and flying with the feeling.

Unfortunately, contemporary society has put a relatively high emphasis on control—especially on the need for control in adult, middle-aged men. One is not supposed to feel too much, not supposed to be out of one's mind with euphoria or joy or even grief or pain.

The definition of "manhood," in terms of excessive self-control, is an unfortunate and interminable legacy of the stiff-upper-lip philosophy of the British. One woman, describing her ex-husband, complained, "Did you ever try kissing that famous stiff upper lip? My old man had one, complete with military mustache. It was a lot like kissing a nailbrush."

The sensuous man will be able, when it is appropriate, to abandon the need for vigilant self-control and just let himself go. He can let it all hang out and float along without feeling the need to push the river.

The folk phrase "tight ass" is descriptive of more than just a way of walking. It is also predictive of stilted, conventional, and dispassionate sex. The tight-ass man has never learned what Mae West kept telling everyone, "Too much of a good thing can be wonderful."

Conformists and

Nonconformists

A man needs a little madness, or else . . .
he never dares cut the rope and be free.
—Nikos Kazantzakis, *Zorba the Greek*

The man who is sensuous, the man who is a sybarite with the gift of passion, is likely not only to be androgynous but also to be a nonconformist.

Of the many kinds of people in the world, those most likely to be conservative are little old ladies, which can refer to little old ladies of both sexes. Old ladies often reflect the conservatism of age, of being raised in a different milieu, combined with the fact that their role as mothers and keepers of the hearth has stressed their function as culture bearers. They are moralists and are more likely to be cautious moralists than are most people.

The role of traditional little old lady is essentially the role of the conformist and, as such, can be assumed by anyone, including some men. In France, for example, it is commonly observed that there are not two sexes but three: men, women, and clergymen.

A man who is at heart a little old lady is a conservative who prefers conventional things. He is likely to believe in the desirability of marriage, meaning monogamous marriage, and he certainly will believe in it for you whether or not he himself conforms strictly to this ideal! He is likely to believe in being good, which is all very well, except that he means very good. He means not getting parking tickets, not walking on the grass when the sign asks you not to, always brushing after every meal, and never being overdrawn at the bank, and always paying your MasterCard before the due date. He tends to favor sensible shoes and will suggest that you wear them, all the while ogling other women strutting about on six-inch heels. He believes in polite language at all times and, when very angry, says things like "Gosh, darn it anyway!"

A man who is at heart a little old lady is not only good but also nice and neat and clean and careful, and he tries very hard not to give offense to anyone. When he gives you advice, which is done frequently and with little provocation, he sounds a lot like your mother: "Be good, be nice, be careful," followed by the all-purpose admonition, "Be ladylike."

Mothers who tend to be little old ladies are likely to love the men you bring home who are, at heart, little old ladies too. The little-old-lady man who meets your mother never forgets to wipe his feet at the door, and when he comes for dinner, he always brings a little gift. The two of them discuss china patterns, the rude behavior of people who cut to the front of the line at the meat counter in the grocery store, and the disturbing lack of manners among young people nowadays. Any one of these traits is, in and of itself, quite laudable or at least harmless. Taken en masse, however, they add up to a conforming, conventional, and conservative state of mind. If you want to select an accountant, you should look for someone who is a little old lady at heart. He would be meticulous, cautious, law-abiding, and reliable.

If you want to select a lover, however, you should look for someone who is more bold, more full of zest, and most of all, full of joie de vivre.

THE BOHEMIAN FACTOR

*The hallmark of Bohemianism is a tendency to
use things for purposes to which they are not
adapted. You are a Bohemian if you would gladly
use a razor for buttering your toast at breakfast,
and you aren't if you wouldn't.*

—Max Beerbohm

The lover relationship, as we have been discussing it, is by definition a new type of relationship. Many places and cultures today would still view it as a deviant alternative albeit not a very serious kind of deviance. It is certainly unorthodox.

Many people are going to disapprove of lovers, or at least disapprove of many of the behaviors associated with a lover relationship. The kind of juvenile who never stole anything is not likely to be very good at what it takes to brazen it out. He will be embarrassed and constrained and generally act as a wet blanket. One need not pick out a criminal or a thug, but one might well consider a man who was and is a bit of a hell-raiser. At least, not one who was and is something of a Goody Two-shoes.

The most promising kind of lover is the man who is, by choice, somewhat out of step with conventional middle-class morality: someone who has chosen to be nonconformist in at least some areas of life and who is comfortable with the choice. The ideologies, which nonconformists espouse, may vary as widely as the ways in which they choose to express their social rebellion.

At one time, these nonconformists might have been called Bohemians. Bohemians were not so different in their worldview than the later beatniks, who were not so different from the hippies or today's Generation X or metrosexuals. They are people who question convention and push the boundaries.

One of the most desirable features of a Bohemian man is his tolerance for a wide range of behavior and his acceptance of a wide range of human foibles.

One simple way to gain some insight into how a man really feels about unconventional people and unconventional sexuality is to watch how he reacts when he hears about those who get into trouble in nondissimilar situations. For instance, the preacher for the Moral Majority who is revealed to have had an affair with a female prostitute or President Clinton and his very public indiscretion with Monica Lewinsky. Almost any newspaper will contain examples of people tripped up by their indiscretion. Although the more conservative members in the community may well condemn the woman who takes a lover, that woman should not also have to contend with a lover who is himself judgmental and righteous.

The promising prospective lover is a Bohemian type who says, in effect, "The flesh is weak, and the public is harsh. There, but for the grace of God, go I."

The not-so-promising lover says, in chorus with the other little old ladies, "Serves them right! Hang 'em high!" And in most cases, little old ladies of both sexes believe that the woman in the plot should be hung slightly higher and sooner than the man.

CHAPTER 4

SCREENING OUT
THE OBVIOUS LOSERS

The game is not worth the candle.
—Michel de Montaigne, *Essays*

You have met a man, an attractive man, an interesting man. He moves with assurance and has a gleam in his eye. He speaks your name like a song and dances like a dream and reminds you of the gypsy rover who was always supposed to be coming over the hill but never did. He is interested but does not press you too quickly. He is attentive, but not overwhelming. Wow! Now what? Well now, you play a game of wait and see. You know what he *seems* like. What is he really like?

The first step in picking a lover is to screen out those men who are obvious losers. As delightful as it may be to have a lover, there are some men who are such unlikely prospects that entering into a relationship with them is not very likely to be worth the costs in terms of emotional distress, disenchantment, or actual danger.

The most obvious of the obvious losers are the mentally unbalanced. Most women are taught from an early age to be wary of strangers who seem to be paranoid or emotionally unstable or who have delusions or obsessions. These men signal, in many ways, that they are not likely to behave as ordinary, sane, and therefore more or less predictable human beings.

More dangerous than the obvious misfits are men who seem to be ordinary citizens but who have some characteristics which render their potential as worthwhile companions and lovers very low. They present hazards because, in some circumstances, a woman may find herself embroiled in an affair before she fully realizes the kind of man she is dealing with.

One young woman I know was attracted to a mysteriously mystic young man, with staring hypnotic eyes, who talked a lot about the occult. Since many aspiring members of the counterculture are interested in the occult, just as they are interested in bean sprouts and granola, she did not pay much attention. It was not until they were in bed together that she discovered a small tattoo in the form of a satanic symbol. And it was not until after she asked him about it that she discovered that he was not only a practicing warlock—a male witch—but was actively involved with one of the more fanatical satanic cults. She was able to make a prudent retreat, but other unaware young women have found themselves accidentally embroiled in rituals and rites far beyond their experience or their ability to cope.

There are many distant early warning signs of impending trouble. Fortunately, except in the case of a true psychopath, men who are going to be trouble usually tell you about it in advance, if you are only wise enough to listen carefully. Psychiatrists talk about "listening with the third ear," which simply means attending to communication on many levels—verbal and nonverbal, explicit and implicit—and taking your own intuitions seriously.

Among the men one might specifically guard against are the misogynist, the closeted homosexual, the predator, and the incipiently violent man. Different women have different levels of tolerance for the bizarre, but for everyone, there is a point where weird and wonderful simply become a bad choice.

As an aside, I am not suggesting that all homosexual men per se are obvious losers. My focus here is on the closeted homosexual. As a straight woman, a lover relationship with a closeted homosexual who has a strong desire to pass as "straight" is not likely to be a positive experience for you or him.

THE MISOGYNISTS

*Regard the society of women as a necessary
unpleasantness of social life, and avoid it
as much as possible.*

—Leo Tolstoy, *Diary*

The social heritage and cultural background on which present-day culture is based is essentially androcentric, that is to say, male centered. As a result, it is almost impossible to find men who are not chauvinistic to some degree. "Chauvinism" simply means the belief that persons like oneself are superior to persons who are different. The word traces back to Nicholas Chauvin, a fiercely patriotic soldier under Napoleon, and has come to describe any behavior in which there is a fierce belief that one's country or belief system—or sex—is superior to any other.

In the early sixties, the epithet MCP—male chauvinist pig—was used to highlight a new awareness of the dynamics of sexism in everyday life. Since then, it has become an overused and not very meaningful cliché. The world of men is not simply divided into pigs and nonpigs. There are degrees of swinishness, and some boars are more boorish than others.

One kind of man almost certain to be a loser as a lover is one who is not only a chauvinist but also a misogynist: a woman hater. The term stems from "mis," meaning hatred, and "gyn," meaning women. Being a misogynist is like being a misanthrope, one who hates mankind, only more specialized. (In English, we have room for many specialized hatreds. "Misandry," for example, is the hatred of men; "misopedia" is the hatred of children, especially one's own.)

A chauvinist may believe that he is superior to women but may still feel affectionate tolerance for them, and even love them in much the same way that people can love children or pets without considering them to be equals. A chauvinist may simply be indifferent to women and womanly things without feeling any particular animosity toward them. He simply does not find them very interesting or worthwhile.

In contrast, the misogynist has an active dislike of women. The roots of misogyny are found deep in our cultural heritage. In the fifteenth century, Pope Pius II described a woman as "a destroyer of youth, pillager of men, the death of the aged, the devourer of inheritances, the destruction of honor, food for Satan, and the reinforcement of hell."

A well-developed sense of misogyny views women as a source of evil, often with reference to the woman as the source of temptation to sin, almost always meaning sexual sins. She is viewed as sapping a man's vital energies as deflecting his attention away from important matters. She is seen as a source of conflict and bitterness, debilitating men by demanding money and attention, thereby draining their resources and dissipating their energies. She is a source of anxiety and discontent. She is, in a word, trouble. Women are, at best, regarded as a necessary evil required for the perpetuation of the species and nothing more.

The Women's Liberation movement has not succeeded in stamping out misogyny. However, it has succeeded in making the expression of overtly antiwoman statements politically sensitive and unwise.

As a result, the misogynist no longer proclaims his views directly. The average man who decides he wants to have a woman, not necessarily to have a relationship but to get laid, is not likely to announce that he cannot stand women. He knows it would likely cause an angry reaction, and in the end, he would not get what he wants. Making such an admission might also result in him possibly being perceived as homosexual, which would be disconcerting to his ego. He therefore masks his feelings.

The kind of statements, which may still be made openly in other cultures, are no longer stated out loud in the dominant North American culture, or they are expressed only in selected company. (As an analogy, consider one embittered African-American man who, commenting on the progress made in overcoming racism, exclaimed, "We have come a long way! We have taught the redneck not to say 'nigger' in public.")

The misogynist does not necessarily wear a lapel button, saying, "Down with women." But since he has such a strong negative view of women, his suppressed rage is buried only millimeters beneath the surface.

To detect a misogynist, all you usually have to do is to listen to him and usually not for very long.

Witches, Bitches, and Broads

If there is no word for shrew or slut in male form,
is it because there were no bad-tempered,
no slovenly men? Or is it because only the male
tongue might safely point out defects?
  —Elizabeth Robins, *Ancilla's Share*

When a man who hates women begins to talk, it soon becomes apparent that all the women he has ever encountered were villainous. Starting with his mother, they are portrayed as promiscuous, untrustworthy, or just downright evil.

The man who hates women has a well-developed lexicon to express his distain. If well educated, he will have discovered words such as "gorgon" (a repulsive woman), "virago" (a sharp-tongued woman), "termagant" (a violent woman), or "harridan" (a hateful woman). He will pepper his conversation with references to "crones" (old women), "shrews" (scolding women), "battle-axes" (aggressive women), "slatterns" (slovenly women), and "gold diggers" (greedy women). There will be a lot of references to women who are too sexual: "sluts," "harlots," "tramps," "hookers," and "tarts." Women who are sexual and who use that sexuality for wickedness or treachery, which is what a misogynist expects, may be called, in biblical terms, Jezebel or Delilah.

Paradoxically, the man who hates women is equally scornful of women who are not sexual or are not sexual enough. He considers them frigid and includes in that category icebergs, ballbusters, castrators, teases, cock-teasers, dykes, lesbians, and nutcrackers. He describes things that are negative as being like the female genitals, usually in four-letter terms. Often in the conversation of a misogynist, there will be lots of references to women in animal terms: chicks, hens, cows, sows, porkers, pigs, broodmares, birds, biddies, foxes, bunnies, and of course, the ubiquitous bitches. The endearment "bed rabbit" is an especially nice touch.

All people, men and women, use some pejorative terms for women when they are saying something negative about a particular woman or a particular situation. The profile, which reveals a misogynist, is that he uses many of these terms. He uses them often, and in his conversation, the situations involving women are so consistently negative that only pejorative terms convey the appropriate connotation.

I know a man who called his former wife the Ex-Witch to distinguish her from his former mother-in-law, who was the Head Witch. Does that tell you something? Was his daughter then known as the Little Witch? And would you be surprised if you were fool enough to be involved with him that, in a short while, you would become known as the New Witch?

If women in general are witches, you can be sure that you, too, will be included and you, too, will be burned.

Hostile Humor:

Sexist Put-downs

A patronizing disposition always has its meaner side.
—George Eliot, *Adam Bede*

The man who feels hostility and contempt for women may not be able to express these feelings directly or may find it prudent not to. Nonetheless, he may still get the point across quite clearly in the guise of being funny.

There is indeed many a truth spoken in jest. By making a joke of his opinions, he is able to say what he really feels; but since it is only a joke, he cannot be held accountable for his attitude. If a woman takes offense, it only proves again, as he suspected all along, that women don't have a sense of humor.

Listen to his jokes. What he chooses to think of as funny can be quite revealing.

Ideally, a lover is a man who loves you as a unique person and who loves you on many levels as a whole person. One common kind of joke which runs counter to such an accepting attitude involves the idea that one woman is just like another and that they are, therefore, interchangeable. It is a variation on President Ronald Regan's infamous aphorism: "If you've seen one redwood, you've seen them all." Pablo Picasso made a similar observation when noting that "there's nothing so similar to one poodle dog as another poodle dog and that goes for women too." Another infamous one is "all cats are the same in the dark."

Such an attitude is bad enough when discussing trees, dogs, or cats; it is infinitely more of a put-down when discussing people.

Another hostile joke, which appears with endless variations, is focused on the theme that women are "only good for one thing." Stokely Carmichael, the flamboyant 1960s civil rights activist and member of the Black Panther Party and Student Nonviolent Coordinating Committee (SNCC), flatly stated, "The only position for women in SNCC is prone."

And the following example of such humor is sufficient to convey the message of the whole genre. "What is the definition of the female body? A life-support system for a vagina."

DIFFICULT SEXUAL PREDILECTIONS

Whatever the origins of sexual preferences—genetic or hormonal or experiential—they are always easier to recognize than to explain and easier to describe than to change.

—Simon Van Velikoff, sexologist

Some men are losers as potential lovers because their particular preferences do not happen to be compatible with your own. With some studied attention, you can discover what your own sexual proclivities are. Once you know that, if you can then find someone with whom you are basically compatible, you may be able to experience a great deal of growth and an extensive development of your own erotic potential. Most people do not find this process very complex. From an early age, they are unambiguously heterosexual and they express that heterosexuality in a nonviolent and nonexploitative way. Others, however, do not.

It is difficult to answer the complex question of why some people prefer one kind of sexuality and other people prefer something else. Even years of soul-searching or psychoanalysis may not yield any very convincing explanations. We do know, however, that regardless of how basic sexual predilections originate, once they are formed, they are very resistant to change. If you want to change your own sexual inclinations, you might consider one of the sex therapy clinics, which employ surrogate sex partners. If you are considering trying to change someone else's sexual proclivities, however, you are wise to think again.

People with unusual sexual predilections are usually more interested in gratifying their unorthodox desires than in changing them. Even in atypical instances when they do want to change, they have great difficulty doing so. Do not attempt to rehabilitate or to reform a would-be lover whose sexual predilections are basically at odds with your own.

Several types of men should be excluded because their sexual predilections will be at odds with your own. Homophiles, because they are not likely to meet your sexual needs, and predators and men who are prone to sexual violence because they are likely to jeopardize your safety.

Looking for a Straight Man

Breathes there a man with hide so tough
Who says two sexes aren't enough?
                    —Samuel Hoffenstein, "The Sexes"

Parallel to the Women's Rights movement and the Black Equality movement of the 1960s and '70s was the Gay Rights movement, which presented the case for equal treatment of homophiles. To say a person is a homophile means that he or she is emotionally bonded and sexually attracted toward people of the same sex. It is not quite the same thing as being homosexual, which implies both that there is homophilic attraction and that such attraction has been acted out in actual behavior.

There is no consensus on how many homophiles there actually are in our society. Everyone agrees that such tendencies are more common among men than among women, but how common remains a matter of debate. This is made more complex by the fact that people are not always exclusively homosexual or exclusively heterosexual but may combine some components of both possibilities in terms of what is sexually appealing and/or in terms of what experiences they have actually had. A conservative estimate would suggest that perhaps about a quarter of all men have had varying amounts of both homosexual and heterosexual experiences; perhaps about 15 percent of all men—one in seven—are predominately homosexual. In some areas, as for example, San Francisco, the proportion is going to be much higher. It is also going to be much higher if you take as your base population men who are currently unmarried and higher still if you consider as your base population that unusual group of men in their midthirties or older who have never been married.

Despite the efforts and significant advances of the Gay Liberation movement, homosexuality is still stigmatized in our society, and people who declare themselves to be gay are still at a disadvantage in many social situations. Perhaps that is not how it should be, but that is how it is.

The pervasiveness of the negative image is readily apparent in the pejorative terms which people use to describe them and in the often malicious humor which is directed their way. Consequently, not all men who are gay or who think they might be gay are necessarily very accepting or happy about it.

Some homosexual men try to deny their status by maintaining that they are straight. Some maintain that they are bisexual and are attracted to both men and women. Tennessee Williams was once asked if he was a homosexual to which he replied succinctly, "I cover the waterfront."

The folklore refers to the possibility of bisexuality in a number of ways: to be a switch-hitter, to be AC/DC, to be ambidextrous, or more precisely, ambisextrous. The idea of a person who is sexually bonded to both men and women is theoretically an interesting alternative, but in real life, it almost never works that way. Comedians at Finoccio's, the famous transvestite cabaret in San Francisco, offer a standing gag line: "You can buy luxuries, you can buy publicity, you can buy influence, but you can't buy bisexual."

Homosexual men may make great friends and fine companions, but as a rule, they do not make satisfactory lovers. If they can manage to have sexual intercourse at all, and obviously many of them must since they do have children, they approach sex with a woman with a marked ambivalence and a lack of enthusiasm.

Back in high school, teenage boys on the make used to urge their girlfriends, "Let's do it and say we didn't." The gay man has a different request, "Let's not and say we did!" He might like to think of himself as capable of being heterosexual, or he might like other people to have the impression that he is, but he does not really like heterosexual acts themselves.

One woman reported a common experience. "He almost said to me right out loud, 'All right, let's get it over with!'"—much the same attitude you might have when approaching an intimate experience with your dentist.

The homosexual man is not rejecting you so much as he is rejecting womankind, or at least the sexuality of womankind. It is all very well to be advised not to take it personally, but it is very difficult not to take it personally. Women have enough trouble learning to accept their bodies and their sexuality without seeking the negative opinion of a man who has rejected both.

Beware of the closeted homosexual. While he may be emotionally appealing, choosing him as a prospective lover is likely to end negatively for both of you.

If you have a homosexual friend, take him to the movies, take him to a party, take him to dinner, but don't take him to bed.

THE CASANOVA COMPLEX

Hunters of women burn to show their skill,
Yet when the panting quarry has been caught
Mere force of habit drives them to the kill:
The soft flesh is less savory than their sport.
—John Press, "Womanizers"

For some men, the most thrilling and most important aspect of sexuality is the ability to persuade a new woman to have sex with them. Some psychiatrists refer to this syndrome as the Casanova complex after the legendary Giacomo Casanova who seduced hundreds of women and detailed his exploits in his memoirs.

Casanovas, who are also sometimes called Don Juans, after another historical figure with extensive seductions under his belt, are usually very attractive to women because they have made a careful study of the components of masculine appeal, and they work diligently at being attractive. They have an excellent and persuasive line or, rather, a series of lines, one for all possible occasions with all possible kinds of women. In some places, they are called scalp hunters. Sometimes, they are said to be concerned with making notches on their gun, like old-time gunmen of the West who were reputed to carve a notch for every man they killed. Casanovas are obsessed with the idea that they can entice any woman into their net. The more unlikely you are as a sex partner, the more of a challenge you present to their supposedly irresistible charms, and the more diligently they will work at wooing you effectively.

The Casanova has a wide repertoire of seductive tricks. He talks a good game, he has practiced hands, he looks at you with melting eyes, and he simply does not take no for an answer. He declares his undying love or his overwhelming passion or whatever other hyperbolic state of affairs he thinks might please you. Heady stuff.

When you finally succumb to the blandishments of a Casanova and let him take you to bed, you are likely to experience a profound sense of anticlimax. For him, the fun of seducing a woman is all in the chase; and in establishing that, his personality and will are dominant over yours. Once you have submitted to his will, you are no longer very interesting.

The Casanova is often an indifferent lover. He is almost never interested in following up a conquest with an encore and certainly not with a relationship. An encounter with a Casanova, should you have been unfortunate enough to have actually believed his line, is a profound disappointment.

How can you recognize a Casanova in advance? Like misogynists, Casanovas do not necessarily wear identity badges, but there are several clues. Usually, their reputation precedes them, especially since they are proud of their conquests rather than ashamed; many may even brag about them. They certainly do not try to conceal their numerous involvements. Scott Fitzgerald described such a man about town as "one of those men who come in a door and make any woman with them look guilty." The Casanova tends to come on too strong too soon, declaring a passion far and above what would be reasonable and predictable in a given situation.

Finally, although a Casanova may have had many women, his is unlikely to have had any one woman for any length of time. When he is thirty-five, and the longest he has ever been involved with one woman is five weeks, beware.

THE WOLF IN SHEEP'S CLOTHING

Wolf: the kind of guy with whom a woman should eat, drink, and be wary.
—Louis Safian, *Two Thousand Insults for All Occasions*

Whether or not you can tell the sheep from the goats, it is quite easy to tell the sheep from the wolves. The folklore is full of jokes about wolves and their erotic aspirations. Wolves are, after all, one of the first types of would-be lovers that a girl encounters since they prey with special enthusiasm upon the young and innocent. A wolf's life is a bed of ruses. He is a man of single purpose and double talk. He has wandering hands that go from touch to worse. He whistles while he lurks. In short, he is the kind of man that men don't trust too far and women don't trust too near.

Alas, men are not easily classified as merely being either wolves or nonwolves. There is another type of man to watch out for: the wolf in sheep's clothing. He is a more exotic type, usually encountered in later life, and he provides a surprise on the order of Little Red Riding Hood.

The wolf in sheep's clothing seems to be a harmless fellow. He is careful not to use bad language in front of you, and if he slips, he apologizes. He scurries around to open the car door for you and insists that you walk on the inside of the sidewalk. He is a model of gentlemanly conduct until you find yourself alone with him in an elevator perhaps or, even worse, in a closed room. And then, with wolflike cunning and a sense of territoriality, he pounces.

The wolf in sheep's clothing is an especially difficult problem if you do like him. Worse yet, if you work with him, you will then have to resurrect some semblance of an ordinary situation after he has pounced and you have reacted negatively. There is only one defense against this kind of wolf, and that is the presence of other people. The instant you are alone with him, the hassle begins again. He has likely had little experience with women, except perhaps with prostitutes, and so has little understanding of courtship. It is unlikely he will learn and even more unlikely that he would be worth teaching anyway.

Take evasive action.

Eros and Erotica:

Vicarious Man

In adolescence pornography is a substitute
for sex, whereas in adulthood sex is a
substitute for pornography.
                                        —Edmund White

Almost all men are occasional consumers of commercial pornography. Perhaps most women are as well although most of the sales pitch is male oriented. Our culture is increasingly blatant in presenting the intricacies of the female body in all forms and poses and costumes. The Playboy bunny of the 1950s, who smiled coyly over mountainous breasts, has been replaced by a new kind of bunny, more like a march hare, who smiles lasciviously while presenting her vagina with spread-eagle legs.

Other magazines, available in every corner grocery store, add trimmings by showing couples, ménage à trois, gay and lesbian couples, whips, chains, handcuffs, spankings, masturbation, and so on in mind-boggling variety. Even the casual customer in search of a dozen eggs and a loaf of bread has to admit that such a smorgasbord is kind of . . . well, at least interesting, if not completely appealing.

The not-so-casual customer can take himself down to the strip in any major city (in Los Angeles, it is the infamous Santa Monica Boulevard; in Toronto, Yonge Street; in San Francisco, the Tenderloin; and in New York City, Times Square). There, he can see everything the pictures portray in living color and living flesh before his very eyes. With table dancing or lap dancing, it is not only before his eyes but only inches away. There is no special significance in the occasional titillation to be gained from such permissiveness.

It may well make the pulse beat marginally faster or inspire an otherwise flagging erection to become stiffer. It may occasionally even suggest to a bored housewife some leisure-time activities which would be less boring.

You may want to think twice, however, if you encounter a prospective lover who has made pornography his avocation. The man who is an aficionado of pornography is quite likely to view sex and sexuality as a spectator sport. For him, it is a sad day when he has to settle for the real thing. Pornographic pictures on the Internet or in books and magazines may be something to aid the private fantasies of masturbation done alone and behind locked doors. Pornographic performances may be sexually suggestive, but they are not really very sensuous.

Remember that the typical strip club attracts middle-aged men, who are either more or less bored with their wives or more or less impotent, watching from a distance young women, more or less lesbian, disrobing with thinly veiled boredom and contempt. The strippers gyrate automatically while wondering what kind of meatloaf to make for dinner on Tuesday. The men in the audience may feel some mild arousal, but it is left unexpressed and unresolved.

The women involved in pornography are deliberately anonymous. The lack of individual identity is only partly to protect the women themselves; it is also a concession to the preferences of the audience. The woman with no background and no personality cannot have any undesirable traits to intrude upon the fantasy preferences of the individual man. Being nameless, she is not a social entity to be taken into account. Often, the woman is viewed as masked or is photographed so that her face does not show, a variation on the common theme which accepts any body as a suitable receptacle if she has a bag over her head.

Photographs of women are presented cropped so that all that is to be seen are disembodied breasts or buttocks or vaginas. The body parts are not only out of any social context, they are also out of context for a whole body, much less a whole person. This dissociation perpetuates the idea of a woman as a sex object and takes it to its logical extreme. She is first reduced to being only a body. That body is then reduced to being only tits and ass.

The anonymous, impersonal, undemanding, idealized body of the pornographic superwoman is an object of fantasy, which almost all men will occasionally find arousing—that is, the nature of the beast. However, the man who appreciates a stripper brought in to enliven a stag party is not the same as a man who papers his bathroom with crotch shots. The dedicated consumer of pornography—who seeks it out, collects a library, and pays money to watch—is also likely to continue the idea of a woman as an anonymous object when he pursues an affair with you.

You may well find that he would rather look at you and talk about *it* than he would actually like to get down to *it*.

MISOGYNIC PORNOGRAPHY:

SEX AS AGGRESSION

A woman reading Playboy *feels a little like a
Jew reading a Nazi manual.*
—Gloria Steinem

One problem in talking about pornography is that not all of the materials and acts popularly considered to be pornographic are actually innocuous. If what is involved is a striptease artist taking off her clothes to the strains of Gypsy Rose Lee (or perhaps Olivia Newton John's "Let's Get Physical"), then this ritual is a repetition of a theme that presumably goes back to the belly dancers of the Pharaohs. The woman merely repeats for men in public what wives do for a man in private. She is more or less enticing, depending on how many ballet lessons she actually took before swapping artistic aspirations for something more practical, like paying the rent. Other pornography, however, caters to quite different tastes.

Misogynic pornography equates sexual feelings toward women with aggression toward them. If sexism can be compared to racism, then this kind of pornography is the equivalent of hate literature. The woman is depicted not only as an object—a disembodied vagina—but as an object of scorn and abuse. She is made to feel pain, and the more pain she feels, the more pleasure to the Peeping Tom.

Women in rough porn are spanked or beaten or whipped. They wear restraints or handcuffs or even dog collars with metal studs digging into the neck. They are made to crawl on all fours and to present their derriere doggy fashion for the buggering cock or bottle or gun. They are hung by the arms or stretched spread eagle, dominated and degraded, usually with some kind

119

of gag or silencer to prevent any protest. Many of the fantasies involved are rape fantasies—and not even the usual kind of rape, but gang bangs and anal assaults.

These kinds of misogynic images of women, combining sexuality with extreme aggression, have been available in Times Square in New York ever since there was a Times Square. For a small fee, you can buy the pictures or watch a movie or even watch the action live. In the past decade, comparable misogynic images have become increasingly available everywhere, particularly on the Internet where rough porn is readily available to the misogynist in his home twenty-four hours a day.

When you find a man who prefers misogynistic pornography—who has an extensive collection, including a library of DVD/videos, and endlessly surfs Internet Web sites for rough porn for hours on end—then beware. Even if he seems to be gentle and, like most people who lead vicarious lives, never actually does any of these things himself and would not, the fact that he has a more than healthy appetite for such kinds of pornography should alert you that he probably does not like women very much. He may not actually be brutal, but he is unlikely to be tender.

You don't actually have to find the magazines in the bathroom or under the bed or catch him on a rough porn Internet site to get some idea of this sort of attitude. Ask him. When you pass a blue movie house, ask him if he has seen it. Gesture to the porn section at the corner grocery store or comment on the ready availability of sex sites on the Internet and see what response you get. He cannot be offended, and the nature of his response or lack of it tells you a lot. You don't want a Puritan who has not come to terms with his own sexuality to the point where he still believes that pictures of stark naked women are obscene. (Stark naked is, well, slightly more naked than naked.) If a naked body in the abstract offends him, you can be sure that he is not the man to celebrate your nakedness or his own. On the other hand, you do not want a lover who is an overly enthusiastic consumer of porn.

The most promising response, showing a healthy attitude, may be bored tolerance: a sign that he is the kind of man who has gone to the strip clubs, but who has not gone very often. He is probably someone who may occasionally look at pornographic pictures in magazines or on the Internet, but who has not taken them seriously since having used them to masturbate when he was a teenage boy. He is the kind of man who is now past the state of abstract titillation and who is now into real women, literally and figuratively.

Men, who have been with real women whom they like, feel no need to garnish them with garter belts and handcuffs, except for when it has some mutual appeal.

THE VIOLENT LOVER

Deeds of violence in our society are performed
largely by those trying to establish their self-esteem,
to defend their self-image, and to demonstrate
they too are significant.
—Rollo May, *Power and Innocence*

One hazard of intimate relationships is that, because of the intensity of feeling which they engender, they may provide the stimulus for violence. Occasionally, that may involve women being violent with men; but when violence occurs, it is most often men being abusive with women.

Male strength is vastly superior to that of women. Even relatively small and frail men have a disproportionate advantage, and when that edge is fueled by fury, then it is a clear and present danger.

Conflict is inevitable in almost all intimate relationships, and some of that conflict is potentially violent. This fact of life, less pleasant than other facts of life, is something that should be taught to all young girls. It is a reality that a woman of experience must learn to accept and to take into account. She cannot avoid it entirely, but she can learn to minimize the odds.

In our culture, as in many other cultures, there is, for many people, an implicit association between sex and violence. It is apparent in some pornography, which equates eroticism with dominance and brutality. This sex-violence link is apparent in much of the old folk wisdom, which endorses wife beating as legitimate and even as necessary under some circumstances. Such attitudes are not restricted to the uneducated or to the unsophisticated. The philosopher Nietzsche offers the questionable advice: "When thou goest to a woman, take thy whip." Noel Coward quips, "Certain women should be struck regularly like gongs." If a man is not free to beat any woman, he is often perceived to be free to beat his own, especially if he is provoked.

Ordinarily, it is not feasible to ask a man directly whether or not he will hit you. Even if you were to ask, his answer would not necessarily be very informative. You can, however, find many occasions where you can ask him how he feels about corporal punishment for kids. The man who feels that it is all right to spank, beat, or whip a child "if he deserves it" may very well feel it is also all right to spank, beat, or whip a woman "if she deserves it." Guess who gets to decide if the deserving child will be improved by abuse? Guess who gets to decide if the deserving woman needs to be corrected?

Some potentially violent men are easy to spot. They tell you outright that they believe that might is right and that their own judgment of the appropriateness of the use of force and pain is justification enough. Do not be surprised if an argument with such a man eventually leads to him emphasizing his point with the back of his hand.

While you are talking about life in the abstract, you can always ask a man about his own parents. If he reports that his old man used to knock Mom around, that is not necessarily a danger signal. Listen to how he describes it. If there is an undertone of pride in his old man, who really knew how to handle women, then do not be surprised if eventually he attempts to handle you the same way. If, however, he is full of sympathy for his mom's plight and if the story ends as such stories often do, with the boy finally challenging his father successfully thereby being able to protect the mother, then he may be more sensitive to violence against women than are other men. He may, in fact, be the kind of man with whom you will be most safe.

Some philosophers would contend that there is a potential for violence in all of us and that it only requires sufficient provocation for it to erupt. This may well be true, but it is difficult to prove or to disprove. If all men are potentially violent, it does not follow that all men are potentially violent in terms of women.

The code of chivalry asserts that although violence is often necessary, it is not appropriate in those circumstances involving assaults on people who are relatively powerless and defenseless as, for example, women and children.

With men living by a chivalrous code, the possibility of violence is virtually negligible. When you fight with them, they will fight back; when you offend them, they make you pay one way or another, but they will not take out their rage physically.

Other men, however, are prone to violence in varying degrees. Many women, at least one in ten, perhaps more, have experienced the violent laying on of hands by a boyfriend, husband, or lover. The violent lover is trouble and is to be avoided no matter what his other attractions may be.

HANDLING THE MANHANDLER

"Hold off! Unhand me, graybeard loon!"
Eftsoons his hand dropped he.
—Samuel Taylor Coleridge,
The Rime of the Ancient Mariner

One important and direct clue that a man is potentially violent is that he likes to throw his weight around literally as well as figuratively. Such a man may have never done anything explicit, such as hit you or threaten to hit you, but he tends to play rough.

Not too long ago, Sheila, a friend of mine, told me about an incident that occurred between her and her boyfriend Mike when they were having dinner in a restaurant. Mike reached over, smiling, and tweaked her cheek between his thumb and forefinger, saying something not very cute about her being very cute. All acceptable, almost, except that the tweak actually hurt. When Mike took his hand away—and he apparently was none too quick about doing so—her cheek tingled from the pain. There was no obvious sign of injury other than that her one cheek was a bit redder than the other one, but not that much redder as her whole face had become somewhat flushed from the anger she was feeling. She could hardly charge him with assault. She could not even make a fuss, but nevertheless, it did hurt. She told me that she knew, and she knew that Mike knew, that it was meant to hurt.

Beware of the arm twister who grabs your wrist in a vise or playfully puts your arm behind your back while making a joke. He is showing power, not love or even affection, and he is showing power based on the undeniable fact that he is bigger than you are and his hands are stronger. A bad sign of a bad attitude.

A man who will be a good lover may occasionally hold you firmly as, for example, when he is insisting that you stop a minute and listen to what he is saying. Sometimes, he may actually hurt you a little, if he does not know his own strength or if he does not realize your sensitivity. Jocks are especially prone to this sort of thing because they are stronger than most; perhaps their own pain threshold is higher than most. However, the good lover who sees your distress lightens up immediately. He stops and apologizes and offers the equivalent gesture of a kiss to make it all better.

Beware the man who scoffs at your protest that he is hurting you or who takes a long time to cease and desist when you ask him to do so. Beware especially of the man who says or implies, "You think that hurts? You ain't seen nothin' yet!"

There is a difference between being held and being held down—all the difference in the world.

Rough Trade

We are effectively destroying ourselves by
violence masquerading as love.
 —R. D. Laing, *The Politics of Experience*

In addition to believing that they have a right to physical domination over women, some men contend that women, in fact, like to be knocked around. They incorporate restraints and/or pain into their sexual routines and project that the woman's protest is a feigned response. Perhaps some women do find some masochistic appeal in pain, but it is certain that most women do not and that very many women who encounter it do their best to avoid or escape it.

Very few men attack physically without warning. One reads occasionally of psychopaths who become violent in the extreme, without warning, and for no apparent reason that makes sense to the rational mind. Fortunately, these types of men are few and far between; and in any case, there is little defense against them. Among ordinary men who are more or less sane, there are many signals that violence is in the offing and that a psychological conflict could escalate to a physical one. It is, alas, a conflict you are almost certain to lose.

The first clue, so obvious that many a woman would ignore it, is that he tells you his intention. "You deserve a belt in the mouth for talking like that!" he says to you, but you do not take him literally and are surprised when a belt in the mouth is what you get.

Another clue of trouble brewing is the acting out of aggression on various objects. The angry man punches pillows, slams doors, and breaks glasses. An especially effective grand gesture is to yank off a tablecloth, scattering dishes and glasses to the floor. A still more serious sign of violence to come are gestures which cause some hurt to the man himself. He might kick the wall or slam his fist into the table. One husband I know became so enraged with his wife that he punched an elevator wall, breaking two bones in his own hand.

After such threatening behavior, the next most likely move will be a real one: a real slap across your very real face, a real punch to your very real stomach. The husband who attacked the elevator hit his wife the next week with the edge of his cast, closing her eye and breaking her nose.

You do not want a violent lover, not if you value your peace of mind, your body, and your life. When you see the signs of violence building, get away as quietly and as quickly as you can.

When you see the signs or indicators of a violence-prone personality, stop thinking of that person as a potential lover and start thinking of how you can get out of the relationship with your skin intact. Whatever else he has or says or does, if he is rough trade, he is not worth the price he will extort.

CHAPTER 5

EROTIC DIALOGUE: SPEAKING OF LOVE

To speak love is to make love.
—Honoré de Balzac

Part of masculine magnetism has to do with how a man looks. But there are other components to his physical appeal: how he moves, how he dresses, how he smiles, how he smells. That is certainly enough to get your attention.

Although these may be the first things that a woman notices, they are not necessarily the most important traits that make one man more or less appealing than another. How he feels is also very important. The best lovers are sensuous sybarites who have the gift of passion and who are Bohemian enough and confident enough to follow through to the full potential of sensuous delights. Even if he does all of this, he also has to have the right attitudes. He must like women in the abstract and in the flesh with an erotic response that is enthusiastic and involved, but not abusive or violent.

Suppose that you have been to a party where you met a handsome man who has since wined and dined you. The conversation has been extensive enough and intimate enough that you feel confident he is sane and reasonable—not a misogynist or a rapist, not a lecher or a bully. Now what? Remember that most men you encounter are likely to meet these minimum criteria.

So while all those characteristics are important, they are still not enough. Now you must listen to him, really listen to him.

The most important feature of a good lover relationship is mutuality: the flow of interaction back and forth from man to woman and woman to man. What is needed is dialogue on all levels: emotional, physical, and intellectual. What is needed is reciprocity.

Mutuality implies a dialogue, and with a lover, that dialogue has two important interrelated parts: dialogue that involves words and nonverbal dialogue that involves a conversation of gestures and facial expressions.

THE SILVER-TONGUED DEVIL

I have been seduced again, by the silver—
tongued devil again. He is the most
cunning linguist of them all.

—Jadah Vaughn

An important part of making love is, or should be, words. You are passionate for a few minutes; you are involved in an intimate embrace for a few hours but may converse and listen all day long and far into the night.

The lover worth loving knows how to talk and to listen. He knows how to make the experience more acute for being put into words and to make feelings more focused for being articulated. He not only knows how to express himself, but he knows how to draw you out to express yourself as well.

His presence is companionate because it is shared; his presence is not boring because it provides a running commentary of observation, thought, and feeling. With luck, such a lover also has the gift of laughter: he provides reassurance while putting things in perspective.

It may sound like a tall order, but all it really means is that this person has learned to communicate verbally and is willing to use that skill to help create a mood and develop a relationship. Pillow talk, intimate talk may be made up of little nothings, but it is of great importance.

The good lover should not only be able to converse about the weather and the price of tea in China, he should also be able to talk about love. An Irish woman would call it blarney, but she would smile when she said it. An English woman would chide him with "how you do go on!" but she would smile too.

Conversation doesn't only establish intimacy. It also helps to imprint sensual experiences and makes them memorable.

The experience of the sensate world is something to be felt and to be enjoyed. However, it is often difficult to know exactly what you are feeling and even more difficult to remember it with clarity. On occasion, some combination of emotion and circumstance may create an atmosphere that you recall in dreams and daydreams for years. But often, the experiences themselves, the sensations are amorphous and are lost to thought and memory.

They say—that is, men say—that women do not really remember the pains of childbirth, or they would never have a second child. Often, even very intense sensations, such as the great pleasure of making love, are difficult to recall in detail. You experience something more acutely for being able to put it into words. People are always lamenting that a feeling is beyond words, and it may well be true. But, at least, trying to put it into words helps to focus on the reality you are experiencing.

Look for a lover who is articulate. If he can verbalize his emotions and yours as well for that matter, he can enable both of you to feel more completely and to remember more accurately. Strong and silent types may have been fine as stars of the silent screen; but they can be boring, boring, boring in bed.

Brevity may be the soul of wit, but that maxim does not apply when someone is saying "I love you."

THE YOU AND ME THAT IS US

Lovers seldom get bored with each other
because they are always talking about
themselves.
— François, Duc de La Rochefoucauld, *Maxims*

It is nice to have a lover who talks. It is even nicer to have a lover who talks to you and with you about himself and about you and about the two of you together. A lover who talks about both Love and Life, with a capital *L*. He does not have to be a great philosopher; but it is gratifying if he is a man who has, at least, examined his own life, has thought about the relationships in it and what they have meant. Having reflected on that, he will be able to be equally reflective about a possible relationship with you.

Talking with a lover is especially important because the role of lover is a relatively new one and is consequently more ambiguous and unstructured than that of husband or boyfriend, for example. The two of you have the freedom—and therefore, the necessity—to make up your own rules. Talking about feelings is both a way of creating and of expressing them, and the experience becomes more real and more memorable.

The stereotype would have it that women want to talk and men want to get on with it: get drunk, get laid, get back to the game. Perhaps many do just that, and many will chat you up for the quite deliberate purpose of getting you to lie down.

If you can find a lover who can talk and who likes to talk, you have found a man who can help you grow and a man who, perhaps, can also be a friend. I do not suggest that constant analysis of interpersonal dynamics is necessarily good. Analysis, yes; constant analysis, no. It is also important to recognize that if positive words can create a mood, then negative words can and will destroy it. If you are about to make love or are making love or have just made love,

131

the last thing that is needed right then is clinical analysis. The more clinical the conversation about who did what to whom and about what should have been done, the more you distance yourself and your partner from what you are feeling. You become self-conscious and objective rather than free and spontaneous. It is important for lovers to discuss the clinical aspects of their lovemaking. Being able to do so openly and honestly greatly facilitates sexual adjustment. Such postmortems, however, should be held while dressed and seated upright in the living room, with no immediate intention of putting theory into practice.

WHERE ARE YOU COMING FROM?

It is a certain sign of love to want to know,
to relive, the childhood of the other.
—Cesare Pavese, *This Business of Living*

To share a loving relationship with someone, it is important to know not only what they are like now but how they came to be that way. The attentive lover is interested in your past as well as your present. "What were you like as a little girl?" he asks. "Do you have any pictures? What were your parents like? Were you happy? Did you ever run away from home?"

The most desirable kind of man is willing to share his past and childhood with you as well. He lets you see where he is coming from and so opens possibilities of a closer understanding and rapport than you could otherwise have. This is not to suggest that a lover's dialogue should sound like "sharing" in an encounter group or a session with a psychotherapist. However, some insight into the person's past is part of the appreciation for the adult they have become.

The lover encourages you to examine your own life and provides a new source of insight and understanding by letting you compare your past experiences with his own. You learn not only about him but also about men in general and, ultimately, about life.

Sharing past experiences is another way of sharing current ones.

MAN OF MIRTH

---

*Among those whom I like or admire, I can find no
common denominator, but among those whom I love,
I can: all of them make me laugh.*

—W. H. Auden

One role of a lover is to increase our allotment of joy. The best of lovers are proficient at sharing and easing pain; but they also have the gift of laughter, and, having it themselves, they can bring it to you.

Poets talk about the music of girlish laughter, which is appealing as long as it does not get too suspiciously close to the inane giggling of a giddy schoolgirl. What about the appeal of the rich, full, joyous laughter of a happy man? His happiness will infect you as well. His happiness will tell you that, at least in some important ways, he has found the secret of living with joy and how to have fun.

A sense of humor does not mean the typical salesman's ability to remember jokes and tell them well. It means, rather, the capacity to respond with laughter to the things that will inevitably go wrong in the course of your affair and its arrangements. It means he's not taking himself and his preoccupations too seriously. If he not only has a sense of humor but also a sense of the ridiculous that matches your own, then you have a lot to share.

A man of mirth will not only make your time together more pleasurable, but he will lighten up the troubles which you encounter.

PILLOW TALK

By the time you swear you're shivering and sighing,
and he vows his passion is infinite, undying—lady,
make a note of this: one of you is lying.

—Dorothy Parker

Making love is like a play. It has a script of sorts, partly dictated by the culture, partly created through the continual revisions made by the couple themselves. It is a play with an overture: an apt analogy because, in this case, even the word is the same.

Making love begins with someone making overtures. It has a first act made up of various kinds of foreplay. It reaches a climax in the second act. It has a third act, an afterword. There are intermissions. And as in the theater, there must be a willing suspension of disbelief.

When watching a play, you know at some level that it is not real life. Actors are killed, but not really. It takes place in the eighteenth century, but not really. The scene takes place deep in the forest, which is, really, only painted trees on cardboard. To enjoy the play, you must willingly suspend disbelief: knowing it is not real, you nevertheless agree to go along with whatever the author and the players tell you, as if you did believe.

Pillow talk, like a play, needs some suspension of disbelief. When he says, "You are the most beautiful woman in the entire world," you don't stop to wonder about his criteria for beauty or what kind of survey he has taken with what kind of international sample. When he says, "I've never been this happy before," you don't ask, "What about when you were sixteen and your father surprised you with a red Mustang convertible?"

You believe that, at the moment, it is true . . . even if it isn't true. Pillow talk exists in the realm of feeling, not fact. It is not a time to be too literal.

One exasperated young man reported breathing into his girlfriend's ear, "I love you," only to have her bolt upright and demand, "What do you mean by 'love'?" There may well be forty-seven meanings of the verb "to love," but this is not the time or place for semantics. The circumstances of pillow talk are not conducive to accuracy. The whispered words and promises, the hyperboles and dreams have to be considered in context.

If you want reality, listen to what your man tells you the next morning while you are sharing coffees and hangovers.

Names, Pet Names, and Endearments

Two people who are in love are attached above all else to their names.
—Walter Benjamin, *One-Way Street*

The attentive lover speaks your own name to you as a way of getting your attention, as a way of giving emphasis, as a caress. He doesn't do it because he read Dale Carnegie and was told it would make a good impression. He does it because he is thinking of you. The sound of your own name is always sweet: the sound of your own name on the lips of a lover is especially sweet. Everyone remembers a love-struck Tony in *West Side Story*, singing, "Maria, I'll never stop saying Maria."

The sound of your name on your lover's lips tells you that right now, he is thinking of you, not women in general and—God forbid—not some other woman. It does for an embrace what engraving does for silverware or monograms do for towels: it tells you that this particular embrace is yours.

One very perceptive and witty radio skit involves only two voices, speaking alternately: a woman's voice saying, "John!" and a man's voice answering, "Martha!" John and Martha keep up their dialogue for quite some time and, by innuendo, manage to convey an erotic encounter usually quite difficult to describe over public radio.

In a developed relationship, one sign of good rapport and special feeling is the creation of pet names for each other: bedroom names, which are used in private, intimate conversation. In a love affair, the man is somewhat different than he is in other relationships and so is the woman.

Let's take, for example, a couple named David and Maria. The David as seen by Maria is not quite the David seen by the rest of the world, and the Maria as seen by David is not quite the same either. David may well make this point by renaming her in effect My-Maria-as-I-Know-Her, and she renames him My-David-as-I-Know-Him.

Many pet names are diminutive and place the lover in a childlike role. For instance, Franklin Roosevelt called the formidable Eleanor babs, as in "baby." Often, pet names are taken from animals. Winston Churchill called his wife pussy cat, a more conventional endearment than her calling him pig. A woman who had been an Elvis fan called her lover hound dog.

Some pet names provide a delicately euphemistic way of referring to the couple's erotic life. In *Lady Chatterley's Lover*, Lady Connie personifies the penis of her gamekeeper, Mellors, by christening it (him?) John Thomas. (Following Lady Connie's example, Trey, Charlotte's husband in *Sex and the City*, referred to his penis as John Thomas.) And Mellors, in turn, refers to Lady Connie's genitalia as Lady Jane. One woman called her man Longfellow, in spite of the fact that he was neither tall nor poetic. He called her Fantasy because he said she had fulfilled all his fantasies.

Although some pet names are obviously complementary and endearing, others don't seem very affectionate, at least not if taken literally. In the markedly successful movie *On Golden Pond*, Katherine Hepburn calls her aging husband, Henry Fonda, "you old poop." One hears such appellations as old shoe, little cabbage, animal, small stuff, titter tits, little donkey, and so on. Strange endearments, but to those using them, very meaningful—and affectionate.

When you think about endearments, they are in fact things which do endear, which do create love; the good lover uses them in addition to using your name and, sometimes, instead of it. Whatever the literal meaning of the term, if it is said with tenderness and feeling, it is symbolic of a special bond.

Other endearments are also warming but, perhaps, in danger of being overused. If a man calls all women honey or sweetheart or "you lovely thing you" or gorgeous, then these terms lose their meaning. Like "yes, dear" and "no, dear," they become almost reflexive politeness.

One woman used the term "darling" with her lover in tender moments of great significance. He then heard her use the term casually as theater people do, "Hello, darling, how are you today?" After that, the term lost its magic for him.

The special terms must be just that: special. They must be private for the couple, and they must not be used so often that they lose their impact.

SAY SOMETHING NICE:

THE ART OF COMPLIMENTS

The best way to turn a woman's head is to tell
her she has a beautiful profile.

—Sacha Guitry

No woman wants to be with a lover who shows a lack of understanding and compassion and never offers her praise or reassurance. Unlike the master of squelch (who we will discuss in more detail later in this chapter), a lover who compliments you is trying to build you up, not bring you down. He bolsters your confidence.

Everyone is in need of reassurance. Even egomaniacs have some doubts. Mae West was certainly self-confident, but she was only five feet tall. She considered this her great "shortcoming" and was always trying to find ways to make herself look taller. Who knows, maybe Barbra Streisand wonders if her nose looks funny? By all accounts, Marilyn Monroe was never sure that she was beautiful enough.

Providing reassurance is something of an art, and part of the art is knowing where reassurance is needed. If a woman knows that she is beautiful, or at least more beautiful than most, then having a man tell her she is pretty is perhaps nice to hear, but it does not have much of an impact. However, if he tells her she is bright, or at least bright enough, he may help her live more contentedly with a room-temperature IQ. Telling a homely girl she is beautiful will leave her thinking him a fool; telling her she has very unusual and expressive eyes, if she does, may make those eyes sparkle even more.

My sister had a new lover who always greeted her with warm enthusiasm, exclaiming, "You look just great!" and she glowed. But then he said it the next day and the next and the next. One morning, after a sleepless, tearful night, she showed up unshowered and uncombed, projecting red-eyed misery and dressed in an old sweatshirt and baggy jeans which were none too clean. He exclaimed with equally warm enthusiasm, "You look just great!" He wasn't really looking at her at all.

His was the same reflexive rhetoric that leads people to say, "Have a nice day!" to a man who is off to be executed.

The impact of a compliment also depends upon the language in which it is conveyed. One woman from England was startled when a cowboy from the Southwest whispered into her ear, "Babe, you are built like a brick shit house!" Phrasing it more politely—as in "a brick outhouse"—would not have helped her to understand that he meant she was especially well built and that he admired her.

Being a silver-tongued devil in a foreign language also has its hazards. There was a Spanish suitor who looked intensely at his ladylove and said with great emotion, "Your eyes are very impacting!" Perhaps it sounds better in the original Spanish.

In contrast, a woman friend of mine once got a billet-doux from a man praising her chatoyant eyes. After she looked it up (it means changing in luster like a cat's eye), she was enchanted. She had had chatoyant eyes for years and never realized it.

The compliment that counts is the one that is true, that shows he has been paying attention to you, and that reassures you that what he notices is worth noticing. With a real silver-tongued devil, there will be a wider range of comments than your head-to-toe physical appeal. He will remember that because a woman lives in a body, it does not mean that she is just a body. He will be cognizant and appreciative of emotion, personality, and experience as well.

Compliments are little love gifts. They tell you that you are worthy of notice.

PRATTLE AND PALAVER:

THINGS BETTER LEFT UNSAID

The real art of conversation is not only to say the
right thing in the right place but to leave unsaid
the wrong thing at the tempting moment.
—Dorothy Nevill, *Under Five Reigns*

Everyone who addresses the issue of relationships between men and women stresses the need for communication. Open communication. Free, honest, deep communication. A fundamental complaint that women have about their men is that they do not talk enough, and when they do talk, they do not talk about the right kinds of things. Personal things. Important things.

While both these points are valid, it does not necessarily follow that all communication improves a relationship. Some opinions, which are true and honest, are nevertheless better left unsaid. Tact requires the ability to keep one's tongue in check. Although talking is an important means of relating, it is not the only one, and it can be overdone. Listening to some men is like listening to a filibuster.

Many lovers who start out with the plea "Talk to me" end up repeating the plaintive request of the poet John Donne, "For God's sake, hold your tongue and let me love!"

Speeches, Lectures, and Sermons

The time to stop talking is when the other person nods his head affirmatively but says nothing.

—Henry S. Haskins

Conversation, good conversation, is essential in a good lover or a good companion, which is why the short freelance writer with no money and an erratic schedule may be seen as vastly superior to the tall stockbroker awash in money and leisurely pursuits.

You ought not to confuse all talk with real conversation. A good conversationalist should amuse and distract, creating a mood and inviting reflection. True conversation does not involve a monologist who explicitly entertains you with a string of anecdotes or jokes, someone who talks at you rather than with you. Dialogue, by definition, requires two. At its best, it resembles a good tennis match with the ball going constantly back and forth and kept in the air at all times.

The nature and quality of a man's conversation is prone to a number of occupational hazards. Professors profess; and often, with them, one is treated to an intensive lecture on the obscure, which provides more information than anyone ever wanted to know about rock formations in the Jurassic period or the spread of Grecian art forms during the Renaissance. Being familiar with the lecture format, in which they talk while others listen, they will not be fazed by your failure to respond. The same applies to politicians who are used to making speeches rather than conversing and to ministers who are used to sermonizing rather than conversing. The purposes of such pontificating are to persuade and reform, not to amuse and distract.

People who monopolize conversations are not like tennis players as much as they are like jugglers; they like to keep all of the balls circling under their own control. Conversation with them becomes a spectator sport, and they expect women to show their love by listening. And listening. And listening.

Such men don't want a lover as much as they want an audience. Unless you want to spend your time being a cheerleader rather than a player, beware.

Even conversation that does move back and forth can have some dulling components. Lawyers are trained to debate. Almost any innocent generalization on your part will call forth a documented case to establish the exception. If you present one side of the issue, they are likely to present the other side. Whether they actually believe it or not, they are oriented toward the case for the prosecution being balanced by the case for the defense. They don't converse; they argue.

Social scientists and would-be social scientists like to play psychiatrist, and you find yourself not so much conversing as giving a case history. Real psychiatrists are so imbued with their own ideology that they do this almost reflexively.

Journalists tend to do interviews rather than to converse and can sometimes seem like investigative reporters. As with psychiatrists and would-be psychiatrists, you wonder if somehow they are not surreptitiously taking notes. Their interest in you tends to last until they have assembled all relevant information about you at which time they become bored and have little to say. Such attention may initially be flattering, but on closer analysis, it is clear that such a dialogue is one in which they take a great deal from you without giving much back. You counter this technique as best you can by playing the game back and making the documentation of case histories at least a reciprocal one.

The best conversation includes the art of telling people a little *less* than they want to know.

INTERROGATIONS

*A question not to be asked is a question
not to be answered.*
—Robert Southey, *The Doctor*

Anybody can ask direct questions; and even when they are overly personal, somewhat rude or premature, in an amazing number of instances, they are answered. Interviewers with an agenda (like paparazzi) will unabashedly ask, "Why did you lose your last job?" "Do you think your wife is having an affair?" "Does it bother you that your daughter is a hooker?" "Since you say you don't believe in God anymore, why do you still go to church?"

With some people, there is almost nothing they won't hesitate to ask for they have discovered that confronted with direct questions, many people will give a direct answer even if they don't want to and even if they resent your asking. That might be an efficient approach if you are doing a survey or if you are a policeman who needs to do an interrogation in a hurry. But if you want to assess another person's character, it is not necessarily the best approach or the politest.

Samuel Johnson reminds us, "Questioning is not the mode of conversation among gentlemen." Nor should it be among lovers, except in the most oblique and subtle form.

Remember that a question is a request for information. Like other requests, it can be granted or turned down. Because a man asks a question does not mean that you have to answer it, provided you say something less direct than "it's none of your business."

Do not be bamboozled into discussing things you don't want to discuss or answering questions you don't want to answer. The counterpart of this, of course, is to be polite in return and not to interrogate your prospective lover.

Listen to what he tells you. He'll tell it all soon enough, and in a better frame of mind than if he has been put on the spot to account for himself.

A direct question is not only often presumptuous and, therefore, rude, but it also puts people on their guard. You tip your hand about what you want to find out, and people therefore structure their answers accordingly.

If you ask a man, "Do you think women should get equal pay for equal work?" he knows that the socially acceptable answer is yes. And so he says yes. That doesn't necessarily tell you a lot about his real attitudes toward women.

In assessing the character and attitudes of a potential lover, it is a good idea to borrow some techniques from psychiatry and use an indirect approach. A good starting point is simply to get the man to talk. You can use anything to stimulate the flow of conversation, keeping in mind as a model the psychiatrist who sits back quietly and occasionally says, "Uh-huh. Hmmm. Very interesting. What happened next?"

Stimulus for such a conversation can be anything, but it is less threatening if it is a neutral subject that has nothing to do with the two of you. For example, you might discuss a movie that the two of you have seen. Rather than ask, "What do you think about men who measure themselves only by how much money they make?" You can ask, "What did you think of the man, Carl, in the movie? Do you think he was happy?" You are asking in effect, "If you were Carl, would you be happy?"

Psychiatrists call this approach a projective technique. You don't ask the person directly; you ask him to project himself into another situation. The assumption is that the projected self is close to the real self.

Another example of projective techniques involves hypothetical questions. "What do you suppose would happen if . . . if Carl found out his wife had had an affair before they were married?" His answer to this tells you something about how he would have felt had his wife had an affair before they were married.

You don't learn things as fast this way, but what you do learn is more accurate than the off-the-cuff answers to direct questions.

THE CRITIC AND THE SNOB

If a critic's work were done by a woman it
would be called nagging.

—Evan Esar

While your man is talking, listen to his reflections on the state of the world and his reactions to his experiences in it. No one over sixteen really wants uncritical acceptance of everything and meaningless optimism that things are wonderful and they are only going to get even better. Neither, however, do you want a constant barrage of criticism from someone who can never be satisfied.

All adults develop a framework of comparison by which they judge their surroundings and rate their companions, and the discerning person finds some more desirable than others. One type of man to be wary of is the man who sets such incredibly high standards that almost nothing ever gets a first-class rating; and even Bo Derek herself, who personified the perfect female physique in the movie *Ten*, would rate a nine at most.

The ultimate critic is always assessing the current situation in the light of the wonderful past or the promising future and, therefore, always finding the present wanting in one way or another. The world is not entirely perfect, and he is getting impatient waiting for perfection.

If you go out for an elegant dinner, he notes that the pheasant is not as succulent as was the Pheasant Veronica he had last year in France. If the view is quite nice, it does not compare with the view from some Swiss chalet in the Alps. The theater production you have just seen was not bad perhaps, but the troupe will never have the professionalism of the performers at the Old Vic in London. Your new Honda Accord is nice, but it is not a Jaguar. A new Jaguar is nice, but it is not as worthy a car as an old Bentley. And so on.

This is the kind of man who is such a snob that if it were available, he would demand only twelve-year-old gin. He has such a wide basis of comparison and such absolute faith in his own judgment that nothing is ever quite up to snuff.

You can expect that you will meet with equally harsh judgments in his eyes. There are, doubtless, flaws in your clothes, your appearance, your career, your lifestyle, your friends, and even your dog; and if you stick around, you can be sure that his appraising eye will assess them all. The verdict of a resounding B+ will be expressed to you, complete with a detailed analysis of what is wrong.

You might learn a lot from this man, but you won't likely have much fun with him. He hardly ever jumps for joy or shouts out with delight. Not being able to savor the moment for what it is, for its own uniqueness, he is more apt to be smiling inwardly (or so he says, but how are you to tell?) while he tolerates the less-than-stellar efforts of the world around him.

How many of us are world-class? How many of us have access to the world-class level of anything?

THE MASTER OF SQUELCH

It is not more blessed to glib than to perceive.
—Louis A. Safian,
Two Thousand Insults for All Occasions

The gift of laughing at fate and at the paradoxes and inanities of life, the gift of laughing even at one's self and one's own pretensions should not be confused with various other ways of being funny. A lot of what passes for wit is really put-down humor, and the implicit message in sarcasm is often quite hostile.

The best of lovers will be able to laugh with you at the foibles of an imperfect world without necessarily laughing at you. Unfortunately, some people get carried away with the role of stand-up comic, playing, in effect, to an invisible audience or, even worse, a visible one. They are funny sometimes, but they always prick your balloon and leave you with a sinking deflated feeling instead of making you feel light and buoyant—which is what love does.

A woman of a certain age—which in her case was quite advanced—was dancing around her apartment with unusual abandon, making love to her mirror and getting off on bubblegum music. Her man, walking in, remarked roguishly, "Aren't you a little long in the tooth for this sort of thing?"

She wasn't, but after that crack, perhaps she will be. In any case, the harmless joy of the moment was effectively squelched.

There is a character in children's literature *Pollyanna* whose chief characteristic is that she is relentlessly determined to always make the best of everything. She has many misadventures, but she remains resolutely cheerful, always putting the most positive spin on the most dire events. She is insufferable. You do not want a man who really believes that all's for the best in this best of all possible worlds—a sort of grown-up Polyandy.

On the other hand, neither do you want a master of squelch. Mordant humor, which is both biting and caustic, may make for brilliant repartee; but it suggests a mentality that may be very hard to live with especially when you are the butt of his humor. Satire, to be comfortable, should be directed at some anonymous other. It is an ominous sign when it is instead directed at you or at those like you—women, for instance. The master of squelch may be more in love with language and with his skill at using it than with the people he describes.

In the gay world, such an approach is called bitch humor; but being bitchy does not require being gay, only a certain unsympathetic attitude and a barbed tongue.

You would do well to leave stand-up humor to the stand-up comedians and to be sure to watch them standing up. They will not likely have the healing grace of gentle humor, which is so often needed when one is lying down.

NONVERBAL DIALOGUE:

THE CONVERSATION OF GESTURES

*For a fine performance only two things
are absolutely necessary—maximum of
virility combined with the maximum of
delicacy.*

—Sir Thomas Beecham, *Beecham Stories*

When the British conductor Sir Thomas Beecham was talking about "performance," he presumably was thinking of musical performance, but his observation is equally valid when applied to sexual performance.

When a couple is together, they communicate in many ways other than with words. The way they meet or do not meet each other's eyes, the way they lean toward each other or away, and the way they touch or fail to touch transmit emotional messages. Body movements, tone of voice, or the inclinations of a person's head all convey specific emotions, ranging from tenderness to reproof. What is done is always interpreted in terms of how it is done. Even a dog knows the difference between being stumbled over and being kicked.

Nonverbal dialogue conveys many clues as to what a man or a woman do or do not want sexually at a particular time. The lover who is skilled at nonverbal communication is able to read your mind or, more precisely, to read your body so that he knows with a high level of accuracy if you do or do not want to go on to the next level of erotic intimacy, and if so, when.

The skilled lover never offers a proposition unless he is certain that the answer will be yes. This basic skill is very face-saving for everyone. Nobody wants to ask and to be turned down. Nobody wants to have to turn somebody down.

In the same way, the woman who wants to initiate sexual interaction should also be skilled enough to read a man's nonverbal communication so that before she makes a move, she correctly anticipates that his response will be positive.

Sometimes, it means that sexual interaction, especially among men and women who do not know each other well, will be tentative and indirect; but it is always better to be oblique than to be offensive. If the message is positive, then it will not take long for you—or him—to get that message.

Pay attention to how he touches you. Look at how he moves when you touch him. Pay attention to the eye contact or lack of it, the inclination of the head, the accidental and not-so-accidental contact of hands and feet. Seductive men will invite you to come closer to share more, but they will invite you in such a subtle way that if you do not choose to accept, you both can gracefully pretend the invitation never happened.

That way, no one can ever be really insulted, and no one's feelings can ever really be hurt.

Good Hands

I want a man with a slow hand
I want a lover with an easy touch
I want somebody who will spend some time
Not come and go in a heated rush
I want somebody who will understand
When it comes to love, I want a slow hand.
—Pointer Sisters, "Slow Hand"

You touch when making love, and making love is touching, in both senses of the word. The first touch is usually with the hands. Pay attention to those hands—not only to when he touches you but to where and how he touches you.

In many sports, the natural athlete is the one who has "good hands" and a spontaneous intuitive skill which is readily recognized but hard to define, much like an equestrian having a "good seat."

The man with good hands touches you in such a way that it makes you feel good. Your automatic response is to move slightly closer instead of drawing slightly back. He does not intrude too quickly on your personal space. The touch of good hands is light and tentative. If you respond with an answering pressure, then his may quickly become more firm. If you do not respond, or if you move away, he does not press the issue, literally or figuratively.

The man with good hands, who has mastered the conversation of gestures, generally begins to touch you in a neutral place. He may stroke your arm or touch your cheek. It is only after you, in some way, purr or show pleasure that he extends his touch.

The man with good hands uses touch for all kinds of communication, not only for the erotic kind. The man who only touches you when making love or when he wants to make love is not apt to make love very well.

The opposite of the man with good hands is the octopus who seems to be all hands. Beware of the groper. He is turned on by what teenage boys used to call copping a feel and teenage girls called having Russian hands and Roman fingers. Like the honey badger, he tends to go directly for the groin or, at the very least, your breasts.

He is concerned with what he feels when he touches you, which is fine as far as it goes, but it does not go far enough. He also needs to be concerned with how you feel when he touches you.

The groper is the man who squeezes your breast until it hurts, who rams his tongue down your throat with a grip that forces your back to bend until it hurts. He leaves you breathless but only because it is hard to breathe under the weight of two hundred pounds of callous, oblivious determination.

Sometimes, the groper is acting with the mistaken idea that what he is doing is being masterful and that women like dominant men. Perhaps some do on occasion, but unless pain is your thing, you would probably prefer to be mastered without being badly bruised.

Basically, the groper is thinking only about what he is feeling. When you can finally protest, he may be genuinely surprised. He mistakes your squirming to breathe for passion and your shrieks of pain for enthusiasm. He doesn't listen, and you will always find it hard to make him listen. He knows what women want or thinks he does, and he will go right ahead and give it to you regardless of your protestations.

This kind of groping is a kind of rape although not the kind that you can take to court. It is an imposition of the will and often of a stronger body as well, and when you can finally get away, you are wise to do so.

LOVE AND KISSES

There's a line between love and fascination
That's hard to see on an evening such as this,
For they both give the very same sensation
When you're lost in the magic of a kiss.
    —Ned Washington, "My Foolish Heart")

The final thing to trust is the kiss. A kiss may feel magically romantic, or sloppily slobbery, or blissfully gentle, or perhaps too rough and toothy. It can either escalate or kill a relationship. No wonder, so much fuss has been made about kissing. Who kisses whom? when? where? how? How precisely does he feel? Do his lips and tongue feel? Kissing occurs in 95 percent of human societies and is believed to have been first recorded in Vedic Sanskrit texts around 500 BC in India.

Little kids think that the real self, the essence, is to be found in the tummy. For adults, however, the real self is found in the head, behind the eyes, and most of all, behind the mouth. In a recent study, 59 percent of men and 66 percent of women said that they had become attracted to a person only after they had kissed the individual. Whereas, 50 percent of men and women reported in another study that their initial attraction to another person ended after the first kiss.

To lie with words is easy, but to lie with kisses is an unusual art. Those not familiar with the mores of commercial sex workers are surprised to learn that, often, a prostitute will do anything sexual that a john wants her to—except kiss him. She views sexual intercourse with kissing to be a more emotionally intimate activity than sexual intercourse without kissing. The mouth, being closer to the real self, is shared with more reluctance and is given with more meaning, not so much for its potential for sexual arousal as for its psychological import. Women are, however, more sexually aroused by kissing than are men.

A man can fake a lot of things—bravery, wealth, power, influence. But he can't fake great kissing. Only a man who does it with unassuming honesty and romantic readiness can achieve great kissing. He is someone who values the pursuit for what it is: a pleasurable end in itself, not a means to an end.

Pay attention to how he kisses you as well as to when and where. Does he savor your skin? Does he wait for your response and your encouragement, or does he grind on regardless? Remember, many men use kissing as a means to an end—namely, to gain sexual access. Just as kisses can reveal the real self, they can also reveal ineptness and a lack of awareness of you and your feelings.

There are few things sweeter than the right kiss at the right moment, and there are few things more oppressive than having to endure a suffocating and slobbering mouth that relentlessly obliterates your own.

ON FOREPLAY AND FEEDBACK

A good example of give and take is to take pains
to give pleasure.

—Evan Esar

Making love is a sensation of the body as well as a fantasy of the mind. To be good, it must be just right—not too fast or too slow, too soft or too hard, too hesitant or too insistent. The professional call girl must be willing to put up with inept lovers and must do so tactfully and cheerfully. She is not seeking her own pleasure; she is working and she gets paid accordingly. However, unless you are using your sexuality like a call girl, there is no need for you to settle for inadequate lovemaking, and it is better for your morale and your self-respect not to. But how do you know the skillful from the clumsy?

The first fact to remember is that no one but you can know what is sexually just right for you. You can feel your response getting better and warmer and more sensational—or not.

Remember as a child when you played Hide the Thimble? As people wandered around the room, they were told that they were either getting warmer or getting colder. Well, a lot of foreplay is just like that. He does something to you, you do something to him; and by gesture or words or little animal sounds, you tell each other if you are getting warmer or not.

To get these messages—assuming you are wise enough to send them out correctly—he must, first of all, be paying attention. He must be concerned with making you feel good. His concern for your comfort, his willingness to do what is needed to make you feel good will show in lots of other ways before you actually end up in bed.

In the film version of Hemingway's _For Whom the Bell Tolls_, Ingrid Bergman tells Gary Cooper, "I did feel the earth move." Sometimes, the earth does move, but you cannot arrange it anymore than you can arrange

156

a conventional earthquake. It requires not only physical passion but also a combination of urgency and romance and adrenaline and perhaps some celestial event such as an eclipse of the moon.

You need not, should not, expect the earth to move every time. But you should expect every encounter to be, at the very least, pleasant and friendly. You should expect every encounter to be emotionally satisfying whether or not it is orgasmic.

You do not have a right to earthquakes; but you do have a right to lovemaking that is, if not wonderful, at least consistently pleasurable.

Making Love To,
Making Love With

One can know nothing of giving aught that is worthy to give unless one also knows how to take.

—Havelock Ellis

The great lover, when or if you find him, is a man who takes seriously the experience of making love to a woman.

When he is with you, you are the center of his experience and you have his complete attention. He listens to your breathing; feels your hands, your body; and—by a blend of intuition, experience, and trial and error—has the uncanny ability to somehow know what you want now and what you want next and where and how and for how long. Marvelous.

The great lover concentrates on making you feel good, on making you have an orgasm, without demanding that you spend so much effort showing passion that you are distracted from feeling it. This kind of lovemaking is a gift to you.

It is the kind of cherishing and communication that is meant in the wedding prayer when the groom pledges, "With this ring, I thee wed; with my body, I thee worship; and with all my worldly goods, I thee endow." Unfortunately, many husbands are more willing or able to give worldly goods than to give this special kind of lovemaking. Some never give it at all; some only give it sometimes. When you do experience it, you recognize it as a present that is better than show tickets, better than a new dishwasher, better than the proverbial dozen roses. Attentive lovemaking is the ultimate gift of caring.

Being made love to is great. The next best thing is a man who can let you make love to him. I doubt that, in this case, it is always more blessed to give than to receive; but it is also a benison, and it is different and in its own way rewarding.

Not all men are comfortable with this kind of role. They need to be taught, sometimes, to lie back and enjoy it, to be passive while they are being pleasured, and to let someone else take responsibility for the staging of lovemaking and control the timing and the sequence of events.

Maybe it is because past generations associated being passive in bed with not being masculine. Maybe it is a sense that no nice woman could possibly enjoy *that*; and so while they could be made love to by a hooker who was later paid, they cannot feel good about being made love to by a nice woman whom they respect. No matter the reason, most men can eventually be taught to lie back and enjoy something that has so much intrinsic appeal. But then . . .

Best of all, for the very lucky, is the level of mutuality when you and he can make love *with* each other. Then there are no favors, no largesse, no performer, and no audience. Instead, there is a kind of reciprocal dance in which there is not one person who leads and another who follows and, if there is a lead, it moves back and forth from one to the other. Maybe that leads to the celebrated mutual orgasm; most likely it does not, but that does not matter. Because both of you do climax eventually, the lovemaking process is, at least, as important as the achievement of orgasm. Or as John Prine says in one of his songs, "The going is as important as the getting there."

Sometimes, it is more important. To have someone with whom you can make love is indeed to be blessed even if the relationship does not last and even if the lovemaking is a rare event.

Making love with someone does not just happen as spontaneously as is often portrayed on television and in the movies. It needs a certain kind of attitude and requires the availability of time, space, and attention—all of which must be planned for and made a priority. Amazingly, many people do not have this as a life goal, even people who have been there and should know better.

CHAPTER 6

"JUST LOOKING, THANKS": SCREENING OUT THE LONG SHOTS

True luck consists not in holding the best cards
at the table: luckiest is he who knows just when
to rise and go home.

—John Hay

Some of the men you meet seem, at first glance, to be quite delightful. They are charming and articulate, responsive and elegant, interesting and interested. When you listen to their spinning of tales, you don't find any trace of the bizarre or the dangerous. They like women, and they can show it. They seem to like you, and they can show it.

By all the conventional criteria, you should be feeling optimistic and enthusiastic. And yet . . . a small voice in the back of your head keeps reciting those words written by the seventeenth-century poet Tom Brown, "I do not love thee, Dr. Fell, the reasons why I cannot tell, but this I know and know full well, I do not love thee, Dr. Fell." On occasion, we all have had the feeling "I don't know why, but I don't like you" when meeting someone for the first time.

A man may have many of the traits that suggest he could be a divine lover for some woman, and yet not be the right one for you. A lover should not only be desirable in his own right, he should also be compatible with your own personality and background.

There are men with whom you *might* be happy but who are, for you, long shots. We are talking about men who are so different from you that their

161

personalities and priorities are hard to understand. This group includes men who want you but for the wrong reasons and men who will share but not very much. It also includes men who live too far away or those whose personality problems are too big for you to solve.

Such potential lovers do not present the same blatant bad-news problems of the obvious losers, but they may prove to be problematic just the same.

Flawed Gems: The Dubious Appeal of Difficult Men

First time you buy a house you see how pretty the paint is
and you buy it. The second time you look to see if
the basement has termites. It's the same with men.

—Lupe Velez

If you meet men with a fatal flaw, your decision is an easy one. The violent or hostile man or the misogynist is not a temptation because he is not to be seriously considered as a lover. The outcome of an affair with a man of this sort is a foregone conclusion, all of it negative.

If you meet a man with an off-putting flaw, or even several off-putting flaws, it is not so clear. An off-putting flaw can have important consequences, some of which seem ominous. All the same, even though there may be many things to suggest that a love affair with such a man might be difficult or challenging or problematic, it is still possible that it would turn out well. Perhaps the positive points outweigh the negative.

There are men who are dubious choices as lovers or, more precisely, men who have some dubious traits but who are not automatically disqualified. A difficult man is, well, difficult. Sometimes, being difficult is something you can accept. There are a few men who are gems. There are others who are gems, but when you look closely with your jeweler's glass, you discover they are flawed. A flawed gem may not be perfect, but it is a gem all the same. It may still be beautiful, and it may still be valuable.

MONOMANIACS: THE MOVERS AND SHAKERS

Music is my mistress, and she plays second fiddle to no one.

—Duke Ellington

When women describe, in general terms, the kind of man they are attracted to, they often suggest that in addition to being tall, dark, and handsome, he should also be successful. "It doesn't matter so much what he does," they will say, "as long as he does it well."

Perhaps a man who is a down-and-out failure is not very appealing and not much fun to be around. It is paradoxically true, however, that at the other end of the scale, the man who is very successful may not be much fun either. He may be rich and share his money with you. Or he may be famous and share his visibility with you. But he often does not share much of himself.

Very successful men are usually driven by a cause. It could be anything: to make a fortune in real estate, to pitch a perfect baseball game, to write a great novel, to make an important scientific discovery, to make a million by the time they are thirty.

The man with a Cause, written with a capital *C*, is a man with a mission; and the very intensity of his desire, no doubt, plays a large part in his eventual success. His energy, his fantasy life, his devotion and dedication are all focused on one project. Such a man is a model for other ambitious people: he has learned a lot of the secrets of getting what he wants, and his track record is likely to far exceed that of other men. When you ask him what he wants, he has a ready and precise answer, and the earlier in life that answer has come to him, the more successful he is likely to be.

The man with a Cause is often a disappointment as a lover. He has a full-time passion already, a demanding mistress in the form of a career or specific goal, and that is likely to be a more pervasive obligation than any commitment to a lover or a wife and family would ever be.

Psychoanalysts believe that a great deal of creative energy is really sublimated sexuality, that the sex drive is channeled and transformed into a quest for art or music or money. Whether or not this is actually true is hard to determine; but it is certainly true that there is, for any one person, only so much time and energy. The man with a Cause, who has a fanatical obsession or career commitment, has little time left over to devote to love. Referring to Henry Kissinger, certainly a man to take his career seriously, Barbara Howar remarked, "Henry's idea of love is to slow the car down to thirty miles an hour when he drops you off at the door."

Love, as we have been discussing it here, is a privilege of leisure. Above all else, love takes time. It needs time for talk, time for self-analysis and feeling, time for making love on peaceful afternoons and well into the morning. Leisure means not only enough money so that one does not need to work and worry all the time but also the wherewithal or freedom to use that leisure for the development of a certain kind of erotic life.

People on more hectic schedules may have the same potential—maybe even many of the same initial impulses—only they are not fully actualized because they are too busy. Their priorities are different. Success has a price, and that price is most likely to be borne in the private sphere of emotion and eroticism. In his book *Wiseguy*, Nicholas Pileggi describes it well, "The men who really wield, retain, and covet power are the kind who answer bedside phones while making love."

The men who are the most dedicated to their careers—be they in the professions, politics, or the arts—are generally the most successful; but they are not necessarily the most successful lovers. You can gain a great deal by association with movers and shakers, but you are not likely to develop a loving relationship and a rewarding reciprocity with them or with men such as these.

Some women are like groupies and get off on being with a celebrity. Unless you are in this category, don't expect very much when you invite a monomaniac into your bed. Assuming he has time to ejaculate, he has done his moving and shaking elsewhere. And never ever expect him to last through to a leisurely breakfast the morning after.

The Charming Con Man

*Charm seems to me to be the ability to captivate other
people without doing anything about it. The "charm" of it is
that one cannot define its ingredients.*
                —Rudolf Bing of the Metropolitan Opera

Women who desire a man to be tall, dark, handsome, and successful may also add "charming" to their list of ideal characteristics. Some men who have the "happy fierceness" associated with presence have an intrinsic appeal in their manner and presentation. Others, who seem to have it, have merely learned to go through the motions, adopting an appealing persona in much the same way that a good salesman or a good confidence man learns to tailor his responses to what his audience or victim wants to hear.

If there was ever a single sentence to alert you to the approach of trouble, it is the apparently innocuous comment: "He can be quite charming, you know." This may not sound like faint praise, but it is. It is quite different from the comment: "He *is* charming." The man who "can be" charming is commented upon, in the first place, because charm is not his natural state and it comes as some surprise to discover that sometimes he has it. Such a reflection also tells you that charm is something which he can deliberately turn on if he wants to, which tells you in advance that he will also turn it off when he is so inclined.

The man who "can be" charming is not only manipulative but is the sort who uses whatever sex appeal he may have as a tool for or a means of manipulation. Rather than feeling warmed and flattered by a woman's response to him, he is likely to be vaguely contemptuous at her being so easily taken in. Real charm in a man stems from his genuine affection for women; acting charming stems from a well-disguised wish to dominate, manipulate, or deflect.

Hire a charming con man as your top salesman, but don't make the mistake of falling in love with his superficialities.

Birds of a (Different) Feather

*A man only understands what is akin to something
already existing in himself.*
> —Frederic Amiel, Swiss Philosopher

One dimension of loving is the feeling that you understand the other person and that he understands you. The more completely you can feel that his actions are predictable and the sources of his emotions comprehensible, the more you can be tolerant of his behavior and appreciative of his actions. Whether or not you *really* understand him, and vice versa, is perhaps of secondary importance to the *belief* that you do.

Some men who would make exemplary lovers for some women may not be quite right for you either because you do not understand the issues which are of prime concern to them or because you do not understand the morality or lack of it which governs their behavior. They remain enigmas to you and may, therefore, be difficult or impossible to relate to satisfactorily.

Although similarly held worldviews can be important for compatibility, some differences are not all that critical. For instance, there is no need to pick a lover who is in the same profession as you are. In fact, there are a number of disadvantages when this occurs, not the least of which is the implicit problem of too direct competition. You can have good relationships with people in diverse fields as long as you have some understanding of what their work involves.

The more passionate you are about your work and the more passionate he is about his, the more important it is that you be in some way fellow travelers. This means that your fields of interests must at least be conterminous—that is, share some boundary where they touch on common ground. Anthropologists are like sociologists, singers are like musicians, chemists are like physicists, and salesmen of any product have a lot in common with all other salesmen.

If there is, at least, some sharing of areas of interest, the work-focused conversation of one party has a chance of striking a spark of sympathy and comprehension in the other.

If a potential lover is in a totally different field, talking about your work will be like speaking Greek to a non-Greek and you must then make the uncomfortable choice between keeping silent or being alternately bored and boring. Of course, you can take the time to learn about your lover's profession; but if he does not reciprocate by learning about yours, you are very likely to be resentful, which is hardly an auspicious foundation on which to build a relationship.

A lover of similar, if not identical, interests is of special importance when one of you is involved in a field of great passion such as religion or politics. If you meet a union organizer who is devoted to the cause and you think that an "agitator" is something in a washing machine, you are headed for trouble. Not only will you not appreciate his greatness and his accomplishments, such as they may be, but you will also be unwilling to recognize the legitimacy in his mind of the many occasions when his passion for the world and its concerns will take precedence over his passion for you.

If your lover is a man of the cloth or aspires to be one, then even if you do not share the same religion exactly, it is important that you, at least, share enough of the spiritual worldview to be sympathetic with matters of conscience and with such psychological dynamics as the inevitable crisis of faith. The happy heathen has no patience with such problems. From the start, you will find such men with their manifold doubts unfulfilling as lovers, no matter how passionate the Elmer Gantry part of them remains.

The Cat Who Walks by Himself

The worst cliques are those which consist of one man.
—George Bernard Shaw, *Back to Methuselah*

North American culture tends to be group oriented. Our psychologists tend to be skeptical of the mental health of the isolate or the hermit. We expect people to seek pleasure in socializing, and we look somewhat askance at the individualist who prefers his own company.

Suspicion of the solitary life may be overdone. The preference for a good book versus a bad party—or even a good one—is a legitimate choice. Many of the most creative and worthwhile people are not very sociable and reserve their time and energy for more cerebral pleasures. In looking for a desirable lover, it is not necessary to seek out a "good-time Charlie" who is always surrounded by people and aims to be the life of every party.

On the other hand, you might think twice about a man who has *no* friends at all. People who are capable of forming good lasting relationships do so. They understand the demands and the rewards of such involvements and are willing to invest in them. For such friendships to persist over many years, they must have learned the fundamentals of give-and-take.

In talking with a prospective lover, ask him about his friends. He may be temporarily friendless if he is living in unusual circumstances, such as having just moved or just come out of a messy divorce. Usually, however, it is gratifying to find a man who has a number of long-term friendships which he values. How long "long-term" is depends, of course, on his age. For a man of twenty, an "old" friend may be someone who has been a buddy for three or four years. For a man of forty, an "old" friend may stretch back for ten to fifteen years or more.

The length of friendships also depends upon how mobile a person has been. If one moves from New York to Los Angeles or some other impossibly long distance, then it is very difficult to maintain even close friendships on more than an e-mail basis.

Friendships are also likely to suffer if one of the friends moves up in the world. There is no reason why a mechanic with a grade-eight education cannot remain friends with his school chum who has since become a nuclear physicist, but it is unlikely to happen. The nuclear physicist, however, if he is the kind of man who values friendships, should have soon made other friends among his peers, as should have the mechanic.

The man who has *no* close friends is obviously a man who does not do well in intimate relationships and probably does not seek them out. He may be saying, like Greta Garbo, "I want to be alone."

Greta claims what she really said was "I want to be left alone," which is quite a different message.

THE SECRETIVE MAN

*Too much secrecy in our affairs and too little are
equally indicative of a weak spirit.*
—Luc de Clapiers, Marquis de Vauvenargues,
Reflections and Maxims

A variation on the man who is a hermit, or would like to be, is the man who is so "closed" about himself and his dealings that you never learn anything about him. You should be especially cautious when you find someone who is secretive out of habit almost like a compulsive liar will lie when there is no necessity to do so.

One man I knew never called any of his acquaintances by name. He would say, "I bet twenty dollars on the game with a guy I know." It would later turn out that the mysterious person was old Harry who he has lunch with at the office several times a week. Why is that a secret? Either he really has something to hide, meaning there is almost nothing about himself that can stand up to scrutiny in the light of day, or he is so insecure that the only way he believes anyone can like or approve of him is if he maintains this extreme secrecy.

I would designate this kind of behavior as pathological privacy. Beware of it as you would other compulsive pathologies.

THE FAN CLUB

Only God, my dear
Could love you for yourself alone
And not your yellow hair.
—William Butler Yeats, "For Anne Gregory"

Consider for a moment the fortunate woman who is blessed with the ability to do something extraordinarily well. It might be playing bridge or running marathons or singing an operatic aria. It might be breathing in and out under a dangerously low neckline or doing Marilyn Monroe imitations or stripping off one's clothes in a bar while pretending to dance or executing a perfect pirouette in a corps de ballet.

Whatever your particular talent, there will emerge from the woodwork some men who are genuine fans and who are extraordinarily impressed with your accomplishments. You don't need to be a movie star to be imbued with starlike qualities by someone who announces his pleasure in worshipping at your feet.

Having fans is great for your ego and is often exceedingly useful for your career or for the pursuit of your particular avocation. It goes without saying that it is a great way to meet men. Stage-door johnnies come in all ages and shapes; there's a wide repertoire.

It is important to remember, however, that having a man as a fan, no matter how enthusiastic and sincere, does not necessarily qualify him as a lover. Members of your personal fan club have a one-dimensional focus. The man is impressed with *one* of your salient abilities, which does not necessarily mean he will accept the whole package when he comes to know you. What you need in a lover is a man who takes genuine pride and pleasure in your accomplishments, even your more modest ones, but who does not consider you only in those terms.

172

Ask yourself: Would he still want to go out with me if I hadn't won the tennis championship, published the book, gotten the scholarship? Would he still love me if I couldn't dance or draw or sing?

The lover who loves you only for your accomplishments rather than for other reasons as well is giving only conditional love. It will be of limited comfort at four in the morning the night before the awards are announced.

The "fan club" lover draws on your accomplishments to add them to his own. He is, in some ways, like a groupie. A man may get satisfaction out of having a beautiful girl on his arm for his friends to admire as a showpiece, but his attitude toward the girl is as a status prop.

Margaret Trudeau, the wife of former Canadian prime minister Pierre Elliott Trudeau, was on the right track when she proclaimed, "I can't be a rose in any man's lapel."

The Faraway Lover

Absence extinguishes small passions and increases
great ones, as the wind will blow out a candle and
blow in a fire.
—François, Duc de La Rochefoucauld, Maxims

One problem faced by the two-career couple is that of being able to pursue their respective professions in the same city. When this is not possible, one solution to the crisis of having to choose between one's marriage and one's work has been to stay married but to live apart in different cities.

The long-distance marriage is a relatively new phenomenon, but from all accounts, it seems to be very difficult to maintain. The constraints of marriage, which are considerable, often outweigh the benefits of being a wife.

However, a long-distance love affair is not as constraining and may be a rewarding possibility. If you are picking a lover, why not pick one in another city? Even in another country? He would not be a good prospect for a husband unless one or the other of you could relocate, but he may be fine for a series of exciting and rewarding encounters.

Some couples have managed to conduct meaningful and erotic love affairs over ten, fifteen, or even twenty years while living thousands of miles apart. It is not an easy alternative, but it can be done. If you have a real ambivalence about marriage, then a marriagelike arrangement in which you are involved intensely but intermittently may be the ideal solution. There is an excitement and a vitality which can be maintained for a long time because you are never around each other long enough to get tired of each other or to get caught in deadly routines.

One such part-time mistress explained, "When Jonathan is at home in Seattle, I'm on my own again, and I love it. I don't have to cook or be home on time. I play my music full blast at all hours and don't pick up my shoes. I leave the car parked in the driveway. I put on a facial mask and chat on the phone for hours. But then I get bored. Bored and lonely.

"Before I get too bored, Jonathan comes back to town. I fly around and make myself beautiful and get everything straightened up. We fall on each other and have a little 'honeymoon' for a week or two.

"Before I get resentful that I have to pick up his shoes as well as my own, he is gone again. Some nights peanut butter, some nights *canard à l'orange*. Contrast is everything. It keeps us up. When we are together, we are always on, and it's been years now. Why get married and spoil it?"

A successful long-distance affair depends a lot on being able to manage the logistics without too much stress. You need to be able to communicate effectively on the telephone and to resign yourself to horrendous telephone bills. It helps a lot if you have learned to write effective e-mails or letters although curling up by the fire to read nice e-mails on your Blackberry or a specially delivered letter is still not the same as curling up by the fire with a more substantial presence.

Couples in a long-distance affair need to have the kinds of jobs that leave their work time flexible. Since few people can work out their own schedules as someone who freelances could, that means a lot of juggling of long weekends and sick leave and holidays. A long-distance affair also demands a high-enough level of affluence to make frequent travel possible.

Not only affluence, endurance is also needed. Commuter travel takes planning and organization and the ability to defer gratification and to tolerate frustration of many kinds. Planes are late, schedules get changed, storms occur, flights get canceled, suitcases get lost. You must be willing to slog along late at night, schlepping your suitcase onto the last airport bus, humming cheerfully the motto of the New York City mail carriers: "Neither snow nor rain nor heat nor gloom of night stays this courier from the swift completion of my appointed rounds." You might add to that "neither strikes nor traffic jams nor airport security checks."

Coming and Going

If I see you sad, my heart breaks and my sadness increases;
if you are gay and silly with your friends, I reproach you with
forgetting so soon that we have been separated three days;
you have a light heart then, not affected by any deep
sentiment. As you see, I am not easy to satisfy.
—Napoleon Bonaparte to Empress Josephine

Parting may be sweet sorrow, but it is a sweetness that can begin to cloy if you have to do it all the time. In a long-distance relationship, you are never quite sure where you are or where you stand; and often, it is literally hard to remember if you are coming or going. You spend a lot of time packing and unpacking. You spend a lot of time wondering how you are supposed to be feeling.

On the one hand, a love affair brings out desire and dependency. "I want you, I need you, I love you," sang Elvis Presley. If you love, then you also need and want. But in the long-distance affair, the person you want is not always there and you have to make do without always getting what you need from him.

On the other hand, you don't want to feel too much desire and too much dependency, or you will be too despondent when you are separated. Supposedly, a mature adult is self-sufficient and self-contained enough to be able to take temporary separations in stride.

Long-distance lovers are often not too sure just what they are feeling. Worse, they are often not too sure what their absent playmates want them to be feeling.

One woman who managed a long-term long-distance affair recounted her sense of frustration with the double messages in the dialogue. "Jeffrey would be away for weeks and come home and say, 'Did you miss me?' The first time, I told him the truth and said, 'Yes, terribly. I was so sad and lonely.' So he gave me a lecture about how I was a big girl and about how women were too dependent on men and did not take responsibility for themselves.

"So the next time he was away, I took a course in jazzercise and met some terrific people and learned how to windsurf and even gave a party. And he came home and said, 'Did you miss me?' And I said, 'Yes, but I didn't pine. I went out and did this and that.'

"And he looked hurt and said, 'What's the point of being lovers if it's just out of sight, out of mind before my plane is even out of sight?'

"So I can't win. If I'm sad, he feels guilty. If I'm not sad, he feels rejected. I'm working on just the right air of wistful melancholy borne with quiet courage."

The Importance of

Being Present

When I can't fondle the hand I'm fond of,
I fondle the hand at hand;
When I'm not near the girl I love,
I love the girl I'm near.
—Yip Harburg, Finian's Rainbow

Conducting a rewarding love affair long-distance is possible, if one has the time and the money and is willing to make the effort. It seems unlikely, however, that one can conduct a monogamous love affair long-distance. To paraphrase a familiar saying, "Absence makes the heart grow fonder—of whom let absent lovers ponder."

If you have a long-distance lover, you probably have a lover you will have to share. There are exceptions to this of course. The dedicated scientist or frantically busy businessman may be quite content to devote all of himself to his work and then, when he does take time off, to devote all of himself to you and to the joy of the encounter. Such a man is either totally at work or totally at play; and as long as he plays often enough, you may find it quite delightful, especially if you also have other priorities in your own life.

A man who is in some way ill or preoccupied or simply elderly may be more or less content to see you when the occasion permits and to be celibate in between those times. It seems unlikely, but it makes a good story; and if you demand an explanation of his extracurricular activities, that is what he is most likely to say.

If you take a long-distance lover, you need to acknowledge the special circumstances of the situation and follow two basic rules. First, you do not ask him to account for his time and for his being with other women when he is not with you. He may or may not have other affairs—as long as you are lovers from a distance, that is not part of your legitimate concern. If you want to have an exclusive listing, then move to where he is or vice versa. Meanwhile, don't ask.

Second, you do not simply arrive in town and assume that he will be overjoyed to see you. You must make arrangements in advance as you expect him to do with you, and you must stick to them. It may be all right to be a little late and to have to postpone your trip for a few days for a good reason. It is unfair to arrive a few days early.

All you can ask of the long-distance lover is that when you are together, for that period of time, you are his first priority and have his complete attention. In his book *The Complete Idiot's Guide to Long-Distance Relationships*, Seetha Narayan offers a lot of insights into how to make a long-distance relationship workable and rewarding. Its practical advice may be useful if you think a long-distance relationship is in your future travels.

Love as Psychotherapy

*Love—incomparably the greatest psychotherapeutic
agent—is something that professional psychiatry
cannot of itself create, focus, nor release.*
—Gordon W. Allport, The Individual and His Religion

Many people are beset with what might be termed mental problems which are distressing to them but not extreme enough to require psychotherapy. They are not insane or clinically depressed or suicidal, but they are unhappy, sometimes desperately so. According to the folklore, the best cure for unhappiness, depression, angst, anxiety, and other sources of sadness is someone to love and someone to love you back.

The folklore may well be right, but the prescription is difficult to arrange on demand. One kind of man who can be very problematic is the man who is unhappy with himself and life, leading some or another version of quiet desperation; he focuses upon you as *the* answer, as the person who will save him from himself. Even if you want to undertake this daunting therapeutic task, you will find that you are unlikely to be successful. His problems with living are in all probability caused by factors other than simply a lack of love, and they will likely require more than love to resolve them.

THE GRAY ITCH

Unhappy middle-aged man to his psychiatrist:
"Here I am at the dangerous age and there's
no danger!"

—Chon Day, Psychology Today

There comes a time in a man's life when something forces him to realize that he is no longer a promising young man who is going to do great things. Rather, he is a man who has—or has not—done something with his time but who, in any case, is unlikely to do very much more. He can see, or thinks he can see, what life will be like for the rest of his life: this job, going only so far in terms of promotion; this income, going only so far in terms of raises; this wife, going only so far in terms of a relationship. There is an awful realization: this is it, this is real life.

The man with such insight is ripe for a midlife crisis or perhaps the first of several midlife crises. In many instances, his urge to do something before it is too late is immediately manifested in the urge to do something to a woman, preferably a much younger woman, preferably a pretty one.

He may want to do something about his marriage and his career as well. But those areas take a lot of effort and planning and may have real and unpleasant consequences as well. On the other hand, the possibility of doing something about his sex life and his virility is as close as the nearest strip club or the Internet.

The man experiencing a midlife crisis is not a rational creature. What he is experiencing is an emotional crisis, which is more than an intellectual one, and it does not leave him in a frame of mind conducive to sound decision making. Such a lover is easy to seduce and has the added advantage of enthusiasm. Since he is emotionally vulnerable, he is ready to fall in love or in lust or in *something*. He is a plum ripe for the picking. Such offerings are often too good to pass up, and they can certainly be very entertaining.

A love affair that begins in a man's midlife crisis is not likely to be very stable, but it can be great fun while it lasts. The man with the gray itch is given to hyperbole. He gets carried away with the situation and the resurgence of emotion he experiences and, under such circumstances, may make rather extravagant declarations. If you are a young woman who's the focus of these attentions, put the diamonds in the vault, but do not take the proclamations too seriously. He loves you, yes; but he would have loved any other sweet, understanding young thing who happened to come along at the right time. He does not love *you* so much as he loves the *idea* of you, which is not quite the same thing. When a man of fifty falls in love with a girl of twenty, it is not her youth he is seeking, but his own.

For the man in a midlife crisis, the young mistress plays the flesh-and-blood incarnation of his fantasies, and many of those fantasies have to do with magically being able to become young again. As the mistress, you can create that illusion at least temporarily. When a psychiatrist helps a distraught patient who is understandably grateful, that patient may fall in love with the psychiatrist, who is viewed as a wonderful savior. This process is called transference and is a well-known phenomenon in therapy, which both psychiatrist and patient have to guard against. If you help to scratch the gray itch, such transference may also happen to you.

When the man of middle years finds in you a congenial young playmate, he may be tempted to consider his problems solved. He can transfer all his trouble and frustration on to you and then sit back and wait to be saved. But when he finds out you cannot save him and when he sees that sometimes you are not even trying very hard, he is likely to be disappointed and then angry. You can explain to him, "I never promised you a rose garden." But since he was hoping for a rose garden, and indeed secretly expecting one, he will not be consoled.

One day, he is likely to wake up and realize that he is *still* fifty-seven years old, *still* in a dead-end job, *still* with a wife he does not like, and *still* with two kids who are flunking out of college. It may well seem to him that his failure to solve these problems has somehow been your fault.

THE OVERWHELMED

If you love me, what is that to me?
—Jadah Vaughn

Every once in a while, you meet a man who thinks you are just fabulous! He takes one look at you and sort of swoons like fair maidens did in melodramatic comedies. He finds you absolutely wonderful from your gorgeous eyes to your delectable pinkies and announces his desire to sit at your feet for the rest of his life and take care of you. Your first reaction is a rush of pleasure. Finally, a man who can see that you actually are a combination of Jessica Simpson, Simone de Beauvoir, Amelia Earhart, and Madame Eve Curie with just a touch of Sharon Stone thrown in.

It should soon occur to you, however, that sitting at your feet does not leave him in a position to support you and that as soon as you try to move, you will trip over him. The man who is overwhelmed by you is a nice change from the vast majority of men who persist in being underwhelmed. Neither, however, makes for a very balanced relationship.

The man who is too impressed and too full of awe is telling you more about his own emotional hunger than he is about your wonderfulness. This kind of reaching out is more like clutching, and it is dangerous. For a man to be smitten is flattering and exciting. If he shows that he is greatly drawn to you and wants to know you better, terrific. But if you find that he skipped all the intermediate steps and is already acting as if he were seriously in love with you, watch out. The lover who is responsive and who is not afraid of feeling is wonderful, but the lover who is too responsive too fast is showing a kind of desperate hunger, which is likely too desperate for a good relationship.

The lover who is too overwhelmed is the lover who is on the verge of an obsession. He is willing to put himself entirely in your hands. You might like the sense of power, but you soon will not like the sense of responsibility.

The emotionally desperate man will make inordinate demands on you, and when you cannot fulfill them, he will be inordinately upset. His excess of feeling is a danger sign of other kinds of excesses to follow: persistence, prying, possessiveness, jealousy, and incipient violence.

Among the classical Chinese, there is a tradition that saving someone's life made you responsible for him. If a man was drowning in the canal and you came along and fished him out, then from that point on, you were obligated to continue to care for him. The man who is overwhelmed is saying, in effect, "Save my life."

If after knowing you for one night he swears that he loves you and cannot live without you and must have you or he will die, do not be warmed: *be warned*.

CHAPTER 7

MÉSALLIANCES: SELECTING EXOTIC LOVERS

It is the addition of strangeness to beauty
that constitutes the romantic character of art.
—Walter Pater, *Appreciation*

When a marriage occurs between two persons who are thought to be unsuitable for each other, as for example between a nobleman and a chorus girl, the French term for such a union is a "mésalliance."

The mésalliance marriage is beset by many perils in addition to those faced by every marriage. The family and friends of one person often fail to accept the family and friends of the other. If the union goes across racial lines, the white spouse faces racism for the first time and has to learn to cope with it and to accept its inevitable impact on the children. The poor person who "marries up" has to learn how to live the lifestyle of the rich; the rich person who "marries down" has to come to terms with the ever-present possibility that he was married for his money. And so on.

However, when a woman and a man from diverse backgrounds come together and become lovers, with no intention of getting married, the situation can be quite different. An exotic man can be acceptable as a lover even though, if you were to marry him, the union would be seen as a mésalliance.

Marriage is always a public arrangement and is everybody's business; a love affair, however, can be a private concern and is assumed to be nobody's business.

THE MAGIC OF MYSTERY

*The boy next door, however exceptional,
always seems like a boy: he is too easily
understood. The mysterious stranger from
Madagascar, however ordinary, always seems
like a fascinating man: you understand
him not at all.*

—Jayson VanVerten

An involvement with an exotic lover allows you the opportunity to expand your experience beyond the limitations of conventional social interaction. The term "exotic" is an appealing one, designating an attractive kind of strangeness. Apart from the use of the term to describe dancers (in which case it merely means ecdysiasts or strippers and has no bearing on what we are talking about), "exotic" has two related meanings.

It can refer to something which is foreign in origin and which has not yet been assimilated. For example, in our culture, the Japanese dish tempura is foreign and exotic; but the ubiquitous pizza, although Italian in origin, has become as all-American as apple pie and is therefore no longer exotic.

It is the second meaning of the term that concerns us here. Something exotic is striking or unusual in effect: it is glamorous and exciting by virtue of being strange. For a given woman, an exotic lover includes anyone who, as a husband, would be considered too different from herself to be the kind of person she should marry.

New Horizons

Yet all experience is an arch where through
Gleams that untravelled world, whose margin fades
For ever and for ever when I move.
                    —Alfred Lord Tennyson, "Ulysses"

Most people spend most of their time interacting in the confines of rather narrow social boundaries. They stick to their own kind and are expected to do so. They interact in ghettos of one kind or another, perhaps not so much because of prejudice as because the kind of people they are most likely to meet turn out to be, by and large, much like themselves.

Several dimensions are involved. White women, for the most part, interact with other white people. They tend to spend time with people of the same social class—be it upper, middle, or lower—that means people with the same levels of education and wealth and with many parallels in terms of lifestyle. Whether or not religion *per se* is very important, Christians tend to spend time with other Christians and Jews with other Jews. Add to that an expectation of age stratification, which creates almost an age ghetto. Except for one's own parents or one's own children, the young associate with the young, the middle-aged with the middle-aged, and the old with the old however these life stages are defined. People in the workplace may interact with various age groups in the course of carrying out their jobs; but at the end of the workday, when socializing outside the workplace, they are likely to do so with those relatively close to them in age.

When you look at your friends, most likely, they will turn out to be a homogeneous group. Most are in the same general age group, most are of the same race and religion, and most have about the same amount of education and money. Often, they are in the same line of work and live in similar neighborhoods. They are people like yourself.

There is nothing wrong with friendships with people like yourself. You understand them easily, you can empathize with their problems, you can make yourself understood. There is nothing wrong with such friendships—except that they can become very predictable. You know these friends so well that they seldom surprise, seldom outrage, seldom enlighten you. The hazard of such homogenized associations can be serious in a friendship and fatal in a love affair. It is the hazard of boredom.

A man who is different from you is exciting because he provides a contrast to you, a new perspective. The exotic man is mysterious, and you are challenged to solve the mystery. He has the additional appeal, and danger, of forbidden fruit. He may be considered too old for you or too young. In a white community, a black man is exotic; in a black community, a white man is. The exotic lover may be, in some way, unpresentable by virtue of what he does or who he is or where he comes from. He is certainly not the boy next door. The contrast between you, the sense of being different, is simultaneously a source of delight and a source of problems.

MUDDLED MOTIVATIONS

A woman is more influenced by what she
suspects than by what she is told.
—Robert C. Edwards

In talking about exotic lovers, it's important from the outset to insert a word of warning. Exotic relationships are by definition "unconventional." They involve relationships which outsiders regard as unsuitable because they violate some major or minor community taboo.

When a girl falls in love with the boy next door, no one asks, "Why him?" Her motivation is taken as being as obvious as the rising of sap in the spring and as the hormonal explosion that sends young blood singing in young veins. If the boy next door loves her back, we are charmed by their innocence and exuberance whether they are shy sweethearts of eight or passionate steadies of eighteen.

However, if that same girl were to fall in love with an older man from India, Saudi Arabia, or Central America, we would instantly demand an explanation of "Why him?" Just being "in love" does not seem to be an adequate explanation. "Is he rich enough to be worth it?" asks your aunt. "Do you think she has a father complex?" asks your cousin who is a sophomore majoring in psychology.

A little psychology goes a long way.

"He just has the usual obsession about white women," declares your bigoted uncle. "Lots of foreigners are desperate to become citizens," reflects your other uncle who is a lawyer.

All of these questionings and ponderings take their toll even if you defend yourself stoutly against such allegations. The toll is that you are forced to examine your own motivations more than most people do and, in the process, you also have to reflect upon the motives of the man in question. An older

190

woman who was happily financing her young lover through his last year of medical school overheard one of his catty friends remark, "Well, it is one alternative if you can't get a scholarship." She knew he loved her for herself alone and not for her tuition fees. Didn't he?

Examining motives raises the specter of doubt. Every time there is an unconventional liaison, the motives of the man and woman involved will be suspect to everyone, including each of the two people in the relationship. This is a fact of life that you must accept if you seek out what others would deem "unsuitable" men. It is the price you pay for being a nonconformist. If you can accept it, then you need only follow two rules. First, pay attention only to your own suspicions, not to those of others. Second, having examined your lover's responses and your own and found them reasonably reassuring, do your best to disregard them.

In Praise of Older Men

*A man is young if a lady can make him happy
or unhappy. He enters middle age when a lady
can make him happy, but can no longer make him
unhappy. He is old and gone if a lady can make
him neither happy or unhappy.*
                        —Morris Rosenthal, at age seventy-five

There is a strong norm in our society, as indeed in most societies, that in any particular couple, the man should be older than the woman. Usually, the age gap is slight, with an average difference in married couples of only two or three years. Sometimes, there is a more substantial difference.

How great a gap in years does it take to make a significant social or psychological difference for a couple? The answer depends in part on the age of the partners involved. If they are quite young, then a difference of only ten years can seem like quite a bit. Consider, for example, a woman of eighteen who is just barely an adult and a man of twenty-eight who has been a man for some time. Later on, ten years is not very much. If that woman is in her late twenties or older, the age gap would need to be closer to a generation to be viewed as a difference. How many years it takes to make a generation is not clear, but usually, fifteen years would represent a significant difference and twenty years even more so.

In only about 10 percent of marriages is the husband ten or more years older than his wife. And only about 3 percent involves a husband fifteen or more years older. If we consider all couples, however, rather than only married couples, the proportion is doubtlessly much higher. There may be many men who would like to have a mistress much younger than themselves without necessarily wanting to marry her.

From the other perspective, having a lover much older than you are may be acceptable, whereas having a much older husband may not be. There is a certain truth to the folk saying that the man who marries a much younger bride is like a man who buys a book for someone else to read.

In addition, there is the very real problem of differential life expectancy. Women tend to live six or seven years longer than men, so even if a couple is of the same age, the woman is more likely to be left a widow than he is to be left a widower. Women who are not especially drawn to the idea of marriage and the "wife" role may still concede that it would, perhaps, be nice in the future to have someone to grow old with and to provide companionship in old age. This is one comfort of marriage the older man is almost certain not to provide. Marriage to a man twenty, fifteen, or even ten years your senior amounts to voluntary widowhood or years of caregiving at a time when you have already reared your children and you want to relax and enjoy life a little.

In the short range, however, such a man may be a satisfying, if unorthodox, choice for a lover.

First Love, Last Love

Men always want to be a woman's first love.
Women have a more subtle instinct: What they like
is to be a man's last romance.

—Oscar Wilde

One advantage of being with an older man is that whatever proclivities he may have had in his youth for sowing wild oats, he is now likely to be past that stage. He may now have become more concerned with the quality of his erotic relationships than with the quantity. While there are no guarantees, he may be more content than a younger man to settle down with one woman and concentrate on one relationship at a time. He is also more likely than a younger man to have come to terms with his work and to be ready to devote more of his time to relationships and to the cultivation of an enjoyable personal life.

The younger man, especially the ambitious young man on the make, has a lot of energy; but he is often too busy trying to be successful to make time for a full private life as well. The older man may have less energy, but he is much more likely to devote his energy to you than to expend it on many other concerns. Young men are great for starting revolutions, given their considerable energy and unbridled ambition; but these traits do not necessarily make them good companions unless, of course, you want to start revolutions too.

An older man has the advantage of perspective. He has the ability, born of experience, to recognize that everything that *seems* to be important is not, in the long run, really that important. He has seen relationships come and go—perhaps even marriages come and go—and he knows that, in spite of it all, most people survive. A large part of the so-called mellowing process is simply a consequence of his lower energy level: he is too tired to be bothered getting all steamed up over every little thing.

If your older man is past middle age and is approaching what must be faced as old age, he will have a "September Song"; but he is, no doubt, thinking that he does not have time for the waiting game. That in itself can add a certain poignancy which can be romantic. Often, the older man is grateful for what he views as a second (or thirty-second?) chance at a love relationship, and that gratitude can be a welcome contrast from the taken-for-granted attitude often apparent among one's age mates.

Virtually, all May-December marriages, and quite a few May-December relationships, involve an unspoken element of exchange in that they just happen to involve a relatively rich older man and a relatively poor younger woman. A real advantage of the older man is that he is usually willing to play the role of sugar daddy to some degree. His accumulated resources, plus his chauvinistic attitudes, combine to make him quite willing to pick up more than his share of checks. As long as you are having a relationship with him for his own sake and not for whatever money he may spend on you, then that seems like a reasonable exchange. It is not so much a matter of men paying for women as older persons with more resources paying for younger persons with fewer resources.

Remember, however, that if you become involved with an older man for his money rather than for his beautiful gray hair, you are likely to discover what seemed to be a sugar daddy really turns out to be a saccharin patriarch.

The older man is, by definition, a man with a past. Do not begrudge him his former lovers or his former wives. Decades ago, some nameless winsome girl began to teach him what he is now showing you. Other women, wiser women, maybe wounded women, have taught him how to love. Out of their experience, their pleasure, and their pain, he may have developed an ability to be tender and a confidence born of maturity.

If you think of the women from his past at all, it should be with gratitude. Peter Ustinov observed that "parents are the bones on which children sharpen their teeth." The same might well be said of first wives. And of first husbands.

The Older Man as Mentor

Every marriage tends to consist of an aristocrat and
a person, of a teacher and a learner.

—John Updike

When you talk to a younger man, you mostly listen. He endlessly tells you about his hopes and dreams about what he is going to be when he grows up and the great things he is going to accomplish. He worries and wonders about whether or not he will be successful and about whether or not he will be as successful as you are or more so or less.

The older man knows what he is going to be when he grows up. His potential is fulfilled, or at least as fulfilled as it is going to be, and he must come to terms with that fact. When he does, then he can help you to fulfill your own potential. The older man needs to play Pygmalion. Let him. Learn from him. Whether he is being magnanimous in sharing his success or is anxious to try and live again vicariously through you, he will be sincere in wanting what is best for you.

All successful people need mentors as well as collaborators. Being a generation older, the older lover is not competing with you as are men of your own age group. The older man will rightly extract some exchange for his help, if only deference to his wisdom, but his help may well be worth it. The role of mentor is not unlike the role of parent or of coach, but those roles can be loving and fulfilling for both parties. Besides, there is some built-in exchange in that you also teach him, if he is wise enough to learn. You share your youth with him, which helps keep him young; and you bring to him a new perspective—the same world, but viewed through the eyes of another generation.

Being independent is very important for women. Some of the lucky ones have had independence training since they were three years old and have learned to manage for themselves very nicely. But always being independent, like always being exactly equal, is both unnecessary and exhausting.

Couples need to lean on each other—at least loving couples should. There is nothing wrong with letting yourself be emotionally or psychologically dependent on your lover at least part of the time. If your lover is as young and as inept as you are yourself, then you may find yourselves like two clinging vines with nothing to cling to.

The older man lets you lean on him sometimes and does not mind your weight. If you are lucky, he will even have learned to lean back sometimes and to draw on your strength, a luxury he can afford because he has nothing to prove.

Any woman who is competent enough to fix whatever needs fixing, most of the time, should also be secure enough to sometimes say, "Daddy, fix it!"

THE TROUBLE WITH OLDER MEN

There are three sexual ages
of man: tri-weekly, try weekly,
try weakly.

—Jayson VanVerten

Young people talk about their mates or almost-mates as "my old man" or "my old lady." These are affectionate, possessive terms; but when the person involved is literally an old man, the connotations are more serious. Maurice Chevalier described the French as the true romantics because they feel that the only difference between a man of forty and a man of seventy is thirty years experience. While this is a kind and an optimistic interpretation, it is often not accurate.

The problem with the older lover is the reality of sex and aging. Sexologists offer repeated reassurance that old people can have an active sex life, that they should do so, and that many of them do so. Perhaps—and perhaps—it hinges on what you mean by "active."

The problem of the older man is one of sexual apathy. He finds making love to be quite a pleasant pastime but wants to wait until after the evening news, the sportscast, and even the damn weather report. It is not that he is not interested exactly; it's just that having sex is no longer one of his priorities. You know without a doubt that apathy has settled into the marriage when the newspaper, a sandwich, and a cold beer preempt your desire for sex. When you combine this apathy with a marriage of long duration, a passionate sex life may cease to exist. Apathy becomes impotence. There are many forms of impotence for many reasons.

When the older man does make love, he may do it as well as he did when he was young. He has, after all, had many years of experience and so can read your responses more accurately than can the neophyte. He knows his own thresholds well enough that he can be patient and pace himself to your responses.

The problem is that he makes love less and less often and with less and less enthusiasm. You may find his lovemaking to be enthusiastic and satisfying if you only get together with him every couple of weeks. If you should decide to live together, don't expect your lovemaking to become any more frequent. It will still be every two weeks. And should you convince him to make love more often, don't expect your lovemaking to have the same degree of passion as when it was limited to every two weeks.

There are early warning signs to alert you that such a pattern may be in the offing. One important one is that when you stop to think about it, you, in one way or another, initiate almost all of the sexual encounters. If you stop initiating and wait to see what happens next, nothing happens. When you ask, he is in varying degrees accommodating, depending on what's on television. It does not take long for any woman, but especially a young woman, to find that accommodation is more tepid than torrid and is, at best, a pallid substitute for the real thing.

Being sensuous is not to be confused with being sexual, and you must decide which of these interdependent traits is most important to you. Sensuality involves the entire realm of the senses and has connotations of leisurely hedonism; sexuality is more urgent and explicit and is more like the hasty kind.

The older man is to be praised for having had the time to learn to savor sensuality; the young man is more likely to be a sexually hungry animal. The young man is great for games. If you want to do it standing up, the athlete's body is strong enough for both of you and he can stand up all night long. The young body is a joy to him and to you—at least, a joy to look at. But what do you do after all the photographs are taken and the bed has been made?

The young man casually flexes his arm for you to admire; the older man carefully curves his arm about you for your comfort. The young man dashes you through a shower after sex; the older man leads you to a scented bathtub and shares it with you. He washes you all over as he would a child and leads you back to bed, squeaky-clean all over and ready to be loved some more. Because he is not as sexually urgent, he can be more patient and he is more cognizant of the elusive joys of vicarious experience.

Ask yourself simply: what is he proud of? The young man is proud of how often he comes; the older man is proud of how often you do.

There is a moral to this story. An old man, as a lover, is great if you want a friend, a confidant, a companion, or a guidance counselor. If you are interested in various kinds of low-key sensuality, he may have a considerable repertoire. However, if you are interested in sex as sex, you usually need to have a young man.

Better a little schooled enthusiasm than the most proficient but perfunctory mate.

In Praise of Younger Men

Here's to you, Mrs. Robinson, Jesus loves you
more than he can say.

— Paul Simon, "Mrs. Robinson"

When thinking of a possible lover, a woman often considers a younger man. This does not involve a woman of eighteen with a young man of sixteen. Rather, it includes those scenarios where the woman is old enough to be considered an adult by any standard, and the man is young enough still to be considered boylike.

When a woman is in her twenties, this might involve a difference of as little as five years; later, it might be more like ten or fifteen. There is considerably more difference in social position and experience between a woman of forty and a young man of twenty-five than between a woman of twenty-seven and a young man of twenty-two.

The "older-woman, younger-man" combination meets with much more social disapproval than does the association of an older man with a younger woman. It is a less likely combination in terms of marriages and probably is also less common in terms of love affairs.

The media image of such involvements has not been very positive. One such example that immediately comes to mind is the relationship between actress Demi Moore and actor Ashton Kutcher. The media has, for the most part, treated their relationship as an aberrant and questionable pairing. On the other hand, the pairing of actress Catherine Zeta-Jones and actor Michael Douglas, an older man and a younger woman, has not received the same negative press, nor has its legitimacy been publicly questioned to the same degree. Another example is the affair in Dustin Hoffman's hit movie *The Graduate* in which the older woman, Mrs. Robinson, was not exactly a heroine. Stephen Vizinczey's novel *In Praise of Older Women* conveys a more positive attitude. Unfortunately, although the book sold well, attitudes change slowly; and outside the world of Hollywood, many people still consider such pairings to be morally unacceptable or, at the very least, subject to ridicule.

When thinking about a possible lover, there is sometimes an undeniable appeal in a beautiful boy-child in his late teens or early twenties who has finally finished growing and is just beginning to find his place in the world. For one thing, his body is still strong and straight. Being strong is not really important most of the time; it is certainly not necessary in order to make love well, but it is a nice plus. The boy-child's skin is smoother, the breath is fresher, and the eyes somehow seem to be bigger and softer.

He is more likely to have the charm of enthusiasm. He can still be impressed by many things and is willing to show it. And he is, of course, more potent than he will be later in life. He may not make love very well, but he will make love and make it often. He can, perhaps, also be taught to make love well; and then his boundless enthusiasm and virility can be a source of great enjoyment.

Sex roles do not change very quickly, but they do change somewhat with each new generation. Today's generation of young men has escaped some of the rigidity of sex roles that their fathers learned. They are more able to express a range of emotions beyond the traditional ones of lust and rage. Younger men have the gift of tears as well as laughter, and that makes them more sensitive as well as more fun.

A young man also helps to keep you young. He is into a different style of dress, a different music and dance, a different language. By osmosis, you absorb more of the current trends in popular culture than you would otherwise. It is somewhat the same function that children have in keeping their parents in touch with the latest fads and fashion—except that the young man is bringing you the more relevant components of adult culture albeit that of the very young adult.

The Younger Man as Protégé

Girls we love for what they are; young men
for what they promise to be.
—Johann Wolfgang von Goethe

If one of the positive aspects about an older man is that he may assume the role of mentor, one of the positive aspects of being with a younger man is that, for a change, you may get to be the mentor. There is an intrinsic satisfaction in having a protégé who admires you and who wants to learn from you.

Women who are in the arts or are involved in creative work are very likely to encounter a young lover who will become a protégé: the young actor who wants to learn to act, the blossoming painter or dancer or writer, the apprentice in any number of fields. Accepting a young man as a protégé assumes that the older woman involved has some valuable knowledge to impart; she is, in some way, in a position to offer real assistance in the form of advice or perhaps more direct sponsorship. She becomes, in effect, a patron.

How do you feel about being in the role of mentor or patron? There is this aspect to consider: there are many circumstances in which teachers are paid to teach. Tutors or coaches or professors are considered to be working, and they deserve to be paid for that work. Often, they are not paid very well, but they are always paid something. Teaching and learning, master and pupil are complementary roles, but when did you ever hear of someone who was paid to learn? In the long run, being the one who learns is more interesting and more fun. So if you are cast in the role of unpaid teacher, you may easily become bored when you find that you are not learning very much and impatient with constantly being the wise person who explains and illustrates things she already knows to a young lover who is an eager protégé.

THE TROUBLE WITH

YOUNGER MEN

Youth is that period when a young boy knows
everything except how to make a living.
—Carey Williams

The problem with the young lover, of course, is that he talks; and when he talks, the naiveté which produces enthusiasm is less appealing. He simply does not know as much of the world as he will later, and so his conversation is more limited. For many young men, their range of interest is not very broad. His world revolves around sex, sports of many kinds, probably fast cars or motorcycles, beer and booze, and many kinds of recreational drugs. His palate is not very developed; so he will, perhaps, be as happy with beer and a burger as with beef Wellington—not a very varied menu, but at least he's easy to cook for. If you let him choose the wine, it will likely be sweeter than you prefer. Instead of having a more acquired taste for good cognac straight, he will prefer a cold beer. In many ways, young men are simply simpler. They are more direct, less devious, with less guile.

And then there is the issue of money. The young man is, in most instances, relatively poor. Certainly, he is poor in relation to what he will have later on in life. He is just getting started and so is restricted in what he can afford and how he can live. Given that women, in general, make less than do men, that may mean that you make about the same amount. However, many women are still used to men who make more and who pick up more than their share of the tabs. With a young lover, unless he has a very rich daddy, you must be prepared at the very least to pick up half the expenses. Often, like the older man with a young woman, you are implicitly expected to provide

204

some subsidy. That is not just woman to man; that is also the expectation of youth to age.

In most cultures, women have not been taught to pay their own way, much less to pay for others. But if you have a younger lover, then you must not only pick up tabs but must do so unobtrusively, graciously, and without resentment. This is easier in the abstract than it is the first time you realize that what seem like ordinary sneakers are in fact special track shoes that cost $250 and are absolutely essential for jogging. The young lover, like the young girl, expects to receive gifts, to have loans cosigned, and to borrow your car. It is not a con job, nor is it exploitation. It is simply the sharing of resources, which is what couples do. Only for a change, you are likely to be the one with more resources.

There is an absolute rule here which is worth emphasizing. If you are not willing to pick up tabs, don't pick up young men. It goes with the territory, and so it should.

When you pick a lover, how long do you want to keep him? For weeks and months certainly, but how about for years? Young men are restless types as are young women and fickle as well. Not having yet developed definite tastes, they are eager to sample a range of new experiences, which will include quite likely other women as well as other terrains. They need to move. They graduate from college—finally. They develop an unquenchable passion to see Egypt by means of a camel caravan. They want to try to make records or movies or to surf in California.

You don't try to tie down the young lover, and you don't follow him in his wanderlust unless you just happen to be going to Egypt or Los Angeles anyway. And you don't whine when you are left behind, pursuing your own life as you were before you met him. You say, "Godspeed and good luck. Send me a postcard." And you drive him to the airport and lend him your carry-on bag and yet another fifty dollars.

Sometimes, he comes back; but usually, he does not, at least not as a lover. If it has been a good relationship between the two of you, he may well come back as a friend, as if you were an aunt, and proudly introduce you to his new girlfriend. She'll probably be a pretty little thing, fluffy and very young. You give them tea and crumpets—or more likely beer and peanuts—and send them on their way. Eventually, you may have to spring for a wedding present as well.

The younger lover is likely to be a bird of passage, and such birds can be of considerable appeal. But do not confuse them with the lovebird who mates for life.

UNPRESENTABLE LOVERS

*A poet may praise many whom he would be
afraid to marry.*
—Samuel Johnson, *Lives of the Poets*

When you select a husband or when you select a lover with whom you intend to live openly and closely, you are selecting someone who will share many aspects of your life. Even if you are not going to be financially dependent upon him, you do have to take into account how he will or will not fit into your social milieu. On the other hand, when you pick a lover with whom you have no intention of living with either openly or closely, you need not pick someone who is acceptable to your mother or presentable to your friends: he need only be acceptable and presentable to you.

If you move in academic circles where almost everyone in the room has a PhD, your lover with a grade-eleven education might seem unsuitable. However, you don't need to have him vetted by the faculty. If you move in moneyed circles where almost everyone in the room makes two hundred grand a year, your lover who is a schoolteacher might seem less interesting. If you move in artistic circles where everyone in the room is some kind of performer, your lover who is a lifeguard might seem uncultured. All such problems would be very serious for a husband or a husbandlike lover who will have to share your whole lifestyle: they are not necessarily problems at all for a lover who will share only your bed and a portion of your time.

In the old days, when a young man came a-courting, a girl's father might legitimately inquire whether or not his intentions were honorable. Was the young man honestly considering his daughter as a prospective wife, or was he just wasting her time? If the man and maid got carried away in their courting, was the young man then prepared to make an honest woman of her?

In entering into a mésalliance, your intentions usually are not honorable in the sense that you do not intend to make an honest man of your lover by marrying him. (Sometimes, of course, an exotic affair eventually does result in an exotic marriage, but that is another story.) Both men and women can live with the situation of love without any intention of marrying, and can do so without too much pain, as long as everyone understands it from the beginning. When the sexy, handsome, unemployed, and unemployable basketball player asks you to go for coffee, it is hard to say, "OK, but I'll never marry you." Nevertheless, it is important to convey that message unambiguously as early in the relationship as possible.

A love affair with a man who is not the kind of man you would marry can be quite wonderful in its own right. It lets you appreciate otherwise inappropriate men who, by some standards, might seem to be beyond the pale as suitors because they have a dubious background or are too rich, too poor, too close, or too far away. Let us consider the pros and cons of some of these unconventional liaisons.

The Lover in the Mob

You can have respect without love, but you
cannot have love without respect.

—Jayson VanVerten

Sooner or later, you are likely to encounter an interesting man who does not seem to fit the usual classifications of jobs and professions. He does not seem to actually work anywhere, yet he is well dressed and obviously has lots of money. He talks a lot about business, but what business and where it is located is very vague. Generally, all he will explain is that he has some business to take care of—business that keeps happening outside of business hours and ordinary offices. Exotic trips happen or carefully planned trips are called off or postponed for no apparent reason. General questions are met with a blank look; detailed questions are met with a blank wall. It should not take long for someone to figure out that what is involved here is what Grandma would have referred to as something shady.

The man who is reputed to have underworld connections or who simply has an unsavory reputation or who lives well with no visible means of support is not considered by the conventional world to be respectable and so is not socially acceptable. Even if he does not look like the stereotype of a gangster, if there seems to be a strong possibility that he actually is a gangster, then your role as his woman, or even as merely his close friend, places you in the role of gun moll.

Some of your acquaintances may find that exotic position to be interesting or titillating, but others will assume that by associating with known criminals, you must yourself have criminal sympathies if not actual criminal inclinations. Most likely, you will find that with a lover from the mob, your social connections are restricted to others who live in the same milieu. He can take you into the demimonde much more readily than you can take him into the company of law-abiding wage earners. Once you are known to have such notorious companions, you may yourself be less welcome if you later wish to return to your more conventional friends.

The underworld is vast and nebulous and operates by quite different rules than the ordinary world. If you are going to accept the many benefits of life on the fringes of respectability, which include for a start the avoidance of routine and access to a ready supply of money, then you must come to terms with the fact that it probably is better that you do not know exactly where the money comes from or what it is for.

One woman who was associated with a professional gambler was quite enthusiastic when he was on a winning streak—and quite derogatory when he started to lose. If you accept what men like this have to offer you, you do not necessarily have to take part, but you have to accept the morality of what they are doing. And you do have to accept the drawbacks as well as the advantages.

You must remember that the man of respect demands just that: respect. If you believe in capital punishment for evil persons who sell soft or hard drugs to teenagers because you think that it is a sin, then you had best back off unambiguously and quickly.

It is also important to remember that men in the underworld, even those on the fringes of the underworld, are used to breaking rules and to getting what they want. Often, they will be more territorial with "their" women than will men who are upstanding citizens, and they are often more ready to turn to violence as an expression of their feelings or as a way of enforcing their demands. There is also the potential danger of "being in the wrong place at the wrong time" with him.

The lover in the mob may be exciting, but he can also be dangerous.

MISCEGENATION: FLAUNTING

RACIAL TABOOS

With the Negro's sexual image, how do
they have time to write spirituals?
          —Godfrey Cambridge, comedian

The sexual revolution, and the revolution in the status of women, are supposed to have occurred in tandem with concurrent revolutions in other forms of inequality, especially with the changes in the inequality of blacks and whites. One result has been an increased possibility of equality across racial and ethnic lines and, with that, an increased possibility of friendship and, ultimately, of romantic attachments.

A lover from a different racial or ethnic background is exotic. Apart from his other qualities, he may be of special interest because his worldview and his experiences are so different from your own. Often, the very fact of difference is an important element in the development of a significant attraction and in the growth of a love relationship.

"Miscegenation" is a technical term used to describe the mixing of different races. It refers to marrying, cohabiting, having sexual relations, or procreating with a partner from outside an individual's racially or ethnically defined social group. The term is now out of favor and is considered offensive by many. As recently as 1965, there were twenty-five states in the United States that had antimiscegenation laws that banned "race mixing." The U.S. Supreme Court unanimously ruled antimiscegenation laws unconstitutional in 1967. Changing the law, however, did not necessarily change the attitudes of many people.

It is in the area of sexual relations and family formation where the race issue is most sensitive. The pervasiveness of conservative attitudes about sexuality coexisting with liberal attitudes about other things is well illustrated in a declaration which has now become a cliché: "I believe in equality for blacks, but I wouldn't want my daughter to marry one." Or my sister. Or my granddaughter. Many who hold this opinion are likely to maintain that their opposition to interracial marriage is not born of bigotry but of concern for the children born of these unions. They argue that the children will be discriminated against by those in society who are not as accepting as they are. The children per se, however, are not the real problem. The real problem is their belief that such children are unacceptable to society, and by inference, to them, making it a tautological argument. If the children of interracial unions are unacceptable, then interracial marriage is unacceptable. If interracial marriage is unacceptable, then the children of such marriages are unacceptable and around and around we go. Beware. People who use children as their reason for objecting to interracial unions are bigots dressed in sheep's clothing.

Even Martin Luther King Jr. had reservations about intermarriage. One of his most widely quoted statements was his affirmation: "I want to be the white man's brother, not his brother-in-law."

Although the number of mixed marriages is increasing, the overall number has not increased very dramatically over the past two decades and the incidence is still relatively low outside of large cities. Of all couples, only about one in one thousand consists of a husband and wife from different racial backgrounds. Outside of marriage, cross-racial friendships and love affairs are presumably much more common although many of them remain clandestine.

In some social circles, a racially mixed couple may be readily accepted. In many instances, however, a lover from another racial group is going to mean trouble for both of them. A white woman who is involved with a black man may find that he is considered "unpresentable" to her associates as she is to his. A black woman who is involved with a white man may well be considered by her peers to have sold out to Whitey, and she may find that his associates greet her with, at best, stony silence. These realities of contemporary social life do not necessarily mean that you should avoid such relationships, but it does mean that you should be aware of the possible consequences.

The kind of mixed couple which seems most threatening to the greatest number of people is the stereotypic one of a white woman with a black lover. If you enter into such a liaison, you must be prepared for the unpleasant fact that many people who are sexually liberal and tolerant, and who seem to be racially liberal and tolerant, will not necessarily tolerate miscegenation and will sometimes go out of their way to make life difficult for you. Being part of a mixed race couple, or in some places a mixed Jewish-Christian couple, can be seen as a political act.

To sort out your romantic motivations from your political ones, ask yourself this question: If the exotic trait of your lover were to be magically removed, would he still be as interesting? If the answer is yes, then you are probably responding to the man and not the social category he happens to belong to.

Taking a lover because he is black and you are white reflects as much prejudice, albeit in a different way, as rejecting a potential lover because he is black and you are white. Both alternatives deny the person the right to be assessed in terms of his own personal traits.

BROTHERS AND SISTERS:

THE LAST TABOO

The incidence of incest is much higher than
we thought, and its consequences are much
less pernicious.
— Simon Van Velikoff, sexologist

You can learn what is really taboo by looking for those things that nobody jokes about. There are endless raunchy jokes about premarital sex, about adultery, about homosexuality. There are comparatively few about incest. Only two jokes are in common circulation. One defines an Appalachian virgin as "any girl under six who can run faster than her brother," which may be more of a comment on the fragility of virginity than about brother-sister incest. The other defines incest as "the game the whole family can play." Most of the books of jokes or quotations do not even mention it as part of the folklore. It is the last taboo.

Although there is no one universal incest taboo, some kind of prohibition against some kind of incestuous behavior is found in almost all societies. The most stringent taboos are against mother-son incest, followed by father-daughter relationships. The emotional saliency of mores and laws prohibiting these kinds of relationships has two sources: in part, they stem from the fact of incest per se; and in part, they stem from norms against the sexual involvement of any adult with any child.

There are many theories of the origin of incest taboos. One important element in their perpetuation is the perception that a child born of a union between persons in too close a blood relation to each other would have an unfortunate genetic structure and would run a higher than average risk of being deformed or retarded or at least of having some kind of congenital defect.

Taboos about incest are beginning to change. One source of change is more effective birth control so that unfortunate genetic consequences can be prevented. A second source of change is the changing nature of the family. As long as a man and a woman married once and only once, it was very clear who was related to whom. Biological parenthood coincided with legal parenthood; and that, in turn, coincided with social parenthood as manifested by living together and by assuming the roles of mother and father, son and daughter.

However, with today's high rates of divorce and remarriage, who is related to whom and why is no longer so clear. Suppose a woman is married and has a daughter and then remarries a man who has custody of his son by his first marriage. If the remarried couple then has a child together, we can imagine a family of five persons. The three children grow up together as if they were siblings, but there is a girl who lives with a man who acts like a father but is biologically unrelated; a boy who lives with a woman who acts like a mother but is biologically unrelated; and a boy and girl who seem like brother and sister but are genetically unrelated and have a half sister in common.

This kind of hypothetical family can become even more complex when you add in such ordinary possibilities as children who are adopted and parents who marry more than twice. It is made more ambiguous when such unusual arrangements are made when the children involved are no longer babies but are becoming miniature adults. If boys and girls have been raised apart for some time, they do not necessarily feel like brother and sister just because their parents marry. If a man remarries a much younger woman, his son does not necessarily feel that the new wife, who is close to him in age, is exactly like a mother.

What all this means is that what used to be an absolute and taken-for-granted taboo that clearly designated certain people ineligible as lovers has now become a relative taboo open to interpretation in each new and unique situation.

The kind of incestuous relationship which is least objectionable is that between brother and sister who are approximate age mates. Some research on incest suggests that, perhaps, one in ten of all people have, at some time in their lives, had sexual intercourse with at least one sibling on a least one occasion.

Ask yourself: Who do you love and why? And is one of the young and handsome and affectionate men who you love your own brother? Philosophers using quill pens in silent rooms readily draw the line between Agape, which is spiritual or platonic love, and Eros, which is sexual love. It is not so clear in the real world of the flesh and the psyche.

You cannot marry flesh of your flesh for many good and sound reasons, nor should you have children with them for other reasons that are good and sound. But to love them, that is something else. And if on occasion that love is expressed as men and women tend to express it, then lie down in silence and discretion.

In some cultures, opposite sex twins are allowed to become lovers because it is believed that they have already been intimate in the womb. How could two people be more intimate than that? Brothers and sisters of the ordinary kind do not have that much in common, but they have been sharing many of life's circumstances for years. They may understand each other exceptionally well in that they completely relate to one another through their shared background and upbringing. The brother-sister love may be the ultimate kind of self-love in that each sees in the other a reflection of his or her own eyes and features and personality.

A liaison between a bother and a sister is not to be advised as the best choice of a lover relationship—but neither is it necessarily as traumatic or as unfortunate as is commonly believed.

CHAPTER 8

THE WANTON FACTOR: ON LUST AND WOMANHOOD

The great question ... which I have not been able to answer, despite my thirty years of research into the feminine soul, is: "What does a woman want?"
—Sigmund Freud,
The Life and Works of Sigmund Freud

Poor old Freud never figured it out. Neither did lots of women who, after even more than thirty years, are still having trouble with the same question.

Over the past few pivotal decades, women have both wanted to learn and learned to want. One thing they have learned to want is to explore and to savor their full erotic potential. And what they want to learn is just what that potential is and how to seize the opportunity to experience it. As women begin to realize the possibilities inherent in sexuality, they feel increasingly entitled to partake of this important element of life. They feel entitled not only to be sexually active but to be sexually active in the ways which are most rewarding to them.

If you asked men why they want to have a mistress, they would reply almost to a man, "To get laid, of course!" They might phrase it more delicately and might hasten to add that that was not the only thing they wanted; but it would be obvious that a prime motivator, if not the prime motivator, was to expand their erotic experience. For many men, especially young men, the desire for sexual expression is a constant urge needing little, if any, prompting

217

from outside stimuli. The desire seems to come directly from the hormones, and it is not only constant but relatively urgent.

It should no longer be very shocking to discover that spontaneous sexual urges may also be a prime mover for a number of women, some married and some not, some happy and some not. The erotic poet Irving Layton makes this point when he opines, "A woman who is attractive, well educated, and sensible has only one thing on her mind—to get laid."

Layton is given to hyperbole and so overstates his point. One can be forgiven for suspecting him of optimistically projecting his own feelings. Even adolescent boys occasionally have their minds on football, hamburgers, motorcycles, and cold beer.

Nevertheless, it is important to remember what should be an obvious point: in many *cases*, if not most, the erotic component is one factor, and an important one, in what contemporary women want.

DISCOVERING FEMALE SEXUALITY

*The man's desire is for the woman; but the
woman's desire is rarely other than for the
desire of the man.*
—Samuel Taylor Coleridge,
Specimens of the Table Talk of Samuel Taylor Coleridge

In Victorian times and, indeed, well into the twentieth century, the dominant view of sexuality in the Western world was the Puritan Christian view. Sex was considered to be evil, albeit a necessary evil. Sex was evil not only in and of itself but also because it caused other evils. It was a sinister force to be denied, sublimated, and suppressed as much as possible. It was an impulse to be controlled through both the law and the moral codes associated with Christian marriage. The drive for sexual expression was believed to be a masculine trait, and the problem in controlling sexuality was viewed mostly as a problem of repressing the lust and lasciviousness of men.

Most men in the Victorian era believed that most women did not have sexual feelings. More amazing than that, most women seem to have believed it as well. Sexual involvement for women was not supposed to be intrinsically enjoyable, at least not for respectable women. Good women were believed to be sexually motivated only by the desire to please their husbands, or at least to appease them, and by the desire for children alongside a sense of Victorian duty. We now laugh at those by-gone days when mothers advised their soon-to-be-deflowered daughters to "lie back and think of England." Thinking of England wasn't a ruse to get the virgin to dissociate from what was happening to her; it was a strong reminder of her duty to populate England and, particularly within the aristocracy, to provide "an heir and a spare" so that the land holdings remained in the family and increased its prestige and wealth. Bad women, who were whores or fallen women or women of the demimonde, were motivated by money or other kinds of exchange for their sexual favors.

The tradition of sexual repression began to be modified by major thinkers writing at the turn of the twentieth century. Havelock Ellis had a major impact with his seminal work *Studies in the Psychology of Sex*. The writings of Sigmund Freud placed the libido at the center of human experience and interpreted a wide range of behavior in terms of sexual impulses. Bertrand Russell expounded a philosophy of sexual expression and challenged Christian tradition with the publication of his controversial *Marriage and Morals*.

By the time the Roaring Twenties started to roar, the secret was out. Men were sexual creatures but so were women. Sex was not all that bad; in fact, sex was a creative force.

Rather than acceptance of an ideology of sexual repression, there arose an intensive quest for an ideology of appropriate sexual expression. Rather than being viewed as an evil, sex came to be seen as a positive force valuable not only as an end in itself but also as a means of contributing to personal growth and development.

Sadly, even with all the positive changes, sexual expression continues to face strong opposition as we approach the end of the first decade of the twenty-first century—as witnessed by the impassioned crusade of Evangelical Christians to ban premarital sex and demonize same-gender relationships.

Turning On: The Big O

When modern women discovered the orgasm, it
was (combined with modern birth control) perhaps
the biggest single nail in the coffin of male dominance.
—Elaine Morgan, *The Descent of Women*

Once it was finally established that women could have orgasms and that even good women could have good orgasms, there began an intensive search for the Big O. We became less concerned with "does she or doesn't she have sex" and more concerned with "does she or doesn't she have orgasms."

The tone of many discussions divided women into two classes: those who were sexually aware and those who were frigid. It was as if sexual feeling was something a woman did or did not have, the way she did or did not have blue eyes or big breasts, and the lucky ones were those who happened to have it. Frigidity was a problem in the woman.

It was then discovered that frigidity was perhaps in the situation, not in the woman. If women could have orgasms and had a right to have them, then it was the obligation of the man to give them to her. His task was to please her, and if she was not pleased, it was somehow his fault. A common saying of this time was: "There are no frigid women, there are only women with incompetent husbands." In some ways, this attitude has not changed all that much as evidenced in an episode of *Seinfeld*, in which Jerry learns Elaine faked her orgasms while she was in a romantic relationship with him. He feels emasculated by Elaine's revelation and accuses her of "sexual perjury" and having orgasms "under false pretenses." To restore his wounded masculinity, Jerry begs Elaine for another sexual opportunity to prove he is capable of giving her an orgasm.

Sex under these circumstances, evaluated in terms of an important but vague criteria for satisfactory performance, became a difficult and rather joyless task. It was especially threatening for the young and inexperienced boy who was justifiably worried that he might not do it "right" and would thereby fail to meet his partner's expectations. Thinking along these lines, a curious double standard evolved. The man was considered proficient if he could delay orgasm for a long time: the woman was considered proficient if she could accelerate it.

The whole task was made more difficult by the folk belief that if men and women did everything correctly, they would achieve not only orgasms but simultaneous orgasms. Anything short of this ideal was some kind of failure. No wonder Andy Warhol concluded that "sex is work!" It was not until the sexual revolution of the sexy sixties that we came around to more enlightened views.

The sexual freedom of the sixties was fostered by the introduction of the Pill and the freedom from worry that it granted. It was accelerated by the seminal work of William Masters and Virginia Johnson in *Human Sexual Response*. Their laboratory study of female sexuality finally produced real data to dispel speculation.

Masters and Johnson established that all (or nearly all) women were capable of sexual feelings and of sexual feelings leading to orgasm. They further established that an orgasm is an orgasm and that the clitoral kind is no more or less real, or more or less mature, than the vaginal kind.

More important than these clinical insights, Masters and Johnson taught us that each individual should take responsibility for his or her own sexuality. The man was not held accountable for the woman's failure to have a climax; the woman was not held accountable for his failure to become erect. Instead, the sexuality of each individual was defined as something unique to the person, stemming from his or her background and experiences and an aspect of life with which he or she must come to terms. Frigidity and impotence were renamed merely "sexual dysfunctions" and were considered something that should and could be cured.

The new perspective on sexuality minimized performance aspects and stressed sensuality and mutuality. The women's magazines stopped talking about whether or not women could have orgasm and went on to talk about how women might have multiple ones. Increasingly, it was possible to define sexual encounters not as obligatory tasks to be performed but as opportunities for shared delight. Women were finally becoming empowered to take a more active role in their own sexual pleasure—feeling comfortable enough to touch themselves, to guide their partner's hand, or to tell their partner what felt pleasurable.

VANQUISHING VIRGINITY

There was a young girl from a mission
Who was seized by a dreadful suspicion,
That "original sin"
Doesn't matter a pin
In this era of nuclear fission.

—Rev. J. A. Davidson

In the not too distant past, a good girl—the kind fathers and mothers wanted for a daughter—was chaste and pure. If she did not marry, she remained virginal as her status slowly changed from nubile maid to simply old maid.

The good girl modeled her virginity on such celebrated celibates as the Virgin Queen, Elizabeth I. Whatever Good Queen Bess did or did not do with Leicester or her other courtiers, the official story was that she remained unsullied. To suggest otherwise was treasonous; to suggest the defloration of any good girl was libelous.

If the good girl did marry, then she became a good wife, which meant, most of all, a faithful one. She might be unloving and unlovable, an unpleasant companion and an incompetent helpmate; but if she was sexually monogamous, she was, by definition, good.

The counterculture revolution of the sixties and the widespread use of the pill changed such definitions for many people. Helen Gurley Brown dared to talk about *Sex and the Single Girl*. Instead of being pilloried, she became famous and went on to expound the same ideas in the very successful magazine *Cosmopolitan*. Premarital sexual involvement became an open secret. It was no longer considered of great consequence as long as there was no pregnancy and as long as the girl in question permitted sexual encounters only with one man with whom she was in love and whom she planned or, at least, hoped to marry.

223

The Clairol company, which manufactures hair coloring, was immensely successful with an advertising campaign focused around a provocative question with a double entendre: "Does she or doesn't she?" The world has changed, and the question has become less provocative. Most of the time, we assume that she does or has or might.

Now, a more relevant question is, "Will she or won't she?" As it is realized that an affair—or even more than one affair—is not necessarily beyond the pale, the open secret of premarital sexuality has become simply open.

California psychologist Irene Kassorla affirmed that "nice girls do" and no one has to ask, "Do *what?*"

THE EXTRAMARITAL CONNECTION

We don't call it sin today—we call it self-expression.

—Baroness Stocks, British politician

At the same time that premarital sex was becoming increasingly tolerated, there was a gradual recognition that nice people—even otherwise normal, moral, and successful people—did have affairs and had them without necessarily suffering dire consequences. In 1948, Alfred Kinsey and his associates published *Sexual Behavior in the Human Male,* followed in 1953 by the equivalent book for the human female. The implications were shocking. If the data were accurate, nearly one-half of married men had had extramarital sex at some time in their lives. Worse, of all wives, about 20 percent did so. That represents one in five. Suburban housewives were shocked and surreptitiously viewed each other with suspicion and each night faithfully checked their husband's coat pockets.

Albert Ellis and other liberal psychologists of the 1960s began to suggest that under some circumstances, extramarital sex could be beneficial to the individual and even to the marriage. In 1966, John Cuber and Peggy Harroff published *Sex and the Significant Americans,* which showed that many supposedly successful marriages involved covert liaisons often of long duration. Moreover, even when these affairs were exposed to the light of day, their revelation did not necessarily precipitate a divorce. The flower children of the day were beginning to bloom and to talk openly about such unheard-of alternatives as "swinging" (couples having sex with other couples) and "open marriage" (where one or both partners in a marriage permit their partner to have lovers outside the marriage).

The jig was up. Americans began to understand what the French seemed to have known all along. Marriage is one thing, involving a long-term partnership for children and real estate and social status. Sex is something else, and love is something else again.

Sometimes, love *and* sex *and* marriage go together; sometimes, only two are found together; and sometimes, they are totally separate. Sometimes, they start out together with love's young dream and get separated later on.

A very few lucky people find sex *and* love *and* marriage all at once in one relationship; a few unlucky ones never really find satisfaction in either sex or love or marriage.

THE DECLINE OF THE DOUBLE STANDARD

*Liberated sex means an end to the double standard about
who can enjoy sex and who can't, and how much, or who
can initiate sex, and who can't . . . It means an end to
"nice girls don't" and "real men must."*
—Charlotte Holt Clinebell, *Meet Me in the Middle*

In Victorian mentality, although marriage vows were considered sacred, they were considerably more sacred for wives than they were for husbands. Adultery for him was more or less expected as a regrettable but understandable consequence of the male sex drive; adultery for her was an unpardonable sin. The major issue of her adultery was the possibility of pregnancy and the resultant suspicion that any child born might not be the husband's.

With the emergence of recognition of female sexuality and with the birth control revolution, it has become increasingly acceptable for women as well as men to be sexually involved with someone other than their mates. However, it still falls outside the range of acceptable behavior for many people; and like most sexual behavior, it is less acceptable for women than for men.

Married men have often had mistresses while remaining attached to the women who were the mothers of their children. The wife-mother, loved as she may have been, fulfilled other kinds of needs than did the girlfriend, who was perhaps also loved but in a more erotic sense. It now became possible to *think* the unthinkable: if married men could have lovers, maybe married women could have lovers as well.

The sexual revolution of the sixties introduced the second wave of feminism which raised consciousness concerning the unfairness and chauvinism of the double standard in sex as well as in other things. Well, if men could have sex without marriage, they had to have it with someone. Given the new sexuality, why couldn't that someone be a good girl as well as a hooker? If men did not have to give up all other women when they married, maybe women did not have to give up all other men. Maybe a married woman could have a lover or lovers without necessarily destroying her marriage or her life.

Many wives thought about such things late into the night, but they kept their opinions to themselves. Their fantasies were furtive. They existed in a kind of pluralistic ignorance: each one looked at herself in her bedroom mirror and believed that she alone felt this way, and that, if anyone else guessed the scandalous nature of her thoughts and fantasies, they would be shocked.

The outspokenness of the second wave of feminism that washed through the 1960s swept women into consciousness-raising groups where they began to talk. One thing they talked about was the sexual poverty of many of their lives. For every wife who actually strayed, there were many others who thought about it and many others who were tempted and vulnerable.

Men and women still tried to divide the good women from the not-so-good ones, but sexuality per se did not seem to be such an absolute standard anymore. Instead, there evolved a standard of judgment whereby the good woman came to be defined as one who had sex selectively and for the "right" reasons whereas the not-so-good one had sex promiscuously and for the wrong reasons. It was a distinction very hard to perceive from the outside.

Kate Millett, the feminist-activist who wrote *Sexual Politics*, summarizes this way of thinking accurately when she observes, "Love is the only circumstance in which the female is ideologically pardoned for sexual activity."

THE QUEST FOR FULFILLMENT

Until it is generally possible to acquire erotic
personality and to master the art of loving,
the development of the individual man or woman
is marred, the acquirement of human happiness
and harmony is impossible.

—Havelock Ellis

The discovery of female sexuality and the description of the potential pleasures that were involved was touted with considerable publicity. Women were portrayed as being as capable as men of passionate sexuality. They were described as able to experience strong desire and ecstatic orgasmic release. All of the women's magazines, both the cheap pulp ones and the expensive slick ones, offered the same promise: "It can happen to you!"

These days, every time you go to your corner convenience store for milk and eggs, you encounter displays of soft porn magazines—and some not-so-soft—which show women apparently enthralled with sexual feeling and delighted with their sexual prowess. This propaganda tends, by implication, to create very high expectations. Women begin to wonder about themselves and to wonder how their actual experience compares with their potential. "Is what I am feeling an orgasm? Am I having enough orgasms? Are they the right kind? Do I have a G-spot? Where, oh, where is it? What'll happen if I find it?"

Even if you find your sexual relationship with your current boyfriend or husband to be tolerable or acceptable or even pleasurable, you may still wonder, "Is this all there is? Am I missing something."

And many of you are right to ask such questions. You are missing something.

"All She Really Needs . . ."

The human spirit sublimates
the impulses it thwarts:
a healthy sex life mitigates
the lust for other sports.

—Piet Hein, *Grooks*

There is an old husband's tale about what old husbands tend to call "those women libbers," and the essence of it is that "they're all frustrated old maids and all they really need is a good fuck." Albeit misguided, an old husband's tale, like an old wives' tale, may have some germ of truth to it.

A full and rewarding sex life is not only good for your complexion; it is also good for your disposition. The contented body predisposes one toward calmness and serenity. Good lovemaking can generate a kind of peaceful euphoria that carries over into other areas of life, creating feelings of placidity and benevolence. Conversely, a bad sex life, or no sex life at all, predisposes either man or woman to a dour, pessimistic, judgmental view of the world. If you are not having fun, there is nothing more infuriating than to watch other people having fun. If you don't deserve it, neither do they.

Whether or not men and women in such a plight are consciously aware of being frustrated, they are more likely than others to view the world with a jaundiced eye. It is not the absence of orgasms that does it. Orgasms are easy to produce or, if necessary, buy. Orgasms are not the point. If orgasms were all that women wanted, vibrator manufactures could not keep up with the demand. Feeling good or feeling bad relates more to the sense of having this vital and revitalizing human experience or of being denied it.

The absence of physical love erodes the soul and dulls enthusiasm. Your skin gets skin hungry, your dreams are troubled, your temper is sharpened, and your body feels malnourished. You may not have a lean and hungry look, but you will have a hungry one, and you will be more dangerous. Dangerous in the sense that you will feel alienated and isolated from the people around you, and your zest for life will be greatly diminished.

Among other things, making love well, with satisfaction and pleasure, dissipates irritation and petulance. It induces a sense of centeredness and benevolence that is difficult to duplicate. The afterglow is like that of a good meal, but more so; like that of a hot bath, but more so; like that of a massage, but more so; like that of a bottle of wine, but more so, and without the hangover. The afterglow is not only difficult to duplicate, it is difficult to do without—especially if you are among the privileged few who know what you are missing.

And so the old husband's tale may be true after all. Sometimes, a satisfactory sexual interlude *does* render you less acrimonious. Without resolving basic discontents, it does make you more placid and therefore more patient and reasonable.

SAMPLING THE WILD RHUBARB

Variety is not only the very spice of life,
it is also the very spice of sex: the relish
and the zest of all erotic life.
— Simon Van Velikoff, sexologist

Everyone knows that boys will be boys and that when boys are busy being boys, the one thing they do is sow their wild oats. To "sow wild oats" refers to sowing bad grain, that is to say, wild grain rather than the good, cultivated kind. The phrase encompasses a variety of youthful excesses which, under the circumstances, meet with greater permissiveness and indulgence than those same boys could hope for later in life.

Since it is also indisputably true that girls will be girls, we need an equivalent term for their experimentations conducted in a spirit of frivolity and exuberance. Shall we describe such behavior as merely "sampling the wild rhubarb"? (Rhubarb, incidentally, really does grow wild. It has a familiar color and a straight turgid stalk, and although some parts of it are known to be poisonous, other parts are purported to have medicinal properties.)

Sampling wild rhubarb is quite unrelated to long-term goals, such as falling in love and getting married and having children. It is simply fun and merriment for its own sake.

While sampling the wild rhubarb may, at first, be enticing, it is not likely to do well as a steady diet. Like other kinds of youthful excesses, it is likely to be a self-limiting condition, succumbing to boredom or fatigue if nothing else. As Jessamyn West observes in *South of the Angels*, "Enough tomcatting sooner or later acts as its own cure. There are more reformed rakes than reformed celibates."

Sowing wild oats and sampling wild rhubarb in today's world of HIV/AIDS, combined with the resurgence of sexually transmitted diseases, presents risks that cannot be ignored. We will discuss the perils and risks of sexually transmitted disease in chapter 14.

THE EROTIC AFFAIR

What is it in men that women do require?
The lineaments of Gratified Desire.
What is it women do in men require?
The lineaments of Gratified Desire.
—William Blake, *The William Blake Notebook*

How is one best advised to proceed in the quest for sexual fulfillment?

Although both men and women may ultimately end up preoccupied with the dynamics of sex and love, it seems possible that given differences in socialization and differences in physiology, they reach their quest by different routes. One maxim frequently cited states that among men, sexual desire begets love whereas among women, love begets sexual desire. In the nineteenth century, the French novelist Rémy de Gourmont put it somewhat more precisely: "Man begins by loving love and ends by loving a woman. Woman begins by loving a man and ends by loving love."

Although many things have changed since then, our cultural traditions are strong enough that this pattern still holds true for many women. For some women, there may be a spontaneous urge of sexual desire, parallel to that which men experience, which is not appeased by masturbation or by conjugal sex. For many others, however, the inclination toward an erotic affair is not so much a generalized randiness as a wish for a man who would inspire randiness. It is not that they are full of desire, but rather that they want to find a man who would make them feel desire. The libido is there, but it needs to be aroused. They suspect, often correctly, that with a different man or a different kind of man or a man who made love differently, they would be much more turned on. Such inclinations may be difficult to reconcile with how nice, ladylike women are supposed to feel; but it is clear that it is how many of them do feel, whether or not they admit it to anyone else.

Casual sexual encounters may provide a certain excitement or may gratify a desire to seduce or to make a conquest. However, the thrill or newness is often counterbalanced by a certain awkwardness and self-consciousness not unlike what people experience in their first encounters. As one woman put it: "The first time with a new man is always a bit like the first time ever." If everything seems right, the best you can usually hope for is the exultant conviction: "This could be the start of something big!" The second time may be better, the third time better still.

The most exceptional erotic experiences are often the result of a long-term evolving relationship in which increased awareness of each other's body and responses improves rapport and empathy and moves the encounter to a higher and higher pitch. There is time for experimentation and time to incorporate what the experimentation teaches you about what works best for you both. It is in a developed relationship that one can best hope for that special magic where an erotic experience approaches a transcendental one. In this instance, practice may not make perfect, but it does make for better and better and better. And yet . . . there is also the Coolidge effect.

THE COOLIDGE EFFECT

One day, President and Mrs. Coolidge were visiting a government farm. Soon after their arrival, they were taken off on separate tours. When Mrs. Coolidge passed the chicken pens, she paused to ask the man in charge if the rooster copulates more than once each day. "Dozens of times," was the reply. "Please tell that to the President," Mrs. Coolidge requested. When the President passed the pens and was told about the rooster, he asked, "Same hen every time?" "Oh no, Mr. President, a different one each time." The President nodded slowly, then said, "Tell that to Mrs. Coolidge."
—Gordon Bermant, *Psychological Research: The Inside Story*

The Coolidge effect is used by sexologists to describe, among animals, the phenomenon of male rearousal by a new female. One wonders if, perhaps, most of the sexologists in question were male because it does not seem to have occurred to anyone that the same effect may be apparent among women.

For most women, the quest for fulfillment involves, in part, a quest for long-term relationships. The crux of the issue, alas, is what is meant by "long-term." There is no doubt that for most couples who have sexual rapport, the quality of that rapport increases with the passage of time. That process may take weeks or months or, for some, years, depending on how often they make love and with what intensity.

There is also no doubt that except for the most fortunate and exceptional couples, the quality of sexual rapport eventually peaks and, from that point on, tends to decrease with the passage of time. As a man and woman become more and more familiar with each other, the excitement and the erotic tension of their first encounters is diminished. The response patterns become too predictable. As the sexual experience becomes routine, there is a loss of intensity. They can still feel pleasure, but they are less likely to feel ecstasy.

The idea of sex with a nice, affectionate, but totally familiar old husband may produce a state of profound sexual apathy. There is no antipathy, but neither is there much interest.

The decline in erotic enthusiasm can be minimized and delayed by incorporating a wide variety of sexual techniques and by using different props and locations. Eventually, however, there may be a sense that one has experienced all of the experiences possible with a given partner. Even the most enthusiastic lovers can become jaded with each other. The idea of making love with a different man, a strange man, may be much more appealing than making love with a familiar lover.

By any objective criteria, a prospective lover may have no more to offer than the current one and, indeed, may actually be less attractive. However, the appeal of a stranger is that he *is* strange. Sometimes, in seeking sexual fulfillment, you want nothing more than what you have experienced with one man; but you crave the added stimulus and excitement of experiencing it with a different man—a man who arouses curiosity and is still mysterious.

ON KNOWING WHAT

YOU'RE MISSING

One can find women who have never had a love affair, but it is rare indeed to find any who have had only one.
—François, Duc de La Rochefoucauld, *Maxims*

For many women for many decades, the repression of sexuality appears to have been amazingly effective in preventing them from enjoying sex. The denial of erotic response, sometimes to the point of sexual anesthesia or a complete absence of sexual feeling, was possible in part because of the pervasive cloak of ignorance and secrecy which surrounded human sexual response in general and female sexual response in particular. Whether due to differences in physiology or hormones or conditioning, it appears that a woman, more than a man, has to learn to develop her erotic potential. She has to be, as they used to say, awakened. However, once a prince has come and kissed her and the Sleeping Beauty has opened her eyes, the arms of Morpheus, the Greek god of dreams, are no longer the arms she dreams of lying in.

As the Roaring Twenties started to roar, people went around singing a ditty which asked *the* critical question: "How you gonna keep 'em down on the farm after they have seen Paree?" How indeed!

SINGLE WOMEN WILL SEEK LOVERS

The difference between an old maid spinster and a bachelor career woman has a lot to do with sleeping on a single cot or in a big double bed.

—Jayson VanVerten

Love is important to most women. With increasing sexual freedom, the importance of love has come to mean granting importance to erotic relationships as well as to affectionate ones. Not all women want a lover. Single celibates do not: Grandma would have called them *good girls*. Traditional wives do not: Grandma would have called them *honest women*. Lesbians do not, at least not the male kind: Grandma probably did not include them in her lexicon at all.

Apart from these three alternatives, there remain those who are *no better than they ought to be*. Grandma would have considered them *fallen*: she would have called them *tramps*. When you think of a man who is a tramp, you think of an unwashed hobo, taking handouts, sleeping on park benches, and living hand-to-mouth on the open road. When you think of a woman who is a tramp, you think of one bold enough to have a man in her life without the honorable permission of being either married or at least engaged. A "real tramp" has more than one.

It is this residual category of women, not a small minority by any means, who are eligible to consider taking a lover or even lovers. They may be tramps from one perspective, but from another, they are emancipated. They are the vanguard of the third wave of the feminist movement, and their ranks are drawn from both unmarried women and married ones.

Unmarried women make up a large part of our population. They include not only those who have never been married but also increasing numbers of those who have been widowed or divorced, sometimes more than once.

Some of these women basically believe in marriage but do not want to get married *yet*. If an unmarried woman in this category were a man, we would say she was sowing her wild oats. All she is doing is having fun. Later, she expects to settle down to one man; and when she makes that decision, she will start husband shopping. Usually, but not always, the basis for her reformation is the desire to have a child and the recognition of the societal benefits of family life versus the single motherhood alternative.

Women of today who expect to remain single for the rest of their lives consist of basically two groups: those who have rejected marriage per se and those who simply predict that marriage, desirable or not, is unlikely.

In the recent past, women who never married were assumed to be either the unchosen who could not get a man or those dedicated to a career who chose to work instead of getting married. Such women became the familiar stereotypes of the old-maid teacher and librarian. Since women now do not experience the same career-or-marriage conflict, modern women who reject marriage are likely to do so on ideological grounds. They would concur with Gloria Steinem's widely quoted maxim: "A woman without a man is like a fish without a bicycle!"

Women who have resigned themselves to not getting married include those who have some unsolvable problem which makes them less marriageable than others. Being six feet six inches tall or having six children or being seriously disabled can be genuine handicaps in the marriage market. Other women, who are by ordinary standards attractive to men, may understand that their chances of finding a husband, at least the kind of husband they would want, are slim. This certainly applies to many young and not-so-young widows as well as to the overachievers who are overeducated and overaffluent compared with the men they are likely to meet. There are simply not enough eligible men available to go around for the women at the top. Statistics showing population distribution by age, sex, and marital status bear out that this is more than a perception. As columnist Maureen Dowd, of the *New York Times*, astutely notes, "Women moving up still strive to marry up. Men moving up still tend to marry down. The two sexes going in opposite directions has led to an epidemic of professional women missing out on husbands and kids."

If there is a surplus of women in the given category and if a number of them therefore cannot marry, what then? Women who do not feel any significant sexual urges or women who are comforted by a deep religious faith and so prefer to devote themselves to God may be content to live celibate lives. Other women who do not meet these two criteria want to experience, if not marriage, then at least something of the potential to be found in man-woman erotic relationships.

One young woman, tanned and glowing and just back from a Mediterranean jaunt with her man of the moment, exclaimed, "I think I've found the secret. Being a wife is a drag, but being a 'bride' is terrific. I think I'll skip committing matrimony and just commit honeymoons. They're probably the best part anyway."

Married Women Will Seek Lovers Too

> There is a proverb, "As you have made your bed,
> so you must lie in it," which is simply a lie.
> If I have made my bed uncomfortably, please God.
> I will make it again.
>
> —G. K. Chesterton

What is it that motivates a wife to take a lover? Those acts, which in retrospect come to be recognized as decisions, have a multiplicity of roots. Some wives are pushed toward an affair by an unsatisfactory marriage. The really unlucky ones are those who were unhappy with their husbands from the start, either because they picked a man with whom they could never be compatible or because they discovered too late that they were not really the marrying kind.

Other wives have had a period of marital happiness, but later find their marriages stultifying and unrewarding. Sometimes, the women have changed; sometimes, their husbands have. A girl who married very young may have found exactly the kind of husband she wanted, only to later change her mind. She may have selected exactly the kind of nice boy who seemed ideal when she was seventeen and then found at twenty-seven that nice boys are boring. Alternatively, the man may have himself changed with time.

In *Fear of Flying*, Erica Jong has her heroine lament, "I longed for him as he was when I first met him. The man he had become was disappointing."

In conventional wedlock, the emphasis was on the "lock." Once a husband had won his wife, she was, in effect, his chattel and she had, virtually, no

242

other options but to remain his wife. He could rest on his laurels until they rusted and still be assured of her presence.

In modern marriage, the relationship is more one of a voluntary partnership. Neither husband nor wife is obligated to stay married—and so neither can become totally secure and complacent that once a mate has been won, that individual will remain his or her possession for life. A husband or wife must not only convince a mate to want to marry but must also continually convince him or her to want to stay married.

Waiting for a husband to change and for a deteriorated relationship to rehabilitate itself is indeed an exercise of faith. In many cases, it is a lot like *Waiting for Godot* who, in the Samuel Beckett play, never shows up even though the watchful and undeterred Valdimir and Estragon wait and wait and wait for him to come.

In pharmacology, there is a category of drugs called palliatives. They do not cure what is wrong with you, but they mitigate some of the symptoms and make you feel better. They are anodynes which relieve distress or pain and soothe the mind and feelings.

In a marriage, there may come a point where a wife has accumulated a whole bale of last straws. Taking a lover may be a desperate palliative before chucking the whole unfulfilling enterprise.

The Apathetic Husband

Never mind "Is there life after death?"
That is too abstract. What I really want to
Know is: "Is there sex after marriage?"

—Jadah Vaughn

One of George Bernard Shaw's often quoted sayings observes that marriage remains popular because it combines "the maximum of temptation with the maximum of opportunity." Usually, Shaw's epigrams are quite pithy; but in this instance, he is mistaken. A honeymoon might well combine temptation with opportunity, but cohabitation does not, especially if the marriage is of long duration. Familiarity need not breed contempt, but it very often does breed sexual apathy.

What was passion in a marriage can become so vitiated, so watered-down, and so dissipated that it is hardly worthy of the name. In some marriages, perhaps in many, the act of love becomes an act of sex and an infrequent one at that. When you have reached the stage where you make love on Saturday nights, and Saturday nights only; when you have reached the stage where you have sex rather than making love, only late on Saturday nights in the dark; and when you have reached the stage when you have sex on Saturday nights only, late at night in the dark and quickly, without words, then you have reached the stage where you owe it to yourself to take a lover.

You owe it to yourself, not only for the desolation you experience now, but also for the desolation you will feel when you are old and look back on thirty years of such encounters—one thousand and forty consecutive Saturday nights of minimal fulfillment.

You owe it to the old lady you will become to give her something better than those passionless encounters to reminisce about and then either exaggerate or deny, depending on her perspective.

THE SEXLESS MARRIAGE

Living with impotence is like sleeping in a shroud.

—Jadah Vaughn

In discussing why husbands stray, it is common to observe that they are looking for something they need which they do not get at home. One hears homilies such as "nobody encourages adultery more than a wife who consistently refuses her own husband's advances." While this may well be true, it is only one side of the coin. Worse than a husband who is sexually incompetent or sexually apathetic is one who has become impotent.

A great deal of impotence, perhaps most of it, is psychogenic in nature. That is, it does not occur because of illness or hormone deficiency but because of depression or some other negative state of mind. It may relate to a loss of self-esteem due to business failure or to the aging process or to a midlife crisis. Fortunately, most impotence that is psychogenic can now be easily overcome with Viagra or Cialis.

Often, however, impotence relates directly to unsatisfactory and unresolved dynamics between the husband and wife. In these circumstances, it is not very useful to tell the wife not to take it personally. It *is* personal.

A sexless marriage may be especially galling to the wife whose husband is impotent with her but who, under her suspicious and watchful eye, appears to be quite potent with other women, which may very well be the case. Impotence may be only an occasional occurrence; even when it happens frequently, it is not usually a permanent condition. In the meantime, however, the disruptive effects for a particular couple may be pervasive enough to permanently affect their relationship.

Almost all couples fight, and some fights are worse than others. After apparently irretrievable things have been said and done, being able to have sex (which under those circumstances can hardly be called making love) does not mean that everything is restored to where it was: it only means that restoration may still be possible. The erotic communication does not solve the problem; but it does keep open, at least, some avenue of communication. If the sexuality itself can be gratifying, the bond of emotional rapport is strengthened, and the reassurance of your own attractiveness is maintained. But when a couple can no longer depend on or use sexuality as a palliative to their conflicts, then the marriage is indeed in big trouble.

Impotence breeds bitterness and insecurity. The wife may need reassurance that she is in fact still attractive and feels quite justified in seeking sex elsewhere. The rejecting and frigid wife triggers much the same reaction in her husband. If neither husband nor wife is particularly sexually oriented, then perhaps the two of them can disregard their impasse and settle for mutual apathy. Refusal to make love is something else. The wife who is bored stiff ends with a husband who is bored limp.

CHAPTER 9

"PLEASE, SIR, I WANT MORE!"

Is that all there is? If that's all there is,
my friend, then let's start dancing, let's
break out the booze, if that's all there is.
— Peggy Lee, "Is That All There Is"

In the classic scene from Dickens's masterpiece *Oliver Twist*, Oliver is emboldened by hunger and proclaims to the headmaster, "Please, sir, I want more!" Women, too, are emboldened by hunger; and they also feel that they want more. Unfortunately, their hunger is more diffuse than hunger for gruel, and many are not exactly sure what it is they want more of.

Until several generations ago, the lives of most women were quite circumscribed. Their options were limited and most of the outcomes of their lives were determined by the choice of a husband, a choice which, as often as not, was practically made for them. The expectations of mother, father, and husband were reinforced by the dictates of religion and by well-established custom.

While such women may or may not have been happy with their restricted horizons, most of them seem to have been resigned to it. They had minimal aspirations; and when they did aspire to life beyond the conventional one, they received little, if any, support. There were early feminists and later suffragettes, but most women lived quietly within the confines of Kinder, Kirche, Küche—children, church, kitchen.

The first wave of feminism, which brought the vote and other legal reforms, saw the beginning of women working for pay outside the home. The second wave, which washed over the country in the 1960s, created a generation of women who not only had the Pill but were led to expect that their lives would blossom beyond the confines of "the feminine mystique."

Betty Friedan posited that prior to the 1960s, an idealized image of femininity, which she called the *feminine mystique*, permeated society. According to Friedan, this ideal image served to confine most women to the narrow roles of housewife and mother, limiting their ability to realize their full human potential and ultimately causing them to feel unfulfilled and unhappy. It was "the problem that has no name," as women did not recognize "the feminine mystique" as the source of their discontent.

While Friedan was ahead of her time, she was more eloquent in describing "the problem that has no name" than prescribing what to do about it. Many young women, and some not so young ones, were left with a pervasive but vague sense of discontent. They did not want to be confined only to Kinder, Kirche, Küche; but neither were they quite self-confident enough to pay their own bills and make their own way for the next forty years, let alone dream of being astronauts. They wanted to be "equal." However, they thought more in terms of equal opportunities than they did of equal responsibilities.

The growing number of women who seek a lover for their own erotic fulfillment, independent of the bonds of marriage and the financial support it may provide, represents the front line of the third wave of the feminist movement.

The Love Factor: The Need for Affection

The greatest happiness of life is
The conviction that we are loved,
Loved for ourselves, or rather loved
in spite of ourselves.

—Victor Hugo

It is convenient to view the emancipation of women as part of the sexual revolution and to consider the changes in women's role in terms of the undeniable changes, which have occurred in her expectations regarding her own sexuality as well as that of men. While these changes have raised the consciousness of a generation in terms of their potential for erotic fulfillment, sensuality is only one part of what women want from men.

If you are considering taking a lover, you may be looking for love as well as for companionship and perhaps for adventure. When you evaluate a particular man in terms of the pros and cons of becoming involved with him, you might want mainly to have sex. You also might want mainly to be loved or to be less lonely or to be less bored. In the best of all possible worlds, you probably want eroticism and love together, with a man who is also an interesting companion. Which need comes foremost in your mind depends upon your own personality and upon the circumstances in which you find yourself.

SINGLE WOMEN HUNGER

FOR LOVE

―――――――

Whenever a woman meets a new man, she wonders,
At least for a few seconds, if might he be the one?
—Jayson VanVerten

Ours is a relentlessly romantic culture. The themes of love and the fulfillment it can bring and the despair that follows its loss, are woven into the warp and woof of our heritage, and permeate many facets of our social experience. Little girls grow up on romantic fairy stories, full of charming princesses and handsome princes, exotic castles and dragons to be slain, and those same handsome princes carrying maidens away on white horses. There are gala balls and magic slippers and starlight and the granting of wishes.

If the culture in general is romantic, then the world of teenage girls is especially so. Their music reiterates the theme of meeting "the one and only" and romanticizes about how the encounter will be. Rock music puts it to a different beat, but the story line is much the same. The teenage girl is programmed to expect that one day she will grow up, fall in love, get married, and have beautiful babies, hopefully in that order. By the time she is eighteen—or sixteen (or even maybe fourteen)—she is ready to fall in love with someone. The television shows she watches, the movies she goes to, the books she reads—all reassure her that this is what is supposed to happen.

When it happens, but she does not exactly live happily ever after, the same gallery of advisors explains that what she thought was love must have been only infatuation. She is encouraged to try again, this time for the real thing. The brass ring.

Most single women, sixteen or sixty, want to be loved. And just as importantly, they want someone to love. Maybe by more than just one man, but at least one man who inspires them to look carefully at cashmere sweaters when they pass a haberdashery, someone they can think about when they are trying on lingerie, someone to care should they lose ten pounds or gain them.

A woman may or may not want to marry, and she may or may not want to have children; but almost without exception, she wants a certain someone to share with her the joys of a loving friendship. She wants, if nothing else, the exquisite vanity of living under someone else's gaze.

Married Women Hunger for Love Too

Where there is marriage without love, there
will be love without marriage.
—Benjamin Franklin, *Poor Richard*

Falling in love and getting married are supposed to solve the problem of the hunger for love. Unfortunately, all too often, it does not quite work that way. Sometimes, a marriage becomes loveless or, at least, is felt by the wife to be loveless because of her husband's distant behavior. The opposite of love is not hatred but indifference.

The indifferent husband does not interact with his wife with much intensity. He has other concerns and preoccupations, be they his work or sports, and his interest in his wife appears to be exhausted. It well may be that he still loves her, but he has ceased to show it in any meaningful way.

One young wife reported that she remembered exactly when she decided to have her first affair. "I was feeling neglected and finally asked him straight out, 'Do you love me?' He looked up from his newspaper and answered, 'Of course, I love you. That's my job.' And he went back to reading his newspaper. That did it. I couldn't imagine having nothing but that attitude for the rest of my life. I'm too young to just give up having a good life."

THE HABITUATION EFFECT

The living together for three long rainy days
in the country has done more to dispel love
than all the perfidies in love that have ever been
committed.

—Arthur Helps

Folk wisdom has it that for most people, marriage starts off with a euphoric honeymoon period of high satisfaction and then deteriorates with the passage of time. The blame is not necessarily assigned to either party: it is the nature of marriage per se which is at fault, and that fault lies in habituation.

The overexposure of husband and wife to each other may not only mean a lessening of their sexual attraction, as in the Coolidge effect, but also a lessening of their emotional interest in each other. They may feel affection, but they cease to feel or to show the kind of love their spouse hopes to receive.

Reflections on how the habituation effect leads to a loss of romantic love in marriage are commonplace and are a staple of folklore homilies and aphorisms: "Married life is like sitting in a bathtub: once you get used to it, it's not so hot." "Marriage is a feast where the grace is sometimes better than the dinner." "Marriage is an unfailing method of turning an ardent admirer into a carping critic." "Marriage is the process of turning an attraction into a distraction."

In this view, changes in men and women after marriage stem, in part, from the demands and restrictions of the husband-wife role: demands and restrictions that do not necessarily exist for nonmarried individuals. For instance, husbands and wives are expected, for the most part, to come home at night, share money, visit relatives, even talk to one another, and have sex. In meeting their marital obligations, couples eventually settle down to a routine of predictable ways of dealing with each other. While such habituation may play an important role in marital adjustment, it may stifle the mystery and spontaneity of romantic love. The British writer Beverly Nichols opines, "Marriage is a book in which the first chapter is written in poetry and the remaining chapters in prose." J. B. Priestly, the British journalist and playwright, reflects, "Marriage is like paying an endless visit in your worst clothes."

Other observations in the same vein reaffirm the general conclusion, "Every man may be unique, but husbands are all alike."

"You Don't Bring Me Flowers"

I remember when you couldn't wait to love me,
Used to hate to leave me,
Now after loving me, late at night,
Well, you just roll over, and turn out the light.
And you don't bring me flowers, any more.
—Neil Diamond,
Alan Bergman, and Marilyn Bergman

Women are indoctrinated in the myth of romance much more so than are men. That is Romance with a capital *R*. They are programmed to want not only sexuality and high-power orgasms but also the specific kinds of trappings which are supposed to signal emotional involvement. They want—and expect—verbal declarations, little love gifts, flowers, perfume, soulful glances, and the holding of hands.

For many women, no matter how modern they are in other ways, an important part of their existence is the feeling of being loved; and that feeling is conveyed in words and touches and gestures. It is not enough to know, cognitively, that a man loves you. It is also important to *feel* it.

The younger you are, the more romantic you are, and the more you yearn for starlight and roses. If your husband does not bring you flowers or their equivalent, it is only a matter of time until you find someone who will.

Bringing Love Back

It requires more charms and address in women to revive one fainting flame than to kindle new ones.

—Jonathan Swift

Wives who find that the love they sought in marriage is no longer there usually try a number of things to recapture their husband's affection. Women's magazines are full of discussions on this problem and of suggestions, remedies, and techniques for solving it. They recommend everything from better meals to black negligees to second honeymoons. If the marriage involves a cycle between the two—in which sometimes he seems indifferent, and she must entice him, and sometimes, she seems indifferent, and he must entice her—then some such strategies may be effective. If the effort is always all one way or even *seems* to her to be always one way, she is not only discouraged but humiliated.

Always having to tug at someone's sleeve is bad for anyone's pride or self-esteem. So such a wife is doubly gratified to find that there are other men who are indeed interested and who continue to pay court to her in the ways she learned to expect and appreciate before she married. The husband in these circumstances may still be a good sex partner, but he has stopped trying to court her.

Women are like fires: they tend to go out if left unattended.

THE LONELINESS FACTOR:
THE VALUE OF SHARING

A great many mistakes are made in the name of loneliness.
—John Patrick, *Love Is a Many Splendor Thing*

There are many pleasures in solitude and many activities and pursuits that one can and does enjoy doing alone. However, we are fundamentally social creatures brought up in a social world where companionship and communication are held to be of prime importance. Paradoxically, however, to derive full value from joy, we must have someone to divide it with.

It is pleasant to watch a sunset, but it is more pleasant to watch it with a friend. The same may apply to watching movies or television or the waves at the beach. It is always satisfying to partake of a well-prepared meal, but it is more satisfying to break bread with someone. This is not to say that we necessarily want constant companionship, but only that most of us who are not hermits want some. Companionship may be available from friends, but since the intensity of our involvement with them is less than that of our involvement with lovers, the presence of a lover may be more important—which is why we often feel forsaken when close friends first embark on a new love relationship.

Sometimes, a woman takes a lover to relieve her loneliness and finds the solace of companionship to be more important than the physical aspects of making love. If you are really in love, you can say, with the Pulitzer Prize-winning author and poet Conrad Aiken: "Music I heard with you was more than music, and the bread I broke with you was more than bread."

BEING SINGLE CAN BE LONELY

The couples wander two by two,
A giant Noah's ark, a zoo,
Not one by one or three by four
But two by two, no less, no more.

— Jadah Vaughn, "Cagemates"

The Western world is organized socially around the premise of a husband-wife pair. Traditionally, almost all activities that are done in the evening or on weekends are programmed to be done by a two-person, man-woman team. This arbitrary organization is not typical of all societies and, indeed, is not typical of our own for adolescents or for the elderly. In the adult years, however, the fact that most people are part of a couple is readily translated into the idea that most people should be. While this viewpoint has been changing slowly over the past several decades, it still influences the behavior of many adults.

The need for companionship may be somewhat more important for women than for men in that their activities are more constrained by social norms, which make some things more comfortable when done with a male escort. A man, being free to take the initiative, is less constrained and can often hustle up someone at the last minute to do things with. A woman can as well; but more often than not, it is more difficult, especially when it comes to activities that take place in the evening or extend late into the night.

If you want to go to the movies, you can always go by yourself and hold your own hand. Or you can go with a friend, and he or she may share your popcorn, but they do not hold your hand and they do not engender in you feelings of romance. Wanting a romantic evening of dinner and a movie may sound like a trivial goal, but in some instances, it may be quite a legitimate motive for taking a lover or even for getting married.

Hostesses have been taught that a proper dinner table should be balanced, meaning that there should be an equal number of men and women. Canadian author Merle Shain observed, "Being single can feel like playing musical chairs, and every time they stop the music, you're the one who's out." Unmarried adults are often left out of social activities not so much from a sense of disapproval as from a residual concern that there will be an unbalanced sex ratio.

Having a lover gives a woman access to a companion who is on tap, so to speak, and who can readily be conscripted to take part in a number of activities such as weddings and bar mitzvahs, in addition to making love. Access to an escort is a problem which a wife does not have to face.

Alas, thinking that all your married friends have it made is much the same kind of error of generalization that married women make in thinking that all their single friends have it made. Just remember that the greener grass you yearn for on the other side of the fence may be nothing more than artificial turf.

BEING MARRIED CAN BE

LONELY TOO

Loneliness is never more cruel than when it is felt in close propinquity with someone who has ceased to communicate.
—Germaine Greer, *The Female Eunuch*

Single people are not necessarily socially isolated. If they live by themselves, they may spend a considerable amount of their time in solitary pursuits, but they do not necessarily feel lonely. Even the divorced or the widowed, who were once used to someone sleeping on the other side of a big king-size bed, are not necessarily lonely in their daily routines. They may have many activities, many friends, and many options. Often, they have social schedules, which are almost too crowded with meetings and entertainment.

When single people are lonely, and they often get lonely on national holidays or with Sunday morning coming down, they may have a fantasy of getting married at some point, so they need not be lonely anymore. It comes as a shock for them to discover, or perhaps to rediscover, that being married is no safeguard against loneliness. In fact, it sometimes makes it worse.

According to Gloria Steinem, "The surest way to be alone is to get married."

The Indifferent Husband

When a girl marries, she exchanges the attention of many men for the attention of one.

—Helen Roland

Having a husband who is physically present does not necessarily guarantee an absence of loneliness. In the world of cartoons, one stock comic situation involves a wife who is trying to talk to a husband hidden behind a newspaper. There are endless variations on this theme which continues to be funny because every woman instantly identifies with it.

The problem is not that husbands read or even that they read the sports page. The problem is that the wife is dependent on the husband for affection and companionship, more dependent than he is on her. If, as is often the case, she has spent her day at home either by herself or with only the children, then she has been waiting for her husband to come home to provide a little adult stimulation. The time which is available for focused interaction is limited by many constraints of the daily round; but she is, of necessity, patient. When, finally, there is time for the two of them to be together, he is with her physically; but his attention is focused elsewhere, so he is not *with* her psychologically.

The wife's frustration with an inattentive husband is made more acute in those situations where the object of his attention—for which she is, in a sense, competing—is something trivial and insignificant. If he were doing something *important*, then it would still be unfortunate to be ignored, but it would be more tolerable. However, if he is reading the funnies or watching television, there is no particular time urgency involved.

A preference for reading the paper instead of conversing with her makes it plain that conversing with her is a very low-level priority indeed.

261

THE CAPTIVE WIFE

Age has left me lonely, as lonely as a wife.
—Jadah Vaughn

It will often happen in marriages that the presence of the other takes away the joys of solitude without replacing them with the joys of companionship. When this happens, both husband and wife may be distressed and lonely. The husband, however, usually has more resources to cope with the situation. Men in general tend to have more freedom of movement and more control of their time. If a married man is lonely, he can easily go out by himself or out with the boys, and he is not judged harshly for having done so or for having enjoyed himself. If a married women is lonely, she cannot as readily take herself out to find companionship even if she has a car and an independent spirit, even if she can find a babysitter, and even if she can afford one.

A single woman who is on her own and who feels at loose ends can call a friend. She can go to a movie or go shopping or take a trip or any of a variety of other plans. A married woman who is on her own, and who feels at loose ends, anticipates that her husband, as part of his commitment to the marital relationship, will provide her with the companionship she desires. However, she often finds that she waits and waits. She waits for him to come home, she waits for him to get ready to go to bed, and in the morning she waits for him to get up and out of the shower. Her time is often organized around the possibility of his making time for her, and she soon gets very tired of waiting. And when she does, she will seek companionship elsewhere: perhaps from her friends or her family or, perhaps, from a lover.

When you listen to the lamentations of wives, they often say, "He never takes me anywhere." An obvious query in response to this is, "Well, why don't you ever take yourself anywhere?" Often, however, she does not really have that option.

"Why is it," asks journalist Lawrence Jaqua, "that in public, a woman without a man looks forlorn, but a man without a woman looks romantic?" Most people view women out on their own differently from men out on their own, especially in small or conservative communities. Women are certainly viewed differently anywhere if they are out on their own late at night. Often, if they do go out alone, they receive so much of the wrong kind of attention that the spotlight interferes with their enjoyment. A wife can go by herself to the supermarket on a Saturday afternoon, but if she goes to the races by herself on Saturday afternoon or to a cocktail lounge by herself on Saturday night, she is conspicuous and seems to be making a come-on statement by her very presence. If a woman goes out, she is supposed to be escorted. If a wife goes out, her escort is supposed to be her husband. If he is seldom available, she will indeed be lonely—lonely and housebound.

Such a woman *needs* a lover.

ALIENATION: SHARING

EXOTIC TASTES

---

*Another circumstance tormented me in those days: that no one resembled
me and that I resembled no one else.*
— Fyodor Dostoyevsky, *Notes from Underground*

If you like to do ordinary or more commonplace things, then it is
relatively easy to find someone to do them with you. Everyone likes a
well-prepared meal; everyone likes to drive through the park and watch the
sunset. Sometimes, however, your passions are so exotic that they are almost
unshareable.

One young wife had, in her adolescence, become fascinated with the
Middle Ages. She devoured history books when her girlfriends were still
devouring *True Confessions*. In college, she found her forte in the study of
Chaucer and went around happily reciting passages in excellent Middle
English. Alas, Middle English is a very exotic tongue and one not widely
appreciated.

To her delight, she found, in one of her classes, a young man as infatuated
as she was with the distant past. He spoke Middle English just as fluently.
They went around delighting each other with outrageous puns no one else
could understand. When she found an error in someone's translation, she
could point it out to him and he was interested and impressed.

Eventually, they went to bed together, and they even spoke Middle
English there. Chaucer can be quite bawdy, but the appeal of this lover was
not his lovemaking so much as his companionate understanding of an exotic
world.

One person who is almost, by definition, alienated is the stranger in a strange land. One young wife, a Puerto Rican living in Alberta, Canada, with her English-speaking husband, an oilman raised in Edmonton, found herself in what seemed to her the subarctic. She was terribly lonesome for strong sunlight and a profusion of plants and the ocean. One day at the market, a countryman spoke to her in Spanish, some casual comment about the weather—which, for them, was not a casual issue. They eventually become lovers; but the lovemaking was of less importance than huddling under the blankets, speaking Spanish instead of struggling with English, and reminiscing about palm trees, real rum, fresh fish, and the spirit of carnival.

She was not unhappy with her husband, and she did not want to go home to the poverty of oppression of her childhood, but she was homesick for her own culture. The Puerto Rican lover could understand her ambivalence in ways her Canadian husband never would.

Being Understood: The Lover as Therapist

A woman loves the man who tends her wounds almost as much as the man who inflicts them on her.
—Richard J. Needham, *A Friend in Needham*

Another kind of loneliness is the very common feeling that nobody understands you as you really are. You go around singing to yourself, "Nobody knows the trouble I've seen." There are many kinds of unhappiness, and at the time that you are experiencing them, each one seems a unique burden invented just for you. If you get desperate enough, then you finally get to a physician, or are taken to one, and some official person provides some kind of intervention. The tranquilizers, which are so often prescribed, are not a long-range solution: they are merely a kind of saltpeter for the mind.

Before you get to that stage, there is an alternative and better intervention in the form of sympathy from someone who loves you. Friends can be supportive; but they are not intimate enough, or committed enough, to provide pervasive comfort.

One important role the lover may provide is that of therapist. He listens, he consoles, he advises. It is no wonder that just as the lover acts as therapist, the official therapist is not infrequently also a lover, giving what is disparagingly known in the trade as penis therapy. It may be unethical, but it often does work. Independent of its benefits, however, it is a serious abuse of power for a therapist to enter into any type of intimate relationship with a patient.

The cliché "my wife doesn't understand me" often used by husbands is just a cliché, but it is just as valid of a cliché when it becomes "my husband doesn't understand me." A lover who is understanding and who provides comfort and insight may be the best kind of therapist for minor depressions and anxieties.

For a number of wives, the role of the lover is not so much as a sexual partner who is incidentally also comforting but more as a therapist who is incidentally also a lover in the physical sense.

THE BOREDOM FACTOR: THE QUEST FOR ADVENTURE

It is not true that life is one damn thing after another . . . it's one damn thing over and over.

—Edna St. Vincent Millay

There is a time in early adolescence when you think that being grown-up, if you ever live that long, will be wonderful. You will do exciting things, meet exciting people, have adventures, make money, and experience other delights which seem reserved for adults only. The acquisition of adult privilege is accompanied by adult responsibilities, and it often does not take long to realize that the promised goodies are either not forthcoming or are just not that wonderful.

Presumably, the sense of disillusionment hits men as well as women. It is certainly acutely felt by young and not-so-young women who find that their aspirations for living are not being met by the circumstances in which they find themselves.

A lover may be, at least, a short-time answer to such boredom.

Being Single Can Be Boring

If your morals make you dreary, depend upon it they are wrong.
—Robert Louis Stevenson

When you think of the life of the modern unmarried woman, she seems to have many more options for excitement than would have been her lot in earlier generations. She does not have to live at home if she does not want to. She is most likely free to go to college or to get a job, and there is a wide range of courses that she can take or occupations she can choose. From the outside, it can seem quite interesting, and so it is for many people. It is also true, however, that even relative emancipation does not prevent quiet desperation and does not cure ennui.

There are many things one theoretically can do, but in actuality, the daily round may be quite repetitive. Going to college sounds like fun until you remember that even with a college degree, very few women who work are international CEOs or fashion buyers just off to Paris to see the spring collections. Most of them are confined to cubicles or small offices working as midlevel managers, executive assistants, or accountants committed to routine and repetitive tasks day after day. Computers may be fascinating, but writing program codes or conducting systems analysis offers limited intellectual creativity or emotional appeal.

When you cannot change the circumstances of your life or are not yet willing to try to do so, then one aspect of your life, which is open to change, is your love life. You can consider a new lover. If as a history major you must spend all of Tuesday morning listening to someone recount the development of the Civil War between the States, then you can at least spend Tuesday afternoon in bed with an aspiring physicist who promises not to breathe a word about reconstructionism or carpetbaggers.

Being an unmarried woman with a career of some sort, or at least a job, may make it less likely that you will be bored than if you are a housewife; but it is no guarantee that you won't. You may still have to work forty hours a week at a boring job that provides few emotional rewards. With the right lover, you can at least look forward to an exciting Saturday night and Sunday morning.

Being Married Can Be

Boring Too

*Love has gone and left me . . . and the neighbors
knock and borrow,
And life goes on forever like the gnawing of a
mouse,
And tomorrow and tomorrow and tomorrow
There's this little street and this little house.*
— Edna St. Vincent Millay

Some women, especially middle-class women who do not work, are condemned day after day to lives of the most exquisite boredom. As noted earlier, Betty Friedan, in her now classic book *The Feminine Mystique*, described them as having "the problem that has no name."

Not true. It does have a name, and the name is boredom.

Consider a young woman who hitched her wagon to a promising young executive's star. After a few years of marriage, she finds that she spends all day in the company of preliterate children, an always-full dishwasher, and an erratic washing machine. She walks through the repetitive, demanding, but unchallenging routine subject to the demands of a preschool family. It is not that she does not love her children or that she finds them uninteresting, but they are not interesting enough. And worst of all, one day is just like the next.

The German poet Goethe is quoted as saying, "A man can stand almost anything except a succession of ordinary days." The ordinary days of the young suburban housewife-mother have been described eloquently in the first part of *The Women's Room.* "Bore"—"ing"—two words. The only light, the only spark to be anticipated, is the nightly return of the husband, trailing clouds of glory from the real world where conversations are literate, and decisions are important, and changes are possible.

The young husband is often not very interested in his young wife and her alien domestic world although, in an abstract way, he is at least willing to support her in dollar terms. He is preoccupied with his own world, the masculine world of commerce, which defines his sense of self-worth and also pays the mortgage. Although an understandable and perhaps even laudatory preoccupation, it is not of great comfort to the woman who is doing two loads of laundry a day and is understandably preoccupied with soap and, by trivial extension, with soap operas as well.

Soap operas may be a satisfactory source of vicarious experience for the retired pensioner of seventy, but they are paltry fare for the young woman of twenty-five, who sees in them a reaffirmation of her own deep suspicion that life is passing her by and passing quickly at that. She might resolve this dilemma in a number of ways. Have another baby who, in being only a baby, will *really* need her in ways her four-year-old already does not. Go back to school and study to become an architect. Get a job, if she can imagine being a receptionist and can arrange day care, *or have an affair.*

The mystique of an affair is that, in part, it is immediate. She is already qualified; her body already knows what to do. And with her husband's tired and indifferent response, she has both motivation and justification, not to mention her speculations about his business trips and late nights at the office.

The young mother is often bored. She needs a lover to show her that she is still an attractive woman, to give her a reason to shave her legs, to make her listen for the phone ringing. Someone to hurry through the housework for, so she can be free by two o'clock. A lover fills up the time, the space, the emptiness. A lover, if he is a lover at all, at least promises to be *interesting.*

GOOD OLD CHARLIE

One would be in less danger
From the wiles of a stranger
If one's own kin and kith
Were more fun to be with.

—Ogden Nash

Consider the plight of the older woman who has happily raised her children for twenty or more years only to find that their need for her has become increasingly limited as they approach adulthood. She anticipates that in a few years, they will have left home for college or marriage and will be busily preoccupied with their own lives.

She looks at her husband, an accountant—let's call him Charlie—who is in pretty good shape for a man his age. He makes sensible decisions about stocks and insurance, works hard and loves his kids and cuts the grass and just wants a little peace on the weekends. He's a nice man. A good man, benevolent, and well-mannered and harmless. There are millions of men like Charlie.

If you live with a man like Charlie you learn to become benevolent and well mannered and harmless as well. You learn how to make casseroles, and you shop carefully for sensible shoes. But your life is frittered away in trivia, and nothing new ever happens except that the bathroom needs to be repainted and the living room needs new drapes.

While you are thumbing through samples of materials to make sure that the drapes match the carpet because you cannot afford to replace that too, it will suddenly occur to you that while Charlie is a good man, it would be wonderful to *feel* again: to feel desirable and dangerous and powerful because of that desirability and that dangerousness. To watch the impact of your beauty and personality on a man, to speculate on how far you will go with him, and to wonder, "Is that really another man watching me from the corner of his eye and biding his time until I'm free to be approached?"

It would be wonderful not to know what was going to happen next. Because with Charlie, who is a good man and is good to you, you know what is going to happen next—the next day, next week, next Christmas, next year.

The Charlies of this world are the salt of the earth, and they get the mail out and make the trains run on time, but they are wedded to routine. Worse, they *like* routine. They like the familiar and the predictable. When they go to the city, they always stay at the same hotel. When they buy a new car, they buy another Toyota. They wear the same kind of white cotton underwear that their fathers wore. They have gone to the same barber for fifteen years. When they dine out, they have roast beef medium. Roast beef medium is not only an entrée, it is a state of mind. The woman remembering her first love is also remembering when men were mysterious, when any damn thing might happen next, when life and relationships were uncertain and unpredictable.

So as a married woman considering taking a lover, you have to ask yourself what it is that you want. Well, for one thing, you want to be *surprised*.

Escape From Ennui: The Lover as Tour Guide

*When you are safe at home, you wish you were having an adventure;
when you're having an adventure, you wish you were safe at home.*
—Thornton Wilder

Sometimes, what you are seeking in a love affair is simply adventure. What does "adventure" mean to you personally?

One of my more adventuresome lady friends may have read too much Ernest Hemingway at an impressionable age as she has always thought of an African safari, complete with lions, tigers, and elephants as the epitome of adventure. In her fantasy, there would be something slithery and lethal in the grass which she almost steps on but then does not because, at the last moment, a great white hunter sweeps her out of harm's way, at least out of the way of the kind of harm that comes from a literal snake in the grass. She imagines the great white hunter looks a lot like George Clooney, but he might also resemble a bearded Matthew McConaughey. Either way, he is the master of his environment, strong but gentle, and his presence allows her the paradoxical privilege of being able to take risks while being quite safe. The adventure is filled with tropical sunsets and tropical nights. Interestingly, the concomitant tropical insects do not get equal time in her fantasy. I suspect my friend might very well fly to Nairobi for safari on two hours' notice should I suggest it to her.

This same friend once took a sojourn to the South Side of Chicago at four in the morning, looking around with big eyes and expecting any kind of hassle to break out at any moment. A funky jazz club on the South Side is an exotic place for a straight white woman and is not all that secure, except that she was with not one but two all-American football types who were African-American with a certain don't-tread-on-me air about them.

She found that situation to be an adventure, just as the time she persuaded a racing car driver to give her a helmet and let her go with him on some early morning practice laps. She reported that even a zoom lens and a three-dimensional screen do not approximate the sense of speed that comes from actually being in the car.

There is a definite appeal to a lover who not only offers you the excitement of a new relationship but also the excitement of doing something quite different from what you could otherwise do. The problem with such fantasies is that a real-life person who offers these enticements may not be a particularly desirable lover in other ways.

If what you are seeking is adventure, then you must accept that specific goal as a priority and not expect to also enter the realm of the senses unless you are very, very lucky.

To sort out these issues, ask yourself a simple question. Do you want to be with him? Do you want to do things and go places with him that have nothing to do with being adventurous? Does the great white hunter become boring when you imagine him tending a backyard barbecue?

Suppose you are finally sailing into the harbor in Tonga after a lifetime of dreaming about the South Pacific. You feel happy and excited especially because you are doing it in the full glory of a tropical sunset. Your euphoria makes you look with great benevolence upon the man who just happens to be standing beside you at the ship's rail. Tonga is exciting, but it is easy to get confused and let yourself believe that the man you have met in Tonga is therefore exciting too. Many ill-fated shipboard romances flounder when you finally realize that the excitement of such a lover was in the exotic situation, not in the man himself.

In spite of such hazards, for some kinds of interludes, the lover who acts as a tour guide can be very appealing.

And sometimes, of course, you do find to your delight that he looks as good over a backyard barbecue as he did at the luau on the beach. It is just as likely, however, that the man with the sun-bronzed body, who strolled the white sand beaches of the South Pacific with you during a glorious sunset, may be far less appealing when he is strolling with you on the cold gray pavement of New York City on a dark winter day bundled in clothing.

An Alternative:

The Platonic Affair

Leisured society is full of people who spend a great part of their lives in flirtation and conceal nothing but the humiliating secret that they have never gone any further.

—George Bernard Shaw, *Overruled*

A couple may be obviously fond of each other. They may seek each other out and laugh at each other's jokes and hold hands whenever they can. He may call her by a silly pet name, and she may respond "oh, you" in a suggestive and intimate voice. They may have many opportunities to have private time together and, presumably, every opportunity to have sex. And yet—they don't.

Month after month, sometimes year after year, what appears to be a courtship, and a successful one at that, drags on and on and is neither consummated nor terminated. Such a wife has a lover in the affectionate and emotional and social sense of the word, but she remains inviolate. She has, in effect, a eunuch lover.

What they share is platonic love. As defined by author T. S. Winslow, platonic love is merely "love from the neck up."

THE EUNUCH LOVER

There are some eunuchs, which were so born from their mother's womb:
and there are some eunuchs, which were made eunuchs of men: and
there be eunuchs, which have made themselves eunuchs for the kingdom
of heaven's sake.

—Matthew 19:12

In the old days in the decadent East, men with kingdoms and sheikdoms had the privilege of keeping harems. The potentate might have as many as up to a thousand wives, and to relieve himself of the burden and responsibility of supervising them all, he would employ eunuchs. The eunuchs involved were castrated when they were young and grew up in a kind of limbo between the male world and the female one. Being sexless, they were allowed to enter the harem and to have direct contact with the wives.

In some modern circumstances, some women elect to have what amounts to eunuch lovers: these men are not sexual partners, but they are more than just platonic friends in that their level of involvement is intense.

What kind of men are eunuch lovers? Obviously, only in the most exceptional cases are they actually eunuchs although such might be the case in our culture if you consider the aberrant situation of transsexuals who are midway in the process of their transformation. Eunuch lovers are often men who are homosexual and who can love a woman in the affectionate and emotional sense without feeling any physical passion for her. The woman gets whatever lovemaking she wants elsewhere. And so does he. And they continue a relationship on other levels. Women who are married to homosexual men are often by choice or by chance in the position of having intimate, affectionate, but asexual relationships.

Not all eunuch lovers, however, are homosexual. Some simply have a very low sex drive, so low that they might be more appropriately termed "asexual." As one man described it to me, "If you think of a pilot light on a gas stove, my drive is like the pilot light, and everyone else seems to be like a big burner on high!"

In other instances, the eunuch lover is an ordinary man with presumably ordinary drives and desires, but he chooses not to express them with this particular woman. The woman in the affair may also be a practicing heterosexual but likewise chooses not to be physically involved with this particular man. These relationships are often marriages of convenience in which the couple derives benefits from one another apart from physical intimacy. For instance, the powerful politician who marries a vibrant, beautiful young wife may benefit from the attention she garners him on the campaign trail and at fund-raisers while she benefits from the social status and privileges bestowed on her as his wife. So they make an agreement. "We will love each other, we do love each other, we will act as lovers, but we will not physically be lovers." While they are not lovers in the conventional sense of the word, they are perceived by most to be in a love relationship.

FLIRTATION: ATTENTION WITHOUT INTENTION

A woman may very well form a friendship with a man, but for this to endure, it must be assisted by a little physical antipathy.
—Friedrich Nietzsche

Why bother to have a lover who is not *really* a lover? Many reasons. There are, after all, a number of historical precedents.

Consider, for example, the good Queen Victoria, who was surely the epitome of all that is moral and proper. After the death of her beloved Prince Albert, she was distraught and sought consolation from one John Brown, who had been an attendant to her late husband. John Brown was made her personal servant; but as depicted in the movie *Mrs. Brown*, featuring Judi Dench as Queen Victoria, Brown obviously far exceeded that modest role. Their relationship was extremely close emotionally, and his privileges at Windsor Castle certainly reflected a great deal of trust and intimacy. Were they lovers? No one knows. There was speculation. There were rumors. If you can't trust Queen Victoria, who can you trust?

We have been discussing the new sexuality as if, in fact, the freedoms now available had transformed women into sexual creatures. Often, this is simply not the case. It may not be a case of moral guilt or psychological hang-ups as much as simply an absence of desire. Certainly, there can be an absence of desire for a particular man, someone whose body does not seem erotic even though he is lovable in many other ways. The woman may prefer not to have to bother with sex. If she doesn't want to bother, such a turn of phrase reveals so much of her attitude that it is probably just as well that she does not.

The lover who is not *really* a lover may be willing to be emotionally involved with a woman, yet unwilling to be physically involved with her, especially if she is married. To love her emotionally is acceptable, but to make love to her is not because that would be adultery. According to the Bible, a man who lusts after a woman has already committed adultery in his heart. There can be, however, a curious kind of doublethink wherein having an affair of the heart, which technically is not consummated, does not count. It is not really adultery and is therefore acceptable. Some women committed to the ideal of premarital chastity may use much the same reasoning so that they may be sexually experienced while technically remaining virgins.

Such an affair may evoke the same jealousy that a betrayed spouse feels when his mate is physically unfaithful. In actuality, such emotional infidelity may be harder for the spouse to accept than would a casual affair, which could be dismissed as an impulsive roll in the hay or a one-night stand.

Be that as it may, as long as the lovers can maintain that *it* did not happen, they have what seems to them an impeccable moral position. When confronted, they will even manage a little sanctimony and lament the kind of world in which simple platonic friendship is disallowed. They will even muster some righteous indignation at what from the outside seem to be perfectly well-founded suspicions.

Once you take a eunuch lover, you need a husband of considerable trust and/or credulity in order to carry off what seems to be flagrant disregard for convention. You then have the freedom to be quite open about your comings and goings with him. What is the husband to think? What are the neighbors to think? One obvious explanation is that the man in question is less than a real man and is a eunuch in his heart, if not in actuality.

One woman came home late to an angry husband who demanded to know where she had been. She confessed that she had been drinking at the Purple Cow, a local tavern.

"I don't want you hanging out with men in bars," he said.

"But I was with Freddy," she said.

"Oh," he said, "well, at least you could have called to tell me that you'd be late."

Being with Freddy didn't count. Freddy was not a real man and so could not be threatening. Once Freddy knows how he is regarded, and he is not gay, then one wonders how it will make him feel. He is the kind of man with whom one's wife is absolutely safe, not because he or she are so honorable, but because he is so—safe.

The decadent East has a treasury of erotic literature in which the roles of the potentate, harem girl, and the eunuch figure prominently. One theme of these tales is the delights which await the man who pretends to be a eunuch in order to get into the harem, but who is not, and is instead a fox among the chickens.

Another theme is the eunuch who is not totally a eunuch in that he is still capable of an erection and of some sexual feeling. Sexologists allow that this is possible if unlikely. The eunuch lover who is presented as such to the world in general and to the husband in particular has an especially provident game plan in that he can have all of the enjoyments with none of the penalties.

He must learn two maxims which both he and his ladylove must say repeatedly, "Deny, deny, deny," followed by "That's my story, and I am sticking to it."

CHAPTER 10

EENEY, MEANEY, MINEY, MOE: DON OR CHARLES OR JACK OR JOE

Between two evils, choose neither;
Between two goods, choose both.
—Tryon Edwards

If you are a woman who is thinking about taking a lover, then you are on the verge of an important decision. Having a love affair can be a source of great joy—or great sorrow. Falling in love can make a big difference in your life and in your happiness, and the biggest difference of all is not the fact of the experience per se, but in the kind of man you choose and how suitable he is for you.

When you pick a lover, pick a lover who will be loving. Pick a sex object who turns you on and whose personality pleases you. Pick a man for his intrinsic intangible appeal who evokes a response in you physically or emotionally or both. Pick him as someone to love and to love you back for the sustaining joy of that relationship. Not for money, not for presents, not for saving face, not even for someone to go to the movies with. Do not pick him as an act of kindness to him or as an act of defiance to your friends or family or to please your mother or to punish her (or your father either, for that matter). Do not pick a lover for anyone's sake except your own and for any other reason than that something about him calls out to something in you and makes you want to explore that calling further. Pick a lover this way, and you have a chance for a new kind of relationship with a wide range of potentially enjoyable experiences.

Choosing a lover implies a selection process. It conveys the image that there are a number of men who potentially might be chosen, whether they know it or not, and that some kind of implicit or explicit criteria are being used to make the critical judgments. Picking a lover is a lot like picking flowers, and sometimes, one wants a bouquet.

Lovers Are Not
for Everyone

Women keep a special corner of their hearts for sins they have never committed.
—Cornelia Otis Skinner

There are many circumstances under which a modern woman might decide that having a lover would increase her quality of life and would bring her a great deal of joy and satisfaction. It does not follow, however, that this is a decision that would be right for all women all of the time. At least three kinds of women will not be interested in the prospect of taking a lover: the woman with homophilic tendencies, the contented celibate wife, and the (presumably contented) wife in a traditional marriage.

Some women who are seeking a lover are not seeking a man at all but are instead looking for another woman. The sexual revolution and the new permissiveness have made the lesbian option an increasingly acceptable alternative to traditional marriage. Some women may be exclusively homosexual. Others who are basically heterosexual may, under special circumstances, find themselves in what amounts to a homosexual encounter. Or they may wish to have a woman lover in addition to a husband or male lovers. The focus of this book happens to be on picking a lover who is a man. It may well be that many of the same principles would also apply to picking a lover who is a woman. The examples here happen to be male oriented: their application is a matter of personal preference and taste.

To borrow a slogan from another context: "Sometimes the best man for the job *is* a woman."

THE CELIBACY OPTION

Some modern cynics make assertion
That chastity's a sex-perversion.
Such a description should go far
To make it much more popular.
                    —Geoffrey B. Riddehough

One woman who is not interested in picking a lover is the woman who prefers to be celibate. Some women simply seem not to have sexual urges of the kind that are felt by almost all men and by most women. Rather than being either heterosexual or homosexual, they are more appropriately designated as asexual.

Some women find the idea of sex repulsive. They do not like to be touched; they are not pleased by erotic attentiveness and are by nature inclined toward a nunlike existence. Often, but not always, their negative attitude toward sexuality is associated with a strong religious commitment or with a very damaging experience the first time they had sex. Other women may find the possibility of sexuality mildly appealing under the right circumstances, but they have little interest in the pursuit of sexual experience per se. The anticipated pleasures are not sufficiently enticing to outweigh their religious or moral scruples.

Some women who have been sexually active and who have enjoyed that part of their life may find that at a particular period of time, they want to take a sabbatical from sex and turn their attention and energies to something else. Such a sex sabbatical may well go with some emotional trauma, such as a broken love affair or a divorce. It might accompany a sense of loss and grief when a loved one dies. It might go with being very ill or with recovering from being very ill.

Experts who discuss male impotence are quick to point out that occasional situational impotence is quite common for many men in circumstances of psychological stress or depression. Depression tends to inflate one's troubles while deflating one's physical apparatus. Being depressed is not conducive to being or feeling sexy. We do not talk about female "impotence" in the same way, but some women may experience essentially the same phenomenon with a temporary loss of sexual desire and/or of the ability to achieve orgasm.

The body has a wisdom of its own and a well-developed sense of priorities. When your body is again ready for an erotic life, it will let you know. You have little to gain, and quite a bit to lose, if you try to force from yourself a response which must come spontaneously and naturally.

There is nothing wrong with being celibate if that is what feels most appropriate for you. Whatever your reasons for not wanting a lover, you have a right to be turned off if you happen to feel turned off, and that decision is your own to make. Better to be celibate than to feel guilty, better to be celibate than to submit to unpleasant experiences, better to be celibate than to delegitimize your feelings by going through the motions without desire.

The fact that there is an increasing permissiveness which allows women to have lovers should not be interpreted as an obligation to do so. Sexual apathy is in itself an excellent reason not to be sexually involved whether that apathy is toward only one particular man or men in general. You *can* take a lover if you want to, but under no circumstances should you feel you *have* to do so.

TRADITIONAL WIVES

I've only slept with men I've been married to. How many women can make that claim?

—Elizabeth Taylor

Another kind of woman who does not seek a lover is the married woman who is committed to being faithful to her husband. Some fortunate wives would never consider taking a lover because they find, in their own husbands, all the affection and sexuality that they desire. For them, there is no need for more love or a different love. As Sir Charles Sedley points out in "Reasons for Constancy," "When change itself can give no more, 'tis easy to be true."

Other wives may think wistfully of men more appealing than their husbands, but they are firmly and irrevocably committed to the principal of marital fidelity. Such a good wife may be inhibited from fully loving any man she is not married to or is not intending to marry. Elizabeth Taylor-Hilton-Wilding-Todd Fisher-Burton-Burton-Warner-Fortensky may not be exactly your idea of a traditional wife, but on this issue, at least she has traditional attitudes.

Other wives may be faithful for a lifetime, not because they are particularly infatuated with their husbands, but because they are not particularly tempted by anyone else. Such women may seem to be very virtuous, but in fact, they are merely apathetic. Their energies have been channeled into other things, such as careers or children, which take precedence over love and romance. The absence of a lover is not a sacrifice for them, and the prospect of a lover does not entice them. They are, in effect, faithful by default.

Finally, there are some wives who would love to have a lover, but they cannot find the kind of man that they want. Or they would love to have a lover, but they don't have the courage. They think of a lover, and they visualize jealous husbands and gossiping aunts and sleazy private eyes. They think of a lover, and they remember the scene of sudden, violent death that was the shocking climax in the movie *Looking for Mr. Goodbar*. In real life, taking a lover can sometimes be hazardous; and drastic consequences can, in fact, occur.

As Mark Twain observed, "There are several good protections against temptation, but the surest is cowardice."

SEXUAL DECISION MAKING

There is a tide in the affairs of women which, taken at its flood, leads—God knows where.
                    —George Noel Gordon, Lord Byron, *Don Juan*

Let us assume that you are not a lesbian. Let us assume, moreover, that whether or not you happen to be married, you have been harboring a secret yen for a lover—or for another lover. Let us assume that the twinkle in your eye has become a gleam. Perhaps your present sex life leaves something to be desired. Perhaps you have no sex life at all except for memories and vicarious experiences, both of which lose something in translation.

If so, when you think of taking a lover, first think very seriously about what you want in a lover. Think about what you want to give to him, as well as what you want from him. Make a list if it helps you to focus your thoughts. Pay special attention to what comes to mind first and to the sort of associations you make.

If you are a woman of experience, let yourself remember when lovemaking was a special event for you. This simple exercise in nostalgia is best done on quiet beaches or on a cross-country train trip or in bed on a Sunday morning listening to the rain.

Think about making love, not just in terms of when it was vaguely good or not so good but in specific terms of whether it was in the evening or the morning or the midday when *it* was just right. Of the many times one makes love, only a few are truly memorable, but those few are very important clues to your own secret garden because they offer very telling examples of the possibility of getting what you want. Who were you with then? What was special about that occasion? What did he do or say or arrange that made it right? Can you visualize him? Do you remember his voice, or do you first of all think about the touch of his hands?

A friend of mine relayed to me an encounter she had had when she had long hair. Her lover lifted up her hair and kissed it and then kissed her neck beneath the hair. He was wearing some exotic scent, and his beard tickled her, and the cashmere sweater he was wearing was incredibly soft and radiant with his warmth, and she was totally undone by the simple gesture. And totally attuned.

Where were you when you made love in special and important ways? What was important about the encounter? If it had been only a narrow bed in a cold old cabin, would that have been OK? Was it after a romantic dinner? Was there music playing? Was there a crackling fire in the fireplace?

When you can remember several of these special events, look for the similarities among them. Was there the breathless urgency and excitement of having a plane to catch? Was there the sense of timelessness that goes with checking into a fine hotel for the weekend when no one knows where you are, so no one can contact you? Were you following up on an extensive soothsaying session about your life and his? Or were you full of the enchantment of being with a perfect stranger? Was there the domestic tenderness of having looked in on your sleeping baby or the exotic madness of a rum-soaked Caribbean beach party?

Even if you are remembering many occasions and many encounters, you will soon recognize a theme to the really special encounters. Subsequent wondrous and wonderful events are often some variation on that theme. What you are looking for in a lover is someone who understands that theme: not necessarily the same man or men, but the same kind of man or men and the same kind of situation.

There is, of course, no guarantee that the resulting experience will be all that great—it might be quite mundane and humdrum. Perhaps your tastes have changed, perhaps your memory is faulty, or perhaps the key ingredient was something you overlooked. Putting yourself in the situation where peak experiences are likely to happen does not assure that they will occur, but it does increase the odds.

Only you can define the kind of love experience you want. And while there are no perfect guidelines to ensure exceptional lovemaking in the future, the best indicator of success would be some reincarnation of what was exceptional in the past. Except for the benison of beautiful blind luck, which does happen, it is only after you know what you want and why that you can go about finding it.

THE RATING GAME

Women are moved by sexual impulses towards particular men, not towards men as a whole, and men will never understand women as long as they do not understand this.
—H. M. Swanwick, The Future of the Women's Movement

When you look around a party or when you go over your Christmas card list or when you count on your fingers and toes men whom you have found attractive, you make implicit decisions about their appeal relative to one other. You also make decisions about their attractiveness to you. You have formed impressions based on appearance and conversations and, perhaps, on reports from other people; and you mesh these together into an overall response to the man. The many factors involved in sex appeal or animal magnetism or whatever *it* is called are difficult to define, but they combine to form an impression that is easy to recognize.

Every time you meet a new man, you form an opinion about him. Sometimes you feel indifferent, sometimes you feel a faint distaste, sometimes you feel drawn to him. In your responses, you subconsciously rank him from terrible to terrific, from fatuous to fascinating, from disgusting to delectable. It is fortunate for everyone that the man who seems exactly right to one woman may not even seem passably attractive to another.

Christopher Marlow in *Dr. Faustus* describes Helen of Troy as having "the face that launched a thousand ships." Some irreverent young men, not attuned to the sacredness of classic poetry, borrow this line to rate their women. Out girl watching, they will say cryptically to each other, "Five hundred ships, huh?" "No, I don't think so. Three hundred at most. But look at that one! Eight hundred easy." The popular 1980's movie *Ten*, featuring Bo Derek wearing rows of corn braids and not much else, was based on a variation of this perennial theme where men rate women on a one-to-ten scale.

Long-distance love affairs call for another sort of rating scheme. Just ask yourself: how far would you be willing to commute for a rendezvous? Some men are attractive enough to draw you across the street. Some are attractive enough to rate a drive across town, if it isn't raining. Some of the spectacular ones are worth a bus trip from Boston to Philadelphia. A few even rate a transatlantic flight.

On the other end of the scale, one woman explained, "Well, if we had twin beds, and his was all the way across the room, it wouldn't be worth the trip."

When you are thinking about rating various men and comparing their pros and cons, there is another problem to be taken into account. In assessing people and the pleasure they give you or might give you, you cannot always average out the good with the bad. Sometimes, the bad is *so* bad that it destroys all of the rest.

In Fats Waller's song, "Ain't Misbehavin'," the man turfs out his girlfriend, complaining, "Your feet's too big!" If shoe size is that important to you, then a beautiful smile and charm won't compensate. However, it's important to learn to overlook unimportant quirks and refrain from making arbitrary judgments over insignificant flaws. The more tolerant you can manage to be, the more people you can find potentially compatible, and the more tolerance you can expect in return.

Except for axe murderers, many of the so-called fatal flaws of physique or character are not all that fatal. Sometimes, however, a potential lover has a trait that makes him beyond the pale as far as you are concerned. He is like a phone number you dial by memory. If you correctly remember six out of seven numbers, your memory is 86 percent correct, but you still don't get the person you were trying to call.

Six correct out of seven is pretty good; but with phone numbers, as with people, it is not good enough.

MAKING MISTAKES

*Love is like mushrooms: One doesn't know if they belong to the bad
sort until it is too late.*

—Tristan Bernard

When you are assessing a man as a potential friend or lover, you
unfortunately do not have a crystal ball to tell you the truth about him. You
cannot look into his past or know what he is thinking or use second sight
to second-guess him. Nevertheless, you do form an impression; and right or
wrong, you have to act on that impression.

Most often, your instinctive reactions to someone are sound; but
sometimes, you will make a mistake. When you are wrong, there are two
kinds of mistakes you can make. Suppose, for a moment, that there was an
omniscient person, a fairy godmother to advise and decide just which men
out there are right for you and which are not. To keep it simple, let's just
divide them into good prospects and bad prospects.

One mistake you could make would be to pick a *false positive*—that
is, you could pick someone who seemed like a good prospect but who,
in fact, turns out to be a loser, a turkey, a real dud. The wonderful traits
you thought you saw might have been wildly exaggerated in your mind
or maybe even made up entirely. It is in this sense that people say love is
blind. It sees things that aren't there and refuses to see alarming signals
that are there.

Alternatively, a second kind of mistake you could make is to not pick a
false negative—that is, you reject someone who would have been great. The
fairy godmother is saying, "Go for it, girl! I conjured him up just for you." You
are saying, "Forget it! I can't stand men with buckteeth!" A false negative is
someone whom you reject before you have a chance to realize that he might
have been a good prospect after all.

To put the same dilemma in a different way: with false positives, you start out thinking that someone is pure gold and then discover that he is actually made of brass. Not only made of brass but with feet of clay as well. You have said yes too soon, and you are disappointed and disillusioned. With false negatives, you reject a prospective lover who seems to be made of brass. Underneath, however, he is really made of gold; and you never discovered it, or discovered it too late. If you had not been so quick to say no, you might have found a worthwhile friend, if not a lover.

Sadly, you never even get to know what you should have done because although you might wonder what would have happened if you had done this or done that, you can never know. The amount of risks you take depends on your personality and your options.

If you are yourself very attractive, sort of a princess who has many suitors swarming around, then you can be very picky. A few lost false negatives won't bother you as there are many more where they came from, and you can be very sure of not getting a false positive. However, if you are not quite a princess but rather an ordinary stepsister of a princess, then you may be more reluctant to waste your opportunities and more ready to take chances.

Taking chances involves taking risks, but as the American philosopher Elbert Hubbard, in his famous *Scrap Book*, warns, "The greatest mistake you can make is to be continually fearing that you will make a mistake."

TAKING CHANCES

*Why not go out on a limb? Isn't that where
the fruit is?*

—Frank Scully

The process of picking a lover is a process of prediction and projection.
You think: "If I were to have Robert as a lover, how would he be? Would we
fit well together? Would he make me happy? How would being with Robert
compare with being with Michael? Who knows?"

No one knows. It is not that we are left with an inexact science. We
have no science at all. Cupid is, by definition, capricious and sometimes
mischievously puts together two people who are complete opposites of each
other. The most unlikely couples can be blissfully happy, drawn together by
a magnetic attraction no one else can understand.

On the other hand, sometimes a marriage which seems made in heaven
is, in fact, a private hell for the man and woman involved. Richard Needham,
a former Canadian humor columnist for the *Globe and Mail*, puts it well when
he points out, "You never know the truth about anyone else's marriage; you
only know the truth about your own, and you know exactly half of that."

Generalizations based on experience and common sense can suggest that
some kinds of men are *probably* a better bet than others. There are guidelines
about the kinds of men who *might* make better lovers for you than others.
Alas, there are no guarantees.

Each man and woman is a complex individual; each relationship unfolds
under unique circumstances. Since predictions must be made without the
aid of a crystal ball, any advice which can be given is less than crystal clear.
You could have selected some men for all the right reasons, men who had
all the right attributes. Nevertheless, your choice led to a disastrous affair
because something unforeseen happened. He crashed his car or lost his job

or succumbed to a numbing midlife depression or encountered some other hazard no one could have predicted.

Or as often happens with young marriages, the man you picked may have been exactly right for you at the time, and then you grew up and changed your mind—or he did.

Sharing the experiences and perspectives of others will not give you absolute answers about what you should do next. It will, however, give you something to ponder as you sit by the phone, waiting for it to ring.

Or in a bolder mood, as you scroll through your BlackBerry or cell phone address book, trying to decide whose number to call.

SINGLE MEN, MARRIED MEN,

AND SORTA MARRIED MEN

---

*No man worth having is true to his wife, or can be true to his wife,
or ever was, or ever will be so.*
                              —Sir John Vanbrugh, The Relapse

The world is always more complex than it first seems. At first glance, it would be natural to consider single men, and perhaps married men as well, as potential lovers. Among single men, we could include those who have never married as well as the divorced and the widowed.

Alas, it is not that simple. A man who is separated is still technically married in that he cannot yet remarry. However, he usually thinks and acts single and is socially considered that way.

A man who is living with someone is outwardly viewed as a married man by society even if he is not legally married. The U.S. census calls him a POSLQ, which is ungainly bureaucratese for "persons of the opposite sex sharing living quarters." He is, perhaps, not quite a common-law husband, which is a matter-of-legal definition, but he is certainly more than a boyfriend.

To make matters even more complex, there are also degrees of being married. Some men seem to be "barely married" in that they come and go as they please and, in general, act as if they were single in spite of a wife and children who technically live in the same place with them. On the other hand, some men are "dreadfully married" in that their wife is a constant presence to be taken into account whether she happens to be physically present or not.

The single woman who selects a single man as a lover has few problems. In this permissive day and age, lovers can be quite open about their affair, and few people are likely to object openly. The end point of the affair is also open: it could easily lead to marriage, or it could easily not. The situation is balanced and relatively uncomplicated.

The married woman with a single man as a lover will find that he presents a number of advantages. If she is constrained by when her husband gets home or by when she can get a babysitter (and many other domestic details), her lover can arrange his time to suit her erratic schedule. The disadvantage is that in a very short time, he will resent having to do so. Men are used to being the ones who make arrangements and call the shots even in such trivial ways as deciding the time for a date. The married woman with an unmarried paramour reverses the roles and must do so with considerable tact. Conveniently, the unmarried man has to live some place; and often, his own home will provide a safe and opportune location for the affair.

The unmarried lover of a married woman is in a relatively powerful position in that his relationship is not balanced by a relationship with a wife. Almost always, that means he will exercise his right to have other women, just as you, as a married woman, have another man. The jealousy you may experience is made twice as hard because you have no legitimate grounds for complaint and because you are never exactly sure whom you should be jealous of or why. On the other hand, with a married man, his wife provides a clear-cut target for any jealousy you might feel.

The most common kinds of affairs, however, involve two other possible combinations: a single woman with a married man and a married woman with a married man.

FIRST WIFE, SECOND WIFE?

Many a man owes his success to his first wife—and his second wife to his success.

—Jim Backus

In traditional courtship, unmarried women were pursued by unmarried men with the explicit intent of getting them paired off and safely wed. When this ideal norm was broken, as it often was, the most common variation was the situation of an unmarried woman being courted by a married man. The triangles that resulted from this pairing have been the subject of many stories, plays, and movies. The wife was compared and contrasted with the mistress, and *the* question was would the man leave his wife and children.

The unmarried woman in this situation was usually advised not to believe any of his stated intentions because in the end, he would be won back by responsibilities and respectability, and the disillusioned mistress would have wasted her time.

It is interesting that a belief that the mistress would be used and abandoned has persisted despite the evidence that in nearly half of all marriages, somebody does leave somebody, and it is not at all uncommon that the precipitating event involves the husband leaving his wife for another woman.

In any case, if the goal of courtship was supposed to be marriage, the man who was already married was a poor risk. From the woman's point of view, his marital status was critical. The same applied to the less common situation of a married woman being courted by a single man. If one begins with a different perspective and approaches a love relationship as an end in itself, then the issue of marital status makes a difference mostly in terms of the logistics of the affair.

The married man who makes a good lover is the one who can handle the complexities of loving more than one person and who gives the mistress a legitimate place in his life. He recognizes the legitimacy of her claims on his time and attention. However, you must cope with the need for secrecy and must adapt to his unpredictable time schedule.

The problems of the backstreet mistress have been documented endlessly. In fact, there was a 1941 film, later remade in the early sixties, called *Back Street*, which, predictably, ended in the mistress being cast aside. However, in fact, an attentive married man might even be preferable to an unmarried one. He will, of necessity, be less possessive; and he does not have the option of trying to turn you into his wife.

If you are yourself married, the main advantage of having an affair with a man who is also married is that he has as much to lose as you do if the relationship becomes public. He will, therefore, be most rigorous in taking precautions and most understanding of your circumstances. The disadvantage, of course, is that instead of having to worry about one set of schedules, you have to worry about two, and both may be relatively inflexible. There is also no safe and obvious trysting place. He has to take you to the no-tell motel, and you can only hope that sometimes, there is truth in advertising.

Freud observed that in every marriage bed, there were really four persons to be concerned with: the bride, the groom, the bride's father, and the groom's mother. In the adulterous affair between two married people, the hypothetical marital bed is even more crowded: we must make room as well for his current wife and your current husband. When four people rather than two must be taken into account, the situation is made more than twice as complex. Add children of various ages, and it becomes a scenario worthy of a double agent.

Fortunately, the rewards for both the errant wife and the errant lover are often so delightful and so sustaining that it is worth it all. Indeed, the very poignancy of an impossible situation and the necessity of love expressed from afar may add intensity and a magic melancholy, which is the essence of romance. The drama of star-crossed lovers may make their occasional coming together that much more marvelous, both literally and figuratively. In the long-running Broadway play *The Fantasticks*, two young lovers are presented with as many deliberate obstacles as possible, so their love for each other will be that much more intense and romantic for having had to overcome them.

These lines,

> Two households both alike in dignity,
> In fair Verona, where we lay our scene,
> From ancient grudge break to new mutiny,
> Where civil blood makes civil hand unclear

begin the prologue of *Romeo and Juliet*, the world's most celebrated star-crossed lovers.

The Borrowed Husband

Husbands are chiefly good lovers when they are betraying their wives.
—Marilyn Monroe

A word on the ethics of involvements with married men. In the first place, you should assume that a man old enough to be married is old enough to be responsible for his own actions. You do not, indeed could not, induce, seduce, entice, or otherwise abduct him away from home and hearth if he did not wish to be waylaid.

Well, to be strictly accurate, maybe you could hornswoggle a husband into a compromising position if you were outrageous enough and if he were drunk enough, tired enough, or provoked enough. The man may be strong, but his flesh is weak. Even if such a seduction could be successfully staged, it is hardly the kind of relationship we have been discussing.

First, if a husband enters into an affair, he must want to enter into an affair. The moral implication of what that does to his promises to his wife and to the nature of his understanding with her are his problems, not yours.

Second, having an affair does not necessarily compromise his marriage, especially when having him for a husband is not among your aspirations. It is a fact, although not a widely acknowledged one, that in a number of cases, a mistress is a stabilizing influence rather than a disruptive one. An extramarital connection may make bearable a situation that would otherwise be unbearable without the emotional underpinnings of the affair.

The most obvious examples of such situations are those where the wife is, in some way, sick or disabled; but these are, by no means, the only instances. Marriage involves many obligations or, to use an old-fashioned word, "duties." A husband may be able to carry out his duties to his wife and his responsibilities to his children better with the help of a mistress than without her. Having a mistress may very well lessen a man's feelings of marital discontent and his overall desire to end his marriage. It is not an argument that many wives are likely to buy, but it may well be true all the same.

It may also be true, of course, that the presence of a mistress raises discontent that did not previously exist in the marriage. I doubt that the impulse for extramarital connections comes willy-nilly from a scene of domestic bliss. The seeds of the liaison are there long before the first introduction is made. You can't "steal" a husband unless he wants to be stolen. Or since wives do not own husbands, and husbands do not own wives, it would be more precise to say, "You can't entice a man into an extramarital connection unless something about his marital connection makes him want to be enticed."

One unrepentant mistress explained, "I've never *stolen* a husband. When one was just sitting around and no one was using him anyway, I may have *borrowed* one once in a while, but I always sent him home when I was done."

ON BEING PERFECT ENOUGH

American women expect to find in their husbands a perfection that English women only hope to find in their butlers.
—Somerset Maugham

Having outlined some of the things that it might be nice to have in a lover, and some of the signs of trouble to watch out for, there is an important qualification to be made: *nobody's perfect*. If you insist on waiting for the perfect lover to come along, you will die an optimistic but inexperienced ninety-year-old virgin.

It might even be admitted, sotto voce, that you are not quite perfect yourself.

The ideal lover would be a complex, composite man. He would, perhaps, have the physique of a Viking, with the sparkling eyes of an Irishman and the graceful eloquent hands of an English nobleman. He would have the wit and repartee of a French jeunesse dorée, with the keen mind of a Jewish intellectual, the bearing of a Spanish matador, and the chiseled muscles of an African-American male. He would have the penis of a Nordic stud, with the clothes of an Italian dandy, and the vitality of an Australian drover.

If you do not like my national stereotypes, you can spend an amusing half hour making up your own. But even the ideal man does not necessarily make for an ideal love affair.

LOVE, OH LOVE,
OH PERFECT LOVE

The centipede was happy quite
Until a toad in fun
Said, "Pray, which leg goes after which?"
That worked her mind to such a pitch,
She lay distracted in a ditch,
Considering how to run.

—Mrs. Edward Craster

Every day women meet men, women and men fall in love, and women and men declare themselves ecstatically happy and walk off holding hands and smiling. Yet when you think of what goes into a love affair, it is, in fact, so complex you wonder how it is that anyone pulls it off. Perhaps like the running centipede, one should not think too carefully too often.

When thinking of a love affair, you must take into account two major components: the affectionate and the erotic. Then you have to think of the affair as consisting of two actors, interacting and responding to each other. From the woman's point of view, what is the best of all possible worlds?

In the first place, a woman wants a man for whom she feels affection. She must like him; it is even better if she loves him. Unrequited affection makes her unhappy, so in the second place, he must be a man who returns her emotional feelings. Third, she wants a man for whom she has erotic feelings, a man who turns her on. Being turned on by herself is merely frustrating, so she also needs a fourth component, a man who responds to her erotically and finds her sexually desirable.

As if all these things were not difficult enough, she also wants to feel that the relationship is balanced. Her affection for him should be returned in the same degree, her desire for him reciprocated with equal passion. Ideally, each one feels for the other exactly the same amount and intensity of love. Moreover, each one starts to love at the same time. If love dies, each one stops loving at the same time. The more you think about it, the more complex and implausible it becomes.

No wonder the course of true love never runs smooth. It is amazing that any love affairs even happen at all! Fortunately, many wonderful things can and do happen with lovers who are less than perfect and in love affairs that come complete with glitches or more serious problems.

Love, Oh Practically Perfect Love

Infatuation is when you think he's as sexy as Robert Redford, as smart as Henry Kissinger, as noble as Ralph Nader, as funny as Woody Allen, and as athletic as Jimmy Connors. Love is when you realize that he's as sexy as Woody Allen, as smart as Jimmy Connors, as funny as Ralph Nader, as athletic as Henry Kissinger, and nothing like Robert Redford—but you'll take him anyway.

—Judith Viorst, Redbook

In the best of all possible worlds, it would be ideal to find that a lover who was just right for you in terms of emotion and affection was also just right for you in terms of erotic fulfillment. Alas, in real life, that is often not the case. The man with overtly tender and affectionate concern for you, the emotional marathoner, may not make love with you at all or may do so very seldom or may not do so very well when he does. The swordsman, who is turned on and gives of himself freely in bed, may not have much love or even much affection once dressed and out of bed.

Many a maiden is still dreaming of the perfect prince who will one day come, who will make her come, and who will love her at all levels all at once. But later, many a woman realizes that love in the many forms she desires is not to be found all at once in the arms of any one man. She gives up on the perfect prince and begins to look around for a make-do prince instead . . . maybe a mere duke, or maybe a mere commoner. The road to love is a series of compromises from the fantasy of girlhood to the world-weary cynicism of old age. There is Mr. Right, but there is also Mr. Right Now, Mr. Right for Me at this Moment, etc. Fortunately, in affairs of the heart, even mistakes can be glorious.

Writer Suzanne Jordan is correct when she asserts that "the perfect mate, despite what *Cosmopolitan* magazine says, does not exist no matter how many of those tests you take." However, Merle Shain is also correct in asserting that "some men are more perfect than others." What is needed is a new oxymoron: things don't have to be *perfect*; they only have to be *perfect enough*. A lover who is perfect enough is just fine. Finding him is a much easier task than finding the absolutely perfect man of your fantasies.

The technology of this country is so proficient that we can get quite carried away with our expectations of what we need—or think we need. With an imposed sixty-five-mile speed limit, we still delight in buying a car that can cruise at a hundred miles per hour without effort. Almost every kitchen has an eight-speed blender when most cooks only need one marked Fast and Slow. Home audio systems can be so elaborate and powerful that only your dog can hear the differences, and the speakers can never be turned up more than one-tenth of their volume capacity. A camera used for family snapshots nevertheless is selected because it is capable of shooting at one-thousandth of a second. This kind of technological overkill produces products which are far more perfect than are necessary. A camera shooting at one-five-hundredth of a second produces satisfactory pictures for half the price. The man who is not perfect but who is perfect enough may well be the one to love you throughout a lovely love affair.

The philosopher Søren Kierkegaard is widely quoted as reflecting philosophically: "If you marry, you will regret it; if you do not, you will also regret it." The same applies to the lover decision. If you take a lover, you may regret it; if you do not take a lover, you may also regret it.

The question you need to consider is this, when you are an old lady of ninety-two, reflecting on the past decades, which will you regret the most: the sins you committed or the sins you omitted? My conversations with old ladies, guarded as they are, usually suggest regret for opportunities lost, for time wasted, for doors not opened, and for experiences not enjoyed.

The poet Robert Herrick gives timeless advice, "Gather ye rosebuds while ye may." He is speaking "to the virgins, to make much of time," but he might well speak to other women too. It is well to enjoy the men of the world while they are as eager to enjoy you. It is well to experience as much as you can of what life has to offer. And the devil take the hindmost, whatever that is.

The philosopher Bertrand Russell offers a sound conclusion, "Of all forms of caution, caution in love is perhaps the most fatal to true happiness." If you must love, love bravely.

CHAPTER 11

THE NEW COURTSHIP

The pleasure of love is in loving. We are happier with the passion we feel than in that we arouse.
—François, Duc de La Rochefoucauld, *Maxims*

For decades, for centuries, for a millennium, men have had the right and privilege of choosing as sex partners women who turned them on. If they wanted a partner who was young or mature, short or tall, blonde or dark, quiet or bold, curved or slender, they could pursue the women most pleasing to them.

Of course, not all men were successful in winning the kind of women they most preferred. And of course, some men did not allow themselves such indulgences but made pragmatic choices of wives who were heiresses or the daughters of bosses or women who were otherwise useful for disparate ends. Such marriages did not necessarily preclude their simultaneous quest for other women who would be mistresses. In most instances, the women selected as sex objects or as love objects were selected because they were judged to be sexy or lovable.

In contrast to this pattern, women for a millennium have selected men for practical considerations. A woman needed a provider for herself and a provider and father for her children. In most instances, the most valuable commodity a woman had, to negotiate with in the world, was her body. She used this marketable asset to her best advantage, offering virginity and then fidelity in exchange for protection and security.

It was not so much that men had to be attractive as that they had to have attractive compensating features, such as money or power. For the good wife, sex was business, and sexual intercourse was work. Many good wives were happy in their work, but it was work all the same. If she refused her husband, she could be out of a job. In fact, she could not refuse him. He provided for her, so he had a right to her body. She had been, in effect, sold to him and could not be used by anyone else without his permission.

Supposedly, North America has experienced a social and sexual revolution. Supposedly, there are now different options for women who are liberated in many new ways and who have given up old stereotypes.

Suppose, then, that we now begin to think about sexual encounters from a new perspective.

Assume for a start that the new woman is enough in tune with her body and its erotic potential to really like sex. Touching feels good, arousal feels good, and orgasms are nonproblematic. Sex for her is or can be joyous. Fun. Wonderful. At a minimum, nice.

Assume further that the new woman is enough in charge of her life and destiny that she can make her own way. If she has enough resources to support herself and her children at a level she considers to be adequate, she can then afford the indulgence of evaluating men as sex objects in the same way that women have been evaluated over the centuries. Whether she works as an executive secretary or is herself an executive, she has a living wage which comes to her in some other way than trading her body for favors or protection.

Such a woman can afford to pick a lover because he is sexy or lovable, not because he owns three apartment buildings in prime locations. She can try to find the kind of man most to her liking, using intrinsic rather than extrinsic criteria. She will have to pay her own bills, but in return, she has control of her own body and a wide range of opportunity for personal and erotic development.

The woman who is not physically or psychologically forced to have sex when she does not want to has a new kind of freedom. She can opt for celibacy if she wants, but she can also opt to have sex for purely sexual reasons. That is a revolutionary idea. That is an idea long overdue. That is an idea whose time has come.

HER SEXUALITY: HIS SEXUALITY

Show business is like sex. When it's wonderful, it's wonderful. But when it isn't very good, it's still all right.

—Max Wall, *The Listener*

The sexual revolution has led to an increased permissiveness regarding many kinds of sexual encounters, including relatively casual ones. The so-called new morality, however, does not yet take into account all of the implications of the discrepancies between male and female patterns of sexual response. Even if 90 percent of young women are now orgasmic and proud of it, there remains another fact of life to be taken into account. The sexual response patterns of most women *are* different from the sexual response patterns of most men. This difference may be innate, or it may be simply due to different socialization patterns. Whatever its origin, it is nonetheless real.

Generally speaking, men tend to be more sexual creatures than do women. His sex drive tends to be stronger than her sex drive; his sexual urges are more frequent and more urgent. The differences that men and women experience in erotic desire are most pronounced when you compare the rapacious enthusiasm which is often characteristic of teenage boys with the reticence often characteristic of teenage girls.

Most young women may very well seek love or affection or contact comfort; but they are, for the most part, less driven by the overt need for sexual release. While recent studies have shown that teenage girls have sex almost as often as teenage boys, they do so for very different reasons. Teenage girls are far more likely to have sex to please their boyfriends or to experiment or because of peer pressure or because they want to feel loved, whereas teenage boys are far more driven by an overarching physical desire for sex.

For the most part, men are more easily turned on than are women. Alex Comfort, the noted British sexologist, observes, "Male sexual response is far brisker and more automatic. It is triggered easily by things—like putting a quarter in a vending machine." At seventeen, a young man may be turned on by anything vaguely suggestive although he may not be able to do anything very effective with all his erotic energy.

The discrepancy in sex drive tends to be less pronounced when you compare older men and women. With age and with lowering levels of testosterone, the male sex hormone, a man's sex drive becomes less compelling. With experience and perhaps with resulting loss of inhibition, a woman's sexual responsiveness may increase with age. She may be more of a sexual creature at forty-five than she was at fifteen or at twenty-five. In spite of this rapprochement, however, for most men compared with most women, sex per se is more compelling and important.

Differences in sex drive also relate to differences in sexual satisfaction. For men who are potent, which is most of them, achieving an orgasm is seldom a problem although postponing one may be. In contrast, for women, having an orgasm is something that has to be learned, and it is not always easily achieved. Except for the very lucky, doing what comes naturally just doesn't work.

A woman, especially an inexperienced woman, often needs a longer time and a particular frame of mind to be able to achieve an orgasm. She needs a lover who is patient and sexually skilled enough to provide the right kind of stimulation. With time, she becomes experienced enough to know what she wants and comfortable enough to tell her partner what works for her. Most often, she also needs a partner whom she trusts enough so that she may feel psychologically secure.

Viewed from this perspective, the shopping list of a woman's sexual "needs" is, in fact, quite extensive. Without all of these components present all at once, having sex may not be all that appealing to her and, on many occasions, she would really prefer not to have sex at all.

The British comedian Max Wall may think that, for him, "when it isn't very good, it's still all right." But legions of women would disagree. For them, when it isn't very good, it can be annoying, intrusive, degrading, painful, or just plain boring.

ON SCORING AND SEDUCTION

The worst sin—perhaps the only sin—passion can commit is to be joyless.

—Sayers

One of the biggest differences between the sexes is that, for him, a casual encounter is almost certainly going to be physically satisfying. Despite how he may feel psychologically, he will be turned on and he will come to a climax almost always. For her, however, a casual sexual encounter may or may not be one which leads to a climax. For many women, especially many young women, sex per se is not all that wonderful; the enjoyment derived from a casual encounter, if any, is often from some secondary aspect of the interaction rather than from the erotic part.

And yet . . . young women do have sex with their young men and with old ones occasionally too. They lie down in parks and are awkwardly supine on the backseats of cars and hide in recreation rooms when no one is home. They are taken to cheap motels and smuggled into dorms. They are often not really being turned on, but neither are they being forcibly abducted. They are not willing, yet they go willingly. Why is that?

Young women have been taught, directly and indirectly, that it *is* more blessed to give then to receive and that sexual pleasure is something she can and should give to the man she loves. The man's desire is for her, but her desire is often only to please him. If she loves him enough, or if she is generous enough, then his pleasure should be all the pleasure she needs.

Many times, women are not that generous. If a woman does not want to give this gift to him when he requests or demands it but does it anyway, then men and women, in general, feel that she should expect some sort of compensation for the act. She is "putting out" for him, and he is "scoring"

313

with her. What's in it for her? The basis of the trading partnership becomes obvious.

Recently on a Los Angeles freeway, I passed a jazzy car adorned with a bumper sticker: "Gas or ass—nobody rides for free!" I didn't notice the driver, but I am sure it was a man and I am equally sure he would not be the kind of man I would approve of for my sister, niece, or daughter. There are still many men in the world who believe that doing you a favor—be it giving you a ride to the local mall or buying you dinner—somehow entitles them to have free access to your body.

In her article "The Dating Game: The Dangers of Cash-Based Courtship," Anne Morse recounts the dilemma experienced by a sixteen-year-old girl named Carrie after she had gone on her very first date ever with a young man named Trent, a senior she knew slightly at the large high school both attended. The pair went to a spaghetti house for dinner and then drove to the mall to see a movie. When the movie was over, they went to a restaurant for dessert. As Trent pulled his car into Carrie's driveway, he asked Carrie for a kiss. Carrie didn't want to go lips to lips with Trent (he was a little bit of a geek), but her first thought was, "He spent all that money on me!" In the end, she didn't kiss him—and he never asked her out again.

Men who think of ordinary gestures on a quid pro quo basis are not usually as explicit as the man who puts up a sign saying Gas or Ass. Dealing with strangers might be somewhat easier if they did. The man who buys you dinner is entitled to polite attention during dinner and a polite thank-you afterward. He may hope for something else, but he is *entitled* to nothing more. Nevertheless, nice girls often find themselves putting out for many nonerotic reasons. They go to bed out of gratitude because a man has been nice to them. They go to bed out of sympathy because a man is sad or hurt or full of self-doubt. They go to bed out of boredom. Or as an alternative to being raped. They go to bed sometimes just to get a little peace, having been exhausted by the impossibility of maintaining an adequate defense against continuous pressure.

Lovers and would-be lovers offer a thousand and one reasons which amount to emotional blackmail but which are, nevertheless, effective.

"Why not?" men used to wheedle. "If you get pregnant, I'll marry you." The offer of marriage was supposed to be the ultimate sacrifice.

"Why not, you're on the pill, aren't you?" "Why not, we will use condoms?" "Why not, I'll pull out just before I come?" "Why not, you're not a virgin, it's the twenty-first century for God's sake!" "Why not, didn't you like the dinner?" Etcetera. The litany is quite familiar even to some fourteen-year-olds.

PUTTING UP WITH PUTTING OUT

There are two things one should never do from a sense of duty, and the other one is to read a book.

—Richard Needham

Consider this cautionary tale. One young woman on the road trying to live as cheaply as possible, but by no means interested in casual hooking, was once offered the opportunity to spend the night on a yacht and thereby save a hotel bill. Since the man in question was a friend of a friend and was by all accounts a respectable and benevolent guy, she took the offer at face value and showed up, backpack in hand.

She was enjoying the tranquility of watching the sun go down over the harbor and listening to the gulls when she suddenly realized that the captain of the boat considered that with overnight guests, he had a kind of droit du seigneur as far as all women were concerned. She could have screamed rape, but there was no one to hear, and she could not swim very well. Besides, the captain was quite sincere in his assumption and genuinely surprised at her reluctance.

"Well," he said, pulling down the strap of her brassiere, "why did you agree to come out here then?"

"Because it was a place to stay."

"And so it is," he said, pulling down her other strap.

She was surprised, confused, and helpless enough that, as they expressed it in Victorian novels, he "had his way with her." She left the next day at dawn after a sleepless night, feeling bewildered and a little soiled, but a lot wiser.

If women's sexual inclinations were assumed to be the same as men's, with her wanting and needing the same kind of sex to the same degree that he does, the entire structure of male-female relationships would have to be rewritten.

315

The sexual revolution has led to many changes, but it has not yet altered this fundamental premise. Both men and women recognize, on a fundamental although implicit level, that for most people most of the time, she is not as sexually driven as he is. Even if she does enjoy having sex (and often she does not) and even if she does have orgasms and cries out with delight (and often she does not), she still does not ordinarily enjoy it as much as he does. More importantly, even if she enjoys it as much, she does not *seem* to need it as much.

We now begin to classify women not so much in terms of whether or not they are sexually active but in terms of *why* they are sexually active.

Good girls, and good women, are compensated for their sexuality by love and affection, by dances and dinners, and eventually, by marriage and children. Bad girls, and bad women, are compensated more directly by presents or favors or cold cash.

TIT FOR TAT: SEXUALITY
AND EXCHANGE

The women who take husbands not out of love but out of greed, to get
their bills paid, to get a fine house and clothes and jewels; the women
who marry to get out of a tiresome job, or to get away from disagreeable
relatives, or to avoid being called an old maid—these are whores in
everything but name.

—Polly Adler, A House Is Not a Home

George Bernard Shaw, who was a master of one-liners, had a widely quoted conversation with a woman of note in which he asked if she would sleep with him for one million pounds. She said, "Of course."

"Well," he said, "would you sleep with me for two pounds?"

"Certainly not," she said. "What kind of woman do you think I am?"

"Madam," said Shaw, "we have already established what kind of woman you are. We are merely haggling about the price."

If we define prostitution in terms of its minimum components, involving merely the performance of sexual acts motivated not by sexual desire but in exchange for some form of gain, then we cast a wide net. The impulse to go to bed, or to be taken to bed, is then based not on anticipation of joyous passion but on some other motive. The incentive may be as blatant as cold cash or as subtle as an improved chance for promotion, but it is for something other than the sexual experience for its own sake.

One of the reasons it is difficult to discuss prostitution objectively is that so many of the terms used to describe it are pejorative. Old-fashioned terms like "tart" or "fallen women" or "harlot" sound strange in modern usage. The term "whore" is straightforward but very negative in tone. The terms "hooker" and "call girl" are less negative, but they refer to very specific kinds of activities.

The most neutral term is one now often used by prostitutes themselves, who refer to each other as "working girls" or "commercial sex workers." By describing themselves as working girls, they convey the neutral attitude that prostitution is an industry like any other industry and that they are merely workers doing a different kind of work.

THE OLDEST PROFESSION

It is a silly question to ask a prostitute why she does it. These are the highest paid "professional" women of America.
— Gail Sheehy, Hustling

There is nothing intrinsically wrong with selling your body. It is, after all, the oldest profession. And it is, after all, your body and you have a right to do with it what you will, including making some choices that others may think unpleasant or unwise.

There are a number of circumstances in which some or another variation of prostitution may be a rational choice. If you are young and powerless, if you are young and powerless and poor, then you use what you have. Eva Peron, who became a political icon in Argentina, was a major spokeswoman for *los descamisados* (the shirtless ones). She herself was born into a slum family and, it is alleged, began her career as a teenage prostitute. Under such circumstances, when all that a woman has is an attractive body, it is difficult to condemn her for doing the best she can with what she has.

On a less dramatic level, the trade-offs involved in sexual exchanges can be very useful. Using your sexuality for nonsexual goals is a question of individual choice and is often a legitimate way to get what you want. In *Gentleman Prefer Blondes*, Anita Loos quite rightly points out that "kissing your hand may make you feel very good, but a diamond is a girl's best friend." It is more or less acceptable for nice girls to prefer men of wealth. While they may be considered gold diggers, they are also considered smart.

Granting sexual favors may not be necessary for survival, but it can be expedient. If the sex acts involved are at least not unpleasant, then having sex can be a convenient way of paying for dinner or of being nice or of exerting control or of creating a useful obligation.

319

If you want to get money from men, then there is no question about the kind of lover you should pick. Pick a rich one. The richer, the better. If you want to get favors from men, then there is no question about the kind of lover you should pick. Pick an influential one.

The exchange of sexuality for other favors can have important consequences. The legendary Hollywood "casting couch" is based on reality and has its equivalent in many other industries. Television celebrity Barbara Walters assures young women, "I didn't get ahead by sleeping with people. Girls, take heart!" Perhaps she did not, but many have.

Many young women have come to realize that like Sally Stanford, the last grand "madam" in San Francisco who later became mayor of Sausalito, they too are "sitting on a fortune." The folk wisdom is full of references to such exchanges, which do not involve explicit prostitution but which do involve the trading of sex for nonsexual considerations.

It is not only that one is advised to "go along in order to get along." Women are also advised to "give head in order to get ahead," and that happens at all levels. In a 1981 book *The Intimate Sex Lives of Famous People*, Irving Wallace reports that when Marilyn Monroe signed her first major contract, she is alleged to have exclaimed, "That's the last cock I'll have to suck."

Don't Be a Working Girl

The prostitute is the only honest woman left in America.
—Ti-Grace Atkinson

While there may be nothing intrinsically wrong with selling your body, there is something wrong in ending up in an exchange of sexuality for some sort of gain when the situation occurs unintentionally.

There is something decidedly wrong in selling your body when you are not fully aware of what you are doing. You are being exploited when you are conned or manipulated into a "deal" you did not want to make.

There is something decidedly unwise, and perhaps also wrong, in selling your body when the rewards are slight and the exchange is unnecessary. Such selling is usually not worth the price in terms of its psychological and emotional costs.

The well-known feminist, Ti-Grace Atkinson, undoubtedly overstates her case when she claims that the prostitute is the *only* honest woman in America. However, it is valid to observe that there are many women who do not think of themselves as working girls who are dishonest about the extent to which they use their sexuality for nonsexual reasons. If you find yourself in a situation where you end up having sex for reasons other than the anticipation of a good sexual experience, then you are in fact acting like a working girl.

Margaret Sanger pioneered the Planned Parenthood movement and fought for birth control to free women from the tyranny of pregnancy. However, she also fought for freedom from sexual coercion. Writing way back in 1917 when such sentiments were not usually expressed, she declared, "A mutual and satisfied sexual act is of great benefit to the average woman, the magnetism of it is health-giving. When it is not desired on the part of the woman and she has no response, *it should not take place.* This is an act of prostitution, and is degrading to the woman's finer sensibility, all the marriage certificates on earth to the contrary notwithstanding."

What Sanger is talking about is nothing like rape in the usual and violent sense of the word. It is nothing like prostitution in the stereotypical sense of streetwalkers standing under streetlights and taking on all comers. What Sanger refers to is the not uncommon practice of women going to bed as a result of feeling sexually intimidated.

Respectable women, who do not think of themselves as working girls, may have sex for many nonsexy reasons: for protection, for a new diamond necklace, for drugs or a fix, for simple companionship. Many young women act like working girls without realizing it. And having accepted this role, they wonder why it is that under these conditions, they do not enjoy sex very much. They are not in helpless situations, yet they continue to use their sexuality as an informal medium of exchange. Or sometimes they continue to put out simply because they feel they don't have a choice.

If a man asks you to have sex with him, you need not be offended, but neither need you be obliging. A working girl may have sex in the absence of desire and may be tactful and cheerful in putting up with men who are unappealing or who are simply inept lovers. As a non-working girl, you don't have to, and you should not. If you do not want to have sex, your negative reply should be as polite as possible but also firm and unambiguous. The absence of desire is in itself sufficient reason to decline.

The correct answer to continued pressure and harassment from someone you do not feel passionate about is quite simple. "Harry, you're a toad. I don't sleep with toads!" But even if the Harry in question *is* a toad, nice girls are too considerate and nice to say so in quite those terms. They might even imply it and have Harry look so injured and tearful they then have to go to bed with him just to provide reassurance that he is *not* a toad.

The correct answer may be that you would rather watch television. That the room is too hot or too cold, and you are too energized or too tired, and he is too big or too small, too young or too old, too this or too that. In any case, the correct answer is simply, "No, thank you, I don't want to."

It is fine to let yourself be seduced, if you decide that is what you want to happen. It is not so fine to let yourself be coerced by force or by emotional blackmail. It is not so fine to let yourself be bribed by presents or trips or dinners or promises of introductions or other benefits. Real sexual freedom, instead of the ersatz kind, is the ability to say no for the simple reason that this particular person, at this particular time, is resistible. When responding to a man's unwanted advances, Helen Gurley Brown, author of *Sex and the Single Girl*, had this witty response, "You're really lovely, but do you honestly suppose I can sleep with every man who asks me?"

If you pick out a man because he really does understand pork-belly futures and has the Swiss bank accounts to prove it, then you don't have a right to complain that those are the only bellies he understands, and he could not find a clitoris even if he had a global positioning system at his disposal.

If you want to enjoy your own sexuality, *don't be a working girl.*

Freedom of Choice,
Freedom to Choose

You cannot decree women to be sexually free when they are not economically free.

—Shere Hite

If you ask a young man his thoughts about being a gigolo, he would likely reply with some scorn that this is not a role for a "real man" and that the man who does take up such a role must not be good for anything else. The same young man, however, would be pleased if his sister were dating a rich man who was generous with her, even if that rich man was of questionable physical appeal and devoid of personality.

If you asked the same young man what he would think of finding a rich woman to marry, he would likely reply with some variation on the aphorism, "The man who marries for money earns it."

For the man who thought of this homily, it was, perhaps, an insight. For women, however, marrying money and then having to "earn" it is a fact of life that every girl of sixteen has already considered to be a clear and present option as well as a clear and present danger. If *she* marries for money, she *expects* to earn it. She is expected to give up control of her life in exchange for a comfortable lifestyle which will be afforded her as long as she submits to her husband's will.

The young man who arbitrarily rejects a money marriage for himself sees no inconsistency in his profound hope that his cherished little sister will have a "good" marriage, which means a marriage to a man of means even if he is a little dull. For the woman of few resources, a husband to take care of things may be the only solution. With limited education and paltry

324

self-confidence, it may well be better for her to marry for money than to work for peanuts.

If a woman is financially dependent upon a man, she is in his power, no matter how generous he is with her. It is the degree of financial dependence which determines, in large part, the degree of power. Women need to obtain their own resources and to be content to live on them, however modest. If they can achieve a minimum standard of living for themselves, then sexual barter is not necessary.

If a woman has sexual freedom and has a degree of financial and social independence, then she has a new option. She has the luxury of choosing someone to love, and perhaps to marry, not because he is rich and not because he desires her, but because she desires him. Or better still because they desire each other.

Billie Holiday says it well when she sings ruefully, "Mama may have, Papa may have, but God blessed the child who's got her own."

SEX FOR THE JOY OF IT

In real life, women are always trying to mix something up with sex—religion or babies or hard cash; it is only men who long for sex separated out, without rings or strings.
—Katharine Whitehorn, Man's Ideal Woman

Back in 1913, H. M. Swanwick speculated in *The Future of the Woman's Movement* that women of the future would have men on only honorable terms—"love and liberty and mutual service"—or would go without. Nearly a hundred years have now passed and the projected future has presumably arrived, but many women are still settling for other terms as well. Many women, but not all of them.

If you can, pick a lover because he is the kind of man who turns you on and for no other reason. If you can pick such a lover, then determine the time and the place where you will make love. If you can pick such a lover, then share with him a mutually responsive and guided experience. If you can do all this, then you have a chance to enter the erotic world in the full sense of the phrase. And if you are very lucky, then you have a chance to explore the other limits of the realm of the senses.

If you think sex is not all that wonderful, then you're not doing it with the right man.

To Choose, To Court,
To Woo, To Win

The pleasantest part of a man's life is generally that which passes in courtship, provided his passion be sincere and the party beloved, kind, and discreet. Love, desire, hope, all the pleasing motions of the soul, rise in the pursuit.

—Joseph Addison

Traditionally, the term "courtship" has been used to refer to something which a man does to a woman. He goes to court her, he pays court to her, he woos her; and if he is successful, he beds her and, maybe, later weds her as well. "To court" is an active verb, but traditionally, it is the man who does the acting.

In the context of the new roles of a lover which we have been discussing, women also have an active part to play in the formation and conduct of relationships. It follows that courtship will become a two-way process. He will still court her sometimes. But on some occasions, she will also court him. The new courtship may be the pleasantest part of a woman's life as well.

If, as we have suggested, men do not yet have enough practice at being sex objects to do it very well, it is also true that women do not have enough practice at courting to do it very well. The process is, or should be, subtle. The result should be flattering and pleasant whether the courtship itself is successful or not. In addition, men need to learn to let themselves be courted; and often that means that you, as a woman, must teach the man in question this role, if it is unfamiliar to him. If you are going to presume to pick a lover, then you must do more than collect applications and sift through them: you must also be willing to pay court to him. Doing this requires essentially the same attentiveness and delicacy that one would hope to find in a lover who is courting you.

The new courtship is a revolutionary idea. Traditionally, women have been trained to seek out relationships by making themselves as attractive as possible and then to wait hopefully to see who might come along and take notice of them. They follow what amounts to a cupcake method of courting: they sit like cute little cupcakes, complete with icing, and wait to be gobbled up. For instance, consider the celebrated ski bunny who wiles away her day in the ski chalet bundled in a fashionable sporting outfit, patiently waiting for the ski wolves, full of adrenaline to return from the slopes to gobble her up.

The new courtship is not so passive. Consider a metaphor from the world of fishing. One way of fishing is called trolling. When you go trolling, you move your bait slowly through the water behind a trawler, and various kinds of fishes may or may not bite. In traditional courtship, women were trolling for suitors. The bait was put out there: some suitors took the bait and were hooked and reeled in; some just swam away.

The new courtship is more like fly casting. In fly casting, you are after a specific kind of trout which is found in a specific location and is tempted by a specific kind of fly. You must make just the right fly dance temptingly before just the right trout to get your fish. In trolling, you have to reel in your line to see what you have caught and then decide whether or not to keep it. In fly casting, if you do hook a fish, you know in advance it will be one you want.

It is worth remembering, while exploring metaphors, that both kinds of fishing require patience. And fishers of all kinds, like women of all kinds, are prone to exaggerate the wondrous qualities of the ones that got away.

SHARING THE INITIATIVE

Courtship consists of a number of quiet attentions, not so pointed as to alarm, nor so vague as not to be understood.

—Lawrence Sterne

The person who makes the first move toward a relationship takes a certain amount of risk. He must declare himself in some way or another so that the stranger knows he is interested in becoming better acquainted with her. If this is done very casually, then little of his self-image is at stake; if it is done more seriously and more deliberately, then the person taking the risk is more vulnerable.

In traditional dating-based courtship, it fell to the man to take all of this emotional risk. The first move was always his. I doubt that this has changed very much even today. The very first move is still likely to be a male move, and both people may be more comfortable with that.

However, courtship is no longer only a one-way process, or it need not be. It is nice to be courted and to passively let a new friendship happen; it is also nice to court and to be more assertive about it. The very best scenario is when the two roles are interchangeable from one point in time to the next as they are when friendships are formed between same-sex friends.

Victor Hugo observed that the first symptom of love in a young man is timidity, but the first symptom of love in a young woman is boldness. The two sexes have a tendency to approach, and each assume the qualities of the other. This move toward androgyny and toward mutuality is certainly conducive to better relationships and to fewer misunderstandings. Yet how to go about it is often less than obvious.

In the initiation of relationships, as in other aspects of sexuality, there remain vestiges of the double standard. The first approach which is made should not be too forceful for either sex. But being obvious and blatant is more or less acceptable for almost all men—or at least all men who have a reasonable claim to being your social equal. While being blatant may be "acceptable," it is becoming increasingly less enticing to women, and a more subtle approach is preferred. Being obvious and blatant is equally bad form for a woman—even an emancipated one. More importantly, it is unlikely to achieve your desired ends.

The woman who sets out to court a man has a double task: how to take the initiative, and how to take the initiative without seeming to take the initiative. She must be explicit without being obvious. She must be evocative without being provocative.

It is no wonder women do not yet know how to act in this role, and men don't know how to respond.

Beware of the Hard Sell

With women worth being won, the
softest love ever best succeeds.

—Aaron Hill

One of the joys of life is that sexual arousal and anticipation are both constantly renewable resources. The person who has turned you on once will very likely turn you on tomorrow and the next day. Unless his regiment really rides at dawn, or his ship really sails with the tide, a love affair is seldom really an emergency that must happen immediately. No matter what Elvis says, sex is never "now or never": it can wait. If a man is so hot to get laid *right now*, one way or another, he presumably can arrange it as the "rosy-breasted pushover" is not yet an endangered species.

The man who presents you with an ultimatum on your last chance to go to bed with him is, in effect, saying that he is not going to waste any more time on you unless you put out. That is unless you pay him back for his invested time and effort by putting out right now. Think about it—unless you are a working girl—do you need that kind of attitude?

And if you say no again, and he stalks away muttering, "Stupid cock-teasing slut," what have you lost? Better to know that kind of bottom line while on your feet than to hear it when you're flat on you back. The man who does not want to spend time on you beforehand is not going to want to spend time on the afterglow either.

The hard sell may not be a bad strategy for doing business, but it is bad business for a friendly love affair. The now-or-never approach is dangerous and counterproductive, whether it is for sex or for vacuum cleaners being sold door-to-door. If the relationship is worthwhile, it will continue to be so while you think it over.

Unless, of course, his regiment really does ride at dawn.

Passive Resistance:

Go Away Closer

Men do not understand, as a rule, that women like to get used to them by degrees.

—John Oliver Holmes

In traditional courtship, a man not only made the first move but also set the pace of the courtship. The onus of acting rested with him.

If a man was enthusiastic about a woman, he might give her the rush and try to instigate a whirlwind courtship; if he was less enthusiastic or simply shy, he might move hesitantly. With each gesture that he offered in order to accelerate the development of the relationship, the woman in question had a choice of responses: she could accede to his wishes, or she could demur. This dance could continue for some time, depending mostly upon the man's feelings and his willingness to press his case or not.

Eventually, the courtship dance would lead either to a proposal, to be accepted or rejected, or to the woman's decision that since the man was not going to propose, she should let herself be courted elsewhere by someone with more serious intentions.

In the new courtship which we have been discussing, the initiative is more reciprocal, and the timetable can reflect his escalations or hers. The decision in question is not whether or not to marry but only whether or not to have an affair. It is a less serious decision, and a more reversible one, but it is still an important decision. Making an important decision requires information and thought. To consider what you are getting into, and whether you really want to get into it at all, takes time—time to interview, to test, to reflect. And all too often, the average man is not at all interested in taking time.

The solution to this problem is simple: stall. Stall, stall, stall.

If you go with him to his hotel room to have a drink and talk things over, you lose a lot of credibility no matter how straightforward your intentions. You can say, "Lie down, I want to talk to you," but at your own peril.

How do you make a man stand still or sit still or even lie still to be interviewed when he has something else entirely on his mind? Long ago, the Spaniards invented a way. The young and virginal were courted at some length but always in the presence of a "duenna," an older woman who trailed along out of earshot but not out of sight and certainly not out of mind.

Get yourself a duenna. Make a deal with a girlfriend, take along a child old enough to watch and talk, lie down and talk in sunlight on a public beach. The combination of being accessible, but not completely accessible, is ideal. The pseudo-intimacy which results is a constraint, but it allows for a certain freedom and permissiveness. Having the outer limits defined helps both of you to relax. That is what double dating is all about for teenagers, but it works well for grown-ups as well.

If your message is one of passive resistance and what you want is for him not to go away but only proceed more slowly, then it is both necessary and fair that you do not confuse the issue with a double message. Some women say no when what they really mean is "coax me." Then when the man takes no for an answer, they are vaguely disappointed. You must, in this kind of situation, make your responses both consistent and unambiguous. You can always change your mind at a later date.

TELEPHONE TYRANNY

Instead of belles-lettres, we have Ma Bell.
> —Donal Henahan

One familiar little dating game ritual played out in the dating market is the ritual of the phone number. If the man who meets the girl decides he likes the girl, he asks for her phone number so he can call her sometime; if the girl who meets the man likes him, she gives it to him. Once this little ritual is complete, he has a right to expect that if he calls her, she will remember who he is and will more or less welcome his call.

There is nothing wrong with this little ritual in itself—except that you will notice that the action involved is again all one-way. He asks or does not; he phones or does not. You may respond in various ways to his actions; but first, you must wait until he asks, and if he does, then wait for your phone to ring.

The game of "don't-call-me, I'll-call-you" is recognized in the business world as a standard status maneuver. Hopeful actors who must audition for parts hear it all the time as do job applicants. It is equally a status game when played with men and women although a man may not immediately recognize it as such. If he offers you his phone number, he has put the ball in your court, and that is an encouraging sign. If he does not, then when he asks for your number, make it an exchange and watch how he responds to that idea.

A promising variation of the telephone game is played by the man who spontaneously offers you his phone number and says, "Please call me if you want to." By giving the number, especially by giving it without being asked, he shows that he expects the interaction will be a two-way interaction. This variation is especially promising if he gives you his number in such a way as to be sure that any attempt at communication with him would be effective.

334

A busy lawyer of my acquaintance, a very genuine man who unfortunately has a most unprepossessing appearance, was in ardent pursuit of a beautiful model. He not only asked for her phone number (she gave him the number for her modeling agency) but gave her his home phone number, his cell phone number, his office number, and a code word to use with his secretary so that, instead of automatically saying he was busy and would return the call, the secretary would actually put the woman through to his desk. The object of the lawyer's affection was not too sure about this man, busy or otherwise, but was convinced of his sincerity. Eventually, she did call him; and while they did not live happily ever after, they did become good friends.

The same game can be played just as easily via e-mail or text messaging. Since e-mail and text messaging do not involve direct interaction with the other person, it is less personal, making it easier to communicate your interest or lack of interest without the risk of having to have a potentially uncomfortable conversation.

Long-distance Gestures

A fox is a wolf who sends flowers.

—R. Weston

With the old customs, the man who came a-courting also brought or sent something other than his charming presence. He arrived with flowers or chocolates or some other little love gift to show his appreciation and his intent. Little love gifts are not the kinds of presents that are almost obligatory on special occasions, such as Christmas and birthdays. They are spontaneous and unexpected and are intended to convey thoughtfulness and concern.

A little love gift is welcome even if it is as unimaginative as flowers, candy, or wine. It is even more welcome, however, if it is somehow uniquely tailored to you or to the relationship. It might be a music CD, which somehow came up in the course of an earlier conversation, or a paperback book. Travelers may bring home souvenirs, people who devour newspapers will bring relevant or cute clippings for your amusement, scholars bring each other book or journal references.

The value of little love gifts is in part that they can be sent so that they arrive in private, through the mail or from delivery services. In this way, no one is put on the spot to come up with an appropriate response on the spur of the moment. If you send a man such a gift, he can then decide at leisure whether to follow up the gesture or to make a token thank you or even to ignore it completely. It helps to save face all around.

The value of a little love gift should be in its thoughtfulness and appropriateness, not in its objective value. Something too expensive is very much like a bribe and conveys a much different message. An expensive present is a significant gesture and is best left for much later in the relationship.

If women are to court as well as to be courted, they too will have to learn about little love gifts. For a while at least, they will have a decided advantage since a man is usually not used to being courted and does not yet take it for granted. One man who received a suggestive card from an acquaintance wrote back in appreciation, "I haven't been so touched since the first time a strange woman patted me on my tushie." Women get flowers all the time, but the flowers you send him may be the first ones he has ever received without having to break a leg or give up his appendix.

THE FIRST TIME YOU SLEEP
TOGETHER, TRY SLEEPING

Breathes there a man with soul so dead
Who never to a girl has said:
"Let's go to bed."

—Evan Esar

You want, in a lover, a man who relates to you on many levels and a man who will not insist on having his own way regardless of your wishes. A lover who understands mutuality.

All married couples know that going to bed together does not necessarily mean they are going to make love. Lots of other wonderful things happen in bed besides sleep. It is snug, dark, comfortable, and private: an excellent place to think or talk or cuddle.

You can tell a lot about how your interaction with a man is going to be by going to bed with him with the expressed, explicit intention of not having sex. You say, "Yes, I'll sleep with you tonight, but I won't have sex with you tonight. All right?"

Some men will bristle indignantly at this; some will be amused, being certain you will change your mind; some will be secretly relieved as this strategy allows the growth of intimacy without any performance demanded on his part or yours.

Without those words, it is understood by everyone that he is obligated to try to make love to you. And you cannot really say no without hurting his feelings and creating misunderstandings. By saying no in advance and meaning it, you create an atmosphere of no pressure. You can be sexually deprived for twelve hours. It helps, in this, to have a good excuse for not making love,

338

something outside the relationship and something non-negotiable. An obvious one is to be having your period. Even if he says he does not mind, it is understandable that you might, at least the first time. Any kind of physical impairment is an understandable excuse. Or you might simply avoid going to bed at all and lie down and eventually sleep on the living room couch. It is not as comfortable, but it is much less ambiguous, and you avoid the critical point of confrontation when you have to negotiate who is going to sleep where and what it means.

If a man agrees to your arrangements and then gives you a night of constant hassle—groping, nagging, whining, and otherwise carrying on—you have lost a night's sleep. You may, however, have saved yourself a lot of trouble in the future because you now know how he is likely to behave on other occasions when he does not get what he wants when he wants it.

There is a pattern of psychological bullying, stemming from incredulity that anyone, any *woman*, could actually oppose him with a will of her own. That attitude is the opposite of mutuality. Whether or not you give in on that particular night and let him have his way with you, as the Victorians used to say, you can know what to expect on future nights should you happen not to feel like having sex.

The best kind of lover acknowledges the fundamental idea that sexual encounters should involve two people who, if not equally enthusiastic, are at least compliant enough to be willingly involved. He does not want to impose himself upon someone who is reluctant. He may be disappointed that the evening is not going to end with you as the dessert, but he is willing to wait for a time of mutual desire.

A man with that attitude usually does not have to wait very long.

The Penultimate Test:

Take Him Home

A woman's home is her hassle!
—Jayson VanVerten

When you have found a prospective lover who seems in many ways to be the real thing, or at least close to the real thing, take him home.

Well, not necessarily home to meet your mother unless you are only seventeen, but home to where you live or work. Contrive some situation in which he will meet your husband or your current lover dangerous as that may initially seem. See him when you are with your children. Put him in the same group with other significant people in your life, be they coworkers or a brother or whomever. This strategy is, of course, irrelevant if all that is involved is a one-night stand or a one-afternoon tumble. It is important for a lover you hope to keep for a longer time.

First of all, you will see how well he behaves under moderate pressure before there is any real pressure. Can he talk baseball scores with your husband without glowering? Does he show deference to your husband and his domain? Does he treat your children as miniature people or as little irritants that get in his way? Can he be cool and poised in a situation in which, you hope, only you and he understand the real nature of the dynamics that are going on?

If a man bungles initial meetings before any events of real significance have occurred, you cannot trust him to be cool and to remain discreet when at some future date there may be more violent emotions and more significant events to cover up. What is really involved here is a test of sophistication but also of potential possessiveness and jealousy. Some unworldly boys of twenty

340

can manage with good grace and good humor; some apparently worldly men in midlife are transparent and awkward.

The good lover must have a certain amount of guile, a certain talent for ambiguity. It is paradoxical, but what you want is a contradictory qualification: the ability to dissemble to the world at large and the ability to project to you that with you, he speaks and shows only the truth and all the truth.

In *1984*, George Orwell called it double think, a dubious trait you must both possess. You must be willing to believe: "Yes, we lie to the outside world, by omission if no other way. But no, we do not lie to each other." Like good theater, a good affair requires a certain suspension of disbelief.

Taking a prospective lover home also helps him to concretize the day-to-day reality with which you have to contend. Not just a husband, but Harry the husband. Not just three kids, but Mollie and Mattie and Maryanne. When you have to get home for a Girl Scout meeting, he knows who it is for and what it will be like. When you have to get home to make cunning little stuffed mushrooms to stuff into your husband's cunning little stuffed business associates, he can visualize the kitchen where you work and the room where they are served.

The obligations are made real, and the more they are made real, the more he is able to take them as seriously as you must.

You also need to take your lover home to demystify him for the people you work and live with. A mysterious gentleman caller is quite romantic and attractive if you are a single girl who delights in collecting beaux just as your grandmother did. But if you are of a certain age and especially if you are married, collecting beaux is not exactly what you are supposed to be doing, however delightful that pastime may be.

When someone finally asks, "Who was that man?" you need to be able to say casually, "Who? Oh, him. You remember him. That's Tony. You met him at the Smith's party. He's in landscaping. He is trying to talk us into a new pool." Or whatever.

The best alibis are those you create before you need them, not afterward.

THE SEAMLESS SEDUCTION

Here is a perfect poem: to awaken a longing to develop it, to increase it, to stimulate it, and to gratify it.

—Honorè de Balzac

When one thinks of the verb "to seduce," one thinks of it as something a man does *to* a woman. More stereotypically, you think of an unscrupulous man, perhaps a villain with a pencil-thin mustache, pressing his attentions upon a young and presumably innocent girl. He suggests, "Have some Madeira, my deara"; and muddled by Madeira and soft talk, she eventually fails to resist and he has his way with her.

In a different kind of world, women, however inexperienced, are not as innocent. Women today do not and need not simply wait for a man to approach and seduce them. Rather, they can themselves select a man they think looks promising and initiate the next stage.

Some men are very indiscriminate and unselective. You can seduce them by the simple strategy of saying, "Wanna fuck?" And they will say, "Of course!" And do so immediately. And when you are done, you will have been, well, fucked. For a man who is the kind of man who is likely to make love seriously, this approach would be, in most instances, a total turnoff.

The kind of man who will be a serious and attentive lover must be approached just as men should approach women: by creating a mood and an atmosphere conducive to the right kind of experience. That means that the communication must be subtle and indirect, with no connotation of obligation, and no suggestion of a need to perform.

Seduction is an invitation, not a command.

The offering of a seductive invitation should be done in such a way that it is possible for the man or the woman to decline gracefully, with neither party losing face. The person who is skilled in sexual matters will never make a pass at someone when the response to the pass is in any doubt. When the time comes to make a definite, unambiguous move, the other person is not going to be surprised and his or her reaction is certain to be positive rather than negative.

Young people make a lot of mistakes in figuring out how to make a pass, how to see one coming, and how to accept or to deflect one. Older people who are not too experienced or those who come from a different tradition can also inflict considerable pain and embarrassment on each other because of their inability to "read" signals and passes.

The strategy for avoiding such confrontation is not all that difficult. In our culture, there are a number of sexual scripts as discussed earlier in chapter 5. Think of the act of sexual intercourse as a kind of theatrical play with the man and woman being both actors and directors. A sexual interlude is a play with an overture at first curtain. It consists of three acts complete with intermissions and ends with a grand finale, followed by a period of denouement.

The sexual script starts with mutual looking. It proceeds, with or without words, to kissing and mutual touching. At each stage, the other person responds with an encouraging gesture (or sound) or a negative one. The skilled lover, male or female, listens to this conversation of gestures, murmurs, and moans and modifies his or her actions accordingly. There should be mutual, if unspoken, consent as to what happens next, if anything.

Because of sexual scripting, the sequence of erotic involvement is generally quite consistent. The man who is seen as a "wolf" or the woman who is seen as "too fast" is merely someone who has skipped some of the expected steps. The sense of affront this creates may not be for the acts themselves but for the failure to prepare the other person by leading up to those acts in the right way. The actual time frame involved has less to do with the script than with the specific male and female involved. If the two are virgin teenagers who have been kept as innocent and uninformed as possible, it may take months; if they are sophisticated New York swingers, it may take only a few hours.

Since men are not as prepared as are women to have someone make a pass at them, it is even more important that the sexual script be followed and that there be no surprises which might create a sense of threat and discomfort. The gestures involved proceed with very small increments and with great attention to the response they receive, if any. No one gesture should be so obvious that it must be acknowledged in a way which could prove awkward for either party.

If the gesture is declined, everyone should be able to walk away without embarrassment. If the gesture is not declined, the sexual interaction should flow smoothly and easily from one stage to the other—right through to the proverbial cigarette afterward.

Pardon My Plurality

In matters of the heart, there may be two kinds of people: those who know that it is possible to love more than one person, and those who know that it is not.

—Jayson VanVerden

If a woman can take a lover, we now come to another nitty-gritty question: can she take more than one lover? What happens to a love affair when one or the other partner—or both—are also involved with someone else.

There has been a lot of material, written mostly by men, implying that men are naturally polygamous whereas women, bless them, are naturally monogamous. The man insists that his passion for another woman does not have anything to do with his feeling for his wife, or at least does not *necessarily* have anything to do with it. The woman typically takes this assertion with a whole pound of salt.

In reality, however, it's not so much that all men are polygamous in intent and all women monogamous as much as it is that there are *some* people—men and women—who can and do simultaneously harbor love and passion for more than one person.

Some people—men and women—can feel love for only one person at a time. If they fall in love with a new person, they must, by necessity, fall out of love with the first. At the very least, they must love the first one less. If they have more than one love affair, therefore, it must be in sequence with the old love being replaced by the new.

In *Marriage and Morals*, Bertrand Russell points out that "the psychology of adultery has been falsified by conventional morals, which assume . . . that attraction for one person cannot coexist with a serious attraction for another. Everybody knows that this is untrue."

Women as well as men may follow a pattern of simultaneous affairs. If you understand in your own heart the possibility of love for more than one person at a time, then when your lover has an affair, you may be hurt and unhappy; but it is comprehensible to you. When you wail, "How *could* you?" it is a rhetorical question, for you know quite well how he could do that and more. You also know, although you may choose to forget it in the heat of the moment, that his having slept with another woman, or even loved another woman, does not necessarily mean that he loves you less.

The one love is different from the other: it has a different place in the psyche, and it fulfills different needs.

A woman has a right to a lover. Indeed, she has a right to more than one lover. While it is quite possible for many women to love more than one man at a time, it is also important to remember that not everybody believes this or is willing to accept it. You have a right to do it, but you must expect a wide range of consequences, some of which will be unfortunate.

To a committed monogamist, male or female, the reaction to infidelity is often a sense of total betrayal, however inappropriate or over-the-top you may find that reaction. If your male lover thinks this way, then love that is really love, in his mind, means love that is exclusively with one person. In deciding to embark on an affair, you need to realize that, for him, even one involvement with one other man will be viewed as an absolute end of your relationship with him. Such an arbitrary stand is quite likely to be associated with a lot of pain and ultimately with loneliness, but the decision may be so fundamental and so emotional that it is non-negotiable.

In most instances, though, the acceptance of the plurality of love and lovers is part of the more sophisticated wisdom that comes with experience. Even with married couples, it may be painful, but it is not necessarily outrageous.

Many people would tend to agree with Oscar Wilde when he asserts, "People who love once in their lives are really shallow people. What they call their loyalty and fidelity is either lethargy of custom or lack of imagination. Faithfulness is to the emotional life what constancy is to the intellectual life, simply a confession of failure."

KEEPING SCORE

How many arms have held you,
And hated to let you go?
How many, how many I wonder
But I really don't want to know.
　　　　　　　　　—Don Robertson, Howard Barnes

Sooner or later, everybody always asks, "How many men have you slept with? How many affairs have you had?"

If you are about to enter your first affair and are still virgo intacta, then you probably should tell your prospective lover that you have chosen him for your first time. The loss of one's maidenhead can be a momentous occasion, and if he knows of your innocence, he may be more solicitous of it.

If you have had one affair, you can say demurely, "Only one." Nowadays, only a minority of men is likely to insist upon a virgin bride although they might prefer such a circumstance. Unless you are about to marry a Mormon missionary, admitting to one previous affair is probably safe.

The trouble with the more-or-less-acceptable answer of "only one" is that you can use it only once. When the truth is that there has been more than one previous lover, the truth becomes more treacherous. Under those circumstances, you might admit to "a passel." This term is appropriately vague, referring to an indeterminate number. And if he insists upon a specific number, then there is only *one* correct answer, which is to give a range: *more than one, less than five hundred.*

Why does your man want to know? What difference does it make to him what your scorecard reads? Why does he want to view a scalp collection?

Don't buy the "I'm-just-curious" answer from anyone except a researcher from the Kinsey Institute for Research in Sex, Gender, and Reproduction and then only after you have seen his interviewer identification badge. The man to whom it is not very important will not press the issue; the man for whom it is very important will keep pressing, and that alone tells you that any answer will be the wrong answer.

Do not be led into the trap of the man who confesses all (all?) of his affairs and then insists that since he has told you, so you must tell him. Wrong. If he wants to confess his sins or brag about his conquests or whatever he is doing for whatever reasons, fine, but that does not obligate you to do the same.

The entire game of "Did you ever . . . ?" is a dangerous one. It leads to other games like "Who all did you sleep with? Did you ever make it with Jack? Did you ever have a black man?" (Or a white man, depending on your race.) That leads to still more games like "Who was the best? Am I the best? Was Jack better than me?" Some conversations are just not worth having, and this is one of them.

It would be nice if teenagers could fall in love once and once only and then live happily ever after, remaining true to each other year after year for fifty years. It would be nice, and it does happen, but it is not the way to bet.

Men, including husbands, have long retained the option of pursuing more than one woman. Women, including wives, are just beginning to realize their potential to do the same. Evan Esar, the American humorist, predicts, "In the future, a woman who sticks to one man will be regarded as a monomaniac."

THE BOTTOM LINE

The bottom line:
it is **my** *bottom that has the honey pot!*
　　　　　　—Jadah Vaughn, "The Bottom Line"

Throughout most of the recorded history of the Western world, there has been an implicit assumption that men owned women and that men especially owned their sexuality.

In the beginning, fathers owned daughters; later in life, husbands owned wives who had been given away by their fathers. The wife was a chattel. It would be an overstatement to say she was a slave, but she was a possession. In effect, she sold her sexual services at the time of marriage for the rest of her life. If a husband was made a cuckold by some other man, he had a right to be aggrieved and sometimes even a right to sue for damages. The law gave him not only a right to his wife's body at all times, and under all circumstances, but an exclusive right to it. The wife had control of the husband's honor. If she was wayward, she brought disgrace to him as much as a wayward daughter would bring disgrace to her father. In some cultures today, "honor killings" are based on that assumption.

Even at the beginning of the twenty-first century, there remains a truism which still needs to be endlessly proclaimed. *A woman owns her own body.* She may decide to share it with a man, or she may not. She may promise to be sexually monogamous, or she may not. She may conceive a child if she wants, or she may not. Having conceived, she may carry that child to term, or she may not. *A woman owns her own body.*

If you own your own body, then the decisions about what to do with it are in fact up to you. You may give your body to someone in an act of love, but you do not deed it to him for time and eternity.

Self-ownership involves two related principles. The first is that you do not have to give your body to anyone if you don't want to; it is a form of rape, even if the man is your husband, if you are taken against your will. The second principle is that you have the right to give your body to whomever you want.

The bottom line: it is *your* bottom that has the honeypot.

CHAPTER 12

SAFE CONDUCT: GUIDELINES FOR AN AFFAIR OF THE HEART

It's a wise man who profits by his experience, but it's a good deal wiser one who lets the rattlesnake bite the other fellow.

—Josh Billings

In times of war, when it is necessary to venture into hostile territory, one is sometimes issued a "safe conduct pass" which is supposed to assure that the bearer can pass through the danger zone unmolested. Women who venture into the uncertainty of new relationships based on new social norms do not have any more guarantees of fulfillment than their grandmothers did. There are, however, some guidelines that can serve as a kind of safe conduct pass which, if followed, will help you to actualize as fully as possible your nascent affair with the new lover you have selected.

Logan Smith, the American epigrammatist, points out, "There are two things to aim at in life: first, to get what you want; and after that, to enjoy it. Only the wisest of mankind achieve the second." There is no foolproof formula for a perfect love affair. There are, however, guidelines which, like other kinds of safe conduct documents, may offer more protection.

In the tradition of commandments, here is a decalogue of rules which you would be wise to consider carefully. Later in chapter 13, there are more rules which apply to the special problems of love affairs involving married women.

DECALOGUE: GUIDELINES FOR AN AFFAIR
OF THE HEART

RULE ONE: ACCEPT RESPONSIBILITY FOR THE AFFAIR.

RULE TWO: ACCEPT RESPONSIBILITY FOR BIRTH CONTROL.

RULE THREE: BE HONEST ABOUT YOUR INTENTIONS.

RULE FOUR: PICK THE RIGHT MAN FOR THE RIGHT REASONS.

RULE FIVE: ACCEPT THE INEVITABILITY OF CHAUVINISM.

RULE SIX: DO YOUR PART TO MAKE THE AFFAIR SUCCESSFUL.

RULE SEVEN: RESPECT PRIVILEGED INFORMATION.

RULE EIGHT: MINIMIZE JEALOUSY.

RULE NINE: BEWARE THE MONSTER THAT IS HABIT.

RULE TEN: TAKE TIME TO SAVOR LOVE.

RULE ONE: ACCEPT
RESPONSIBILITY FOR THE AFFAIR

Responsibility: the high price of self-ownership.
—Eli J. Schleifer

The decision to take a lover, like the decision to get married, is a decision which a woman makes for herself. Except for the aberrant circumstances of rape, she is the one who says yes or no. She decides what she will do with her body. The price of that privilege is that she alone is responsible for the decision.

When women are in a servile position, with no resources and little self-confidence, they may be, to some extent, justified in attributing their misfortunes to something some man has done to them. They were seduced or bullied or beguiled or, in other ways, misled. They were ruined or knocked up or conned or despoiled. Such women adopt the role of victim, playing opposite men who they cast in the role of villain.

While some men certainly are villains and some women certainly unfortunate victims, in many circumstances, women's misfortunes are not so much the result of what men have done to them as they are the result of what women have done to themselves. Children and the very naive are, of course, exempt. Statutory rape is viewed as rape because the teenager is often not yet self-aware enough to give informed consent. For grown-ups, however, the flaws in relationships and the harm that sometimes results must be shared by both men and women.

Once a woman is of age, she must accept responsibility for the consequences of her decisions. The relationship with a lover is an unconventional one. It does not encompass the institutional protections associated with marriage. It

353

does not come with guarantees. The woman must rely on her own judgment about the kind of man she gets involved with, and she must anticipate some negative consequences. She is a willing participant in an affair. If he pressures her in some way and is successful, it is because she *let* him pressure her. If he has seduced her, unless she was drunk or drugged or raped, then she must have *let* herself be seduced.

The relationship with a lover is not only an unconventional one but is something viewed as immoral by many people. It is defined as out of bounds by virtually all of the major religions. Some groups, such as the Unitarians, might regard it with only mild approbation; but none would advocate it as the best alternative. If one is a fundamentally religious person, such a relationship can inspire a considerable amount of guilt.

Some types of guilt are small and nagging and go away in a short while, but others are more consequential, and some stay with you for a very long time or even a lifetime. If thinking about the various moral consequences of an affair makes you feel any guilt whatsoever, then resolve how you are going to feel in the morning *before* the fact, not afterward. Try the idea out in your mind; talk with someone you trust who knows you well. Read some more books.

Above all, do not let someone talk you into a relationship before you are ready. Only you really know how you yourself feel, and you can only know that if you take the time to think things through carefully and clearly examine and understand your own feelings.

When in doubt, wait. Sex is never an emergency. If you change your mind later, there will still be willing men out there.

If, however, you decide to have an affair, then remember that it was, indeed, your decision. You cannot transfer the blame to your lover or your husband or children or even your mother. You must take responsibility for your own sexuality. Once you can do that, you can truly begin to enjoy it.

Rule Two: Accept Responsibility for Birth Control

Without the full capacity to limit her own reproduction, a woman's other "freedoms" are tantalizing mockers that cannot be exercised.
—Lucinda Cisler, Sisterhood Is Powerful

The sexual mores of the later half of the twentieth century and the first decade of the twenty-first century are indeed different from what they were in the past. One important development which permits such differences to flourish with a minimum of harm and maximum of pleasure is that of adequate birth control.

When women were at risk of getting pregnant, then the choice of a lover was usually also the choice of a father for one's child; and a father for one's child, for the sake of all concerned, had better be also one's husband. If pregnancy occurred, then the only acceptable solution was a so-called forced marriage. Better, under such conditions, not to sleep with anyone you would not be willing and able to marry.

However, there is no longer a need for these conditions to apply.

Adequate birth control is available to everyone who seeks it. There are a variety of different techniques for women of different ages, circumstances, and experiences. Whatever you and your physician decide, you should be on the pill or use a diaphragm or a sponge or trust an IUD.

It is, of course, theoretically true that birth control should be the man's responsibility as well; and as a desirable lover, he should be concerned and cooperative. Nevertheless, no matter how unfair it seems to you, he never risks getting pregnant. You do. You run the risk unless he is known to be sterile and has had a doctor say so or has had a vasectomy.

A number of years ago at the height of the "zero population growth" movement, men who had had a vasectomy were proud of the fact and would wear a little male symbol of a circle attached to an arrow, but with a break in the circle. Cute and chic and often done in gold, it was worn as a tiepin or label button. It was not unheard of for a man on the make to borrow his friend's vasectomy pin and wear it as a conversation piece at the local pickup bar. You can't exactly see his scars but . . .

In every instance, getting pregnant should be a deliberate decision, not an accident or an oversight. Retroactive birth control, such as the morning-after pill, is available for situations in which sex may take place without any birth control. And in the case of contraceptive failure, abortion should be considered as a backup emergency procedure.

You run the risk of getting pregnant unless you have had a doctor say that you are naturally sterile or you have been surgically sterilized or you are already pregnant. As long as you are at risk, you must protect yourself and assume responsibility for birth control at the same time that you assume responsibility for your own sexuality.

Rule Three: Be Honest About Your Intentions

You need not tell all the truth, unless to those who have a right to know it all. But let all you tell be the truth.

—Horace Mann

It would be nice to make a rule that everyone should always tell the truth. It would also be hopelessly naive. The social world depends in part on the white lie and, often, on the blackest of the black in order for the daily round to be maintained. And yet . . . with your intimates, it is important to believe that they tell you the truth as they see it.

To your lover, you should tell the truth. You do not need to tell everything, but what you tell should be the truth even if you must say, "I truthfully do not want to answer the question now!" He has no right to cross-examine you, but he should have reason to trust you. Trust in this situation does not mean fidelity in the sense of sexual monogamy. It does mean that you can depend upon the accuracy of what your lover is saying.

It might even mean saying up front that your intentions are not honorable, if indeed they are not. You have a right to change your mind, but meanwhile, you should tell the truth as you see it.

"MARRIAGE REMINDS ME OF DEATH"

I never will marry,
I'll be no man's wife.
I expect to live single
All the rest of my life.
—Fred Brooks, "I Will Never Marry"

In the old days, when a man came a-courtin', a young girl's father might take him aside in the parlor and inquire, "Are your intentions honorable? Are you seriously considering my daughter as a wife, or are you wasting her time?"

In the new courtship, which does not necessarily lead to marriage, the question is still relevant. While you may harbor no intent to commit matrimony, it does not mean that your lover harbors no such intent. If it so happens that your lover is in serious pursuit of a wife, he has a right to know if you would ever consider getting married, and if so, if you would ever consider getting married to him.

The cultural stereotype in our society affirms that, generally, it is the woman who wants to get married and it is the man who must be coaxed or snagged or snaffled into making that commitment. If that was the case in the past, it is not necessarily so today when women alone can lead quite different lifestyles than did the spinsters of the past.

Some women do not want to marry ever. They concur with the spinster aunt in Somerset Maugham's *Mrs. Craddock* who exclaims, "Marriage is always a hopeless idiocy for a woman who has enough of her own to live upon."

Other women, once burned, never want to marry again. Yet despite being misogamists—one who hates marriage—they sometimes find themselves succumbing to social pressures to marry again. Such women should belong to Divorcees Anonymous, modeled after Alcoholics Anonymous. When they feel the urge to get married again, they could call an emergency number, and Divorcees Anonymous would immediately send over a fat man in a T-shirt, with a six-pack of beer, who settles down in the living room to watch football on the tube.

Women who are ideologically opposed to marriage would go along with Gloria Steinem's commonly quoted maxim: "A woman without a man is like a fish without a bicycle." If, whatever your reasons, you are adamantly not the marrying kind, then it is important for you to make that clear to any man who becomes involved with you. The folk wisdom has been justly critical of the man who seems to court a woman but whose intentions are not honorable—that is, he has no intention of marrying her. A woman is equally at fault if she lets a man hope to marry her when she knows from the start that marriage to anyone—or at least marriage to him—is not for her.

Incipient Divorce Potential

Though many, whose church forbids it, believe divorce is a sin, it may be said that aside from these groups, two marriages with a divorce are thought normal; among the rich, three are normal; and in Hollywood four are normal.
—Edmund Wilson, *The Cold War and Income Tax*

If you are already married but are nevertheless contemplating an affair, you need to consider how you feel about maintaining your marriage.

Some women who are not very satisfied with their husbands are nevertheless determined to maintain their households intact. They have other considerations to think about. Often, the main marital glue is a child, but it can also be financial considerations or other family obligations. "How can I leave my husband?" one wife lamented to me. "He's paying for my mother's nursing home care. I could never afford that, and what would become of her?" Some women are simply afraid of being single again and do not think they can manage on their own.

An affair can be the first rebellious step on the way to a woman's freedom. One woman quipped, "Wanting an open marriage is nature's way of telling you that you need a divorce." The affair is a way of testing one's wings or of biding one's time until an opportune moment. One wife confided that she intended to leave her husband and had indeed a definite timetable. She calculated she would be finished graduate school in fifteen more months and would then be graduated and gone in sixteen. Her departure would coincide almost to the day with her first paycheck.

Some of these women are already thinking about what a second husband would be like. Many others have had enough of marriage, at least for now, and are looking for a lover for the sake of a worthwhile affair and nothing more.

For a start, a first requirement that you owe your paramour is to be honest about the state and prospects of your marriage, at least as you understand them at the time. If you are determined to maintain your marriage at all costs, then do not let him hope that someday you will leave your husband and run away with him. Men tend to feel they are irresistible, so if you are serious about remaining married, you cannot stress it too much or too early in the relationship.

On the other hand, if you are more or less looking for an excuse to get out of the marriage, and perhaps are looking for someone who is willing to act as a co-respondent in a divorce action should you be found out, then it is only fair to say this as well. When later you do leave your husband, you have precluded any potential guilt on the part of your lover that he was a home wrecker who broke up an otherwise satisfactory marriage. Being honest here also warns him that you may not always take the need for discretion very seriously.

Love affairs do sometimes change things, and you may decide later that your initial intent needs to be revised. All you can do is to level with him about how you feel at the time.

Rule Four: Pick the Right Man for the Right Reasons

It is more important to be aware of the ground of your own behavior than to understand the motives of another.
—Dag Hammarskjöld

When you approach a new love affair, stop for a long moment to think carefully about what you are doing. Examine your own motives. Interview yourself the way you imagine a psychiatrist or a reporter might. Ask yourself: Why do I want to have an affair? Why now, this month, rather than last month or next month? Why this particular man?

These kinds of questions never have just one answer. Our motives for acting as we do are always complex and are often interrelated. It is important, nevertheless, to at least try to puzzle them out. Are you trying to avoid something you don't like in your life? Are you seeking an affair as a means of running away? Are you simply drawn to an appealing prospect? Would a love affair offer some comfort and consolation when other things have gone wrong? Would it fill an empty place left by a vanished man—or child or job or parent?

If the Freudian psychoanalysts are correct, the motives we think we have for how we act may be superficial and trivial, and the important motives in our lives may be subterranean forces of which we are unaware. The link from motive to action is an endless puzzle. Nevertheless, it is important to try and understand the motives a potential lover may have for seeking you out and the motives you may have for being drawn to him or for rejecting him.

Sometimes, an otherwise promising love affair becomes a long shot because either one or the other of you is approaching it for the wrong reasons.

GETTING EVEN

Revenge is like a boomerang. Although for a time it flies in the direction in which it is hurled, it takes a sudden curve, and, returning, hits your own head the heaviest blow of all.

—J. M. Mason

One of the most usual circumstances that propel women into an affair is the discovery that their lover or their husband has been playing around. Sometimes, they learn only in midlife that while they have been being faithful, their partners have been playing around for years.

It is commonplace to observe that women have the gift of expressing themselves and their emotions whereas men have no such gift and are emotionally inarticulate. While this is often true, there is one major exception: anger. Women who feel sad or hurt can cry more readily than men; however, women who feel rage have fewer outlets for it than do men. Ladies are not supposed to feel rage, and when training little girls to be ladylike, we also train them to deny their anger and to suppress it or turn it inward.

The trusting girlfriend or wife who discovers her man's infidelity is usually enraged as well as hurt. Even people who do not know much Shakespeare are familiar with the idea that "hell has no fury like a woman scorned." However, the woman scorned has few ways of expressing her anger. Lord Byron, in *Don Juan*, contends that "revenge is sweet—especially to women." The sweetness comes in part because of her relative powerlessness.

A woman may be unable to demand justice from her man for real or imagined wrongs. One way she can get revenge, however, is through her sexuality. If her man has a double standard as most men do, then doing the same thing herself will hurt him and will hurt him where he lives. Making him a cuckold gives her a weapon to be used or to be saved and used sometime later.

Revenge can take many forms. Taking a new lover in order to punish the old one may work as an effective punishment, but it is not likely to work as a basis for a satisfactory love affair. The man involved was selected, not for his intrinsic charm but to make a political point in another relationship. The decision process is likely to be one of expedience. The woman may even select someone she does not particularly like because she knows that choice would be particularly galling to her philandering lover or husband.

The popular burlesque performer, Sophie Tucker, had a number of stock comic routines about a boyfriend named Ernie. One of them went something like this: On the occasion of his eightieth birthday, Ernie called and announced, "Soph! Soph! I just married myself a twenty-year-old girl. What do you think of that?"

"Ernie," Sophie countered, "when I am eighty, I shall marry me a twenty-year-old boy. And let me tell you something, Ernie, twenty *goes into* eighty a helluva lot more than eighty *goes into* twenty! So think about that, Ernie!"

The woman who has an affair out of revenge is, in fact, prostituting herself. She is doing sexual things for nonsexual reasons and is not likely to enjoy them very much. The man involved is being used. He may be quite willing to be used, but if he does not understand his role as supporting actor until later, he has a legitimate right to feel resentful.

If you discover that the man you thought was monogamous is, in fact, playing around, you may feel justified in playing the field as well. If and when you do, be sure you do so in order to give yourself the pleasure you deserve, not in order to punish him.

Having an affair out of vengeance may work in that it may inflict reciprocal pain, but it is likely to increase your own disquietude rather than appease it.

The Rebound Effect

A Frenchwoman, when double crossed, will kill her rival; the Italian woman would rather kill her deceitful lover; the Englishwoman simply breaks off relations—but they all console themselves with another man.

—Charles Boyer

One would think that when suffering the pain of having been rejected in love, a rational woman might foreswear love forever and give up on the whole game. At least, one might expect her to walk around for some time muttering, "Never again, never again."

In reality, it is only when a woman has left her man because she is bored with him or offended or outraged that she thinks seriously of giving up men in general. If the man leaves her, then it is quite another matter—even if she did not much want him anyway. If he leaves her, it becomes a matter of pride. To prove that there is nothing wrong with her, that although unloved she is not unlovable, she needs a new love affair—or at least the option of one.

To paraphrase the nineteenth-century novelist Barbey d'Aurevilly, "Next to the wound, what *men* make best is the bandage."

The rebound love affair involves not so much a quest for love as a quest for reassurance. If you are acting on such a motive, it is helpful to be aware of it and to take it into account. When a middle-aged man seduces a young girl in order to prove to himself that he is still young enough to be a macho swordsman, we tend to think that he is exploiting her. Although it often occurs that men use women and hurt them badly in the process, it is necessary to remember that women may also use men and may also hurt them badly.

If your motive in an affair is mainly to seek consolation and reassurance after an unfortunate love affair to bind up your wounds, so to speak, then be sure you do not exploit the lover you pick. He might well delude himself that you loved him for himself alone and not for the incidental fact of his propinquity.

Beware of the Great Ghost Lover

There is sanctuary in reading, sanctuary in formal society, in the company of old friends, and in the giving of officious help to strangers, but there is no sanctuary in one bed from the memory of another.
—Cyril Connolly, *The Unquiet Grave*

There is nothing quite so wondrous, quite so awesome, quite so *interesting* as the first time you fall in love. It may not be with the first man whom you take as a lover . . . indeed, such emotional monogamy is more likely the exception than the rule. The intensity is partly due to ignoring or refusing to accept the possibility that such a feeling can end—not only on his part but also on yours.

If, in addition, the thrill of first love is combined with the thrill of first making love and if that initiation is a satisfactory experience, then it sets up the conditions for a powerful kind of imprinting. Newly hatched goslings will imprint on any moving object they happen to see—a moving wooden cube, the heel of their keeper, a ball of wool—and they will follow that object with all the persistence and devotion that nature intended them to bestow on the mother goose that hatched them. In the same way, a woman whose first love experience coincides with her first sexual experience, or at least her first erotic and wonderful sexual experience, may for the rest of her days be imprinted upon a certain kind of man.

The man who was your first love may provide an idealized model for masculinity in general. If the first eyes that you loved loved you back, and said so, were let's say, slate gray, then twenty years later, slate-gray eyes across a crowded room will still seem more riveting than they actually are. If the first kisses of great passion were enclosed in a full beard, then twenty years later, a full beard is still a special male plumage of particular appeal. Whether he was tall or short, handsome or gnomelike, muscular or slender, there is a body type, a body image, which continues to hold for your extraordinary potential appeal.

If, by chance, you meet someone who seems almost the same as your first great ghost lover from the past, he will almost win your heart just by standing there and breathing in and out. Beware. Looking the same does not at all mean that he *is* the same. You pick him not for what he is but for the man he reminds you of, which is not very flattering to him when he figures it out. You will then project on to him the other traits of the great ghost lover and will be duly disappointed when, quite naturally, he does not live up to these uncanny expectations.

If you find your first great love reincarnated, recognize the source of your attraction. Talk to him if you can't resist the temptation to do so or if you should want to spoil your illusion with a little reality shock. Take his picture. But do not take him to your bed in an attempt to go back in time. Even if he looks the same, he will not *be* the same and you will both be disappointed—you, by his failure to mimic a vanished man he has never met, and he, by your failure to appreciate the fine and unique person that he, in fact, is.

And while you are thinking about your great ghost lover, remember the words of warning from the often-quoted author Bill Vaughan: "It's never safe to be nostalgic about something until you're absolutely certain there's no chance of it coming back."

RULE FIVE: ACCEPT THE
INEVITABILITY OF CHAUVINISM

There are three choices: to be a celibate, be a lesbian, or love a chauvinist.

—Jayson VanVerten

It would be a pleasant change if one could select as lovers only men who were free of chauvinism. Alas, since it is the culture as well as individuals who are androcentric (man centered), there are very few such creatures around.

The misogynist is a man who hates women. The chauvinist is not necessarily full of hate: he simply has a fundamental sense of man's superiority to women and, therefore, a fundamental belief in the intrinsic rightness of existing traditional sex roles. He views the exchange relationship of man the provider versus woman the nurturer as a satisfactory one, perhaps even an exemplary one. Although he may mutter compliance when challenged about equal pay for equal work, he usually does not believe that work done by women is equal to the work done by men.

What are the signs of chauvinism in everyday life? In the early days of consciousness-raising in the women's movement, they used to talk about the click, which was a sudden aha insight into a daily event symbolic of the arrangement between the sexes. Once you start to think in these terms, the clicks are everywhere.

A chauvinist is likely to expect personal services which he does not reciprocate. He tends to make, unilaterally, decisions which should be made jointly; he controls the content of conversations by refusing to participate on topics which do not concern him directly. He seeks emotional support without returning it, he gives unnecessary directions, he assumes that his opinion is more valid and more accurate than a woman's regardless of his expertise or lack of it on a particular issue. Etcetera. The analogy is that a chauvinist tends to treat women in the same way as an adult treats a child: he may be affectionate and even benevolent, but he is not an egalitarian.

If your consciousness is sufficiently raised to be aware of the chauvinism around you, what are you to do about it? You can opt for celibacy and try as much as possible to avoid the company of men. You can opt for lesbianism and the "lavender culture." (Alas, you will find that some lesbian women are sexist as well, but that is another story.) Or you can resign yourself to the fact that chauvinism is endemic and simply try to minimize its effects.

If you decide to become an active feminist and dedicate yourself to reforming and revamping the social system, that is a fine political decision. It is, however, frequently a precursor of disaster in one's personal life. You can end up defining almost everything as a political issue, which is not only exhausting and inefficient but also chips away destructively at even the most affectionate bond.

If you decide to go with the traditional role and model yourself on "total womanhood," you must deny a large part of your selfhood and your intelligence. Total women are the scabs of sisterhood. In the women's movement, they are the equivalent of Uncle Toms in the black movement. We call them Doris Days. Playing this part, even if you were willing to do so, would make you feel most of the time like an actress and a rather miscast actress at that. You might do it but would resent it, and that resentment would eventually sour your love affair.

There is a third alternative. You can learn to live with chauvinism, at least mild-mannered chauvinism, without sacrificing your independence and self-respect. You will not be viewed as acceptable by some chauvinistic men. But you will be increasingly acceptable to enlighten men whose own consciousness has been raised and who, if not exactly feminists themselves, are at least sympathetic to the feminist cause.

Don't Play Pygmalion

Men will never disappoint us if we observe two rules: 1) to find out what they are; 2) to expect them to be just that.

—George Iles

Some people view their intimate associates as promising material from which they can make interesting people. Like the legendary Pygmalion, they want to create others in their own image. This is called teaching or helping or guiding or improving or a number of other euphemisms, but it still boils down to trying to change the other person. People, however, resist being changed . . . especially adult males.

The quest for change has two pitfalls, both equally serious. It is possible, but rare, that you do succeed in changing a person. When that happens, you may have created someone other than the kind of person who attracted you in the first place. Barbra Streisand asks rhetorically, "Why does a woman work ten years to change a man's habits and then complain that he's not the man she married?"

The second pitfall, and one infinitely more common, is that you will keep expecting and hoping that he will change; but of course, he never does. There is a continual sense of rage, which comes down to the demand, "Why can't you be different than you are?" If you want a man who is different, go and find yourself a different man. Don't waste his time and yours to everyone's distress and disillusionment, trying to make a better model citizen of the one whom you have. This is one case in which the most appropriate solution is "love him or leave him."

When you pick a lover, you pick someone who is as close as possible to your ideal man, and remember your ideal lover may be very different from your ideal boyfriend or husband. Once you have done that, learn to accept him for what he is and insist that he accept you in return.

Lovers should be involved in trying to *discover* each other rather than trying to *reinvent* each other in a new image.

Resisting Chauvinism in
Everyday Life

The plain English of the politest address of a gentleman to a lady is, I am now, dear madam, the humblest of your servants. Be so good as to allow me to be your Lord and Master.
—Samuel Richardson

On the one hand, chauvinistic males are everywhere. On the other hand, you are advised not to try to change a man with whom you are having an affair. How then are you to live with chauvinism? The answer is simple: *change yourself, not him.*

The secret to male domination, at one level or another, is that it is domination by consent. If he says, "Be so good as to *allow* me to be your lord and master," you do not have to allow it. Women agree to being placed in a secondary role; they submit to being governed. If you do not comply, he cannot make you obey.

To this generalization, there are two important exceptions. First, obviously, he can make you do anything he wants if you have to deal with physical domination and abuse. You can do nothing in that situation except to leave as soon as possible. Second, and less obviously, he can make you do many things if you are economically dependent upon him. If, however, you have your own resources inside or outside marriage, then most of the domination that is involved is a combination of traditional authority and psychological intimidation.

While each new relationship brings out in a personality something slightly different than any other relationship, the problems you encounter with one man often tend to reoccur in subsequent ones. One young woman used to wail as she found herself in the midst of all-too-familiar hassles, "Why does my life keep repeating itself?" Her not-very-sympathetic friend would respond, "Because, my dear friend, you keep making the *same* mistakes!"

A new love affair gives you a chance to start over. A new love affair gives you a chance to stop making the same mistakes . . . as long as you remain self-aware of your own previous detrimental patterns.

Begin as You Mean
to Continue

Meet the first beginnings; look to the budding mischief before it has time to ripen to maturity.

—Shakespeare

Each new relationship makes its own rules, its own interpretation of the ageless game of man and maid. In effect, by the time you can begin to talk of a relationship rather than merely an acquaintanceship, the rules have already begun. For all the abstract talk about the role of women and the role of men, in real life, all that really exists is the role of a woman as defined by her interaction with one man: her expectations of him, his expectations of her.

The same woman may play several different versions of the so-called role of women with different men or with the same man at different stages in their lives. The tricky part has to do with inertia. Whatever the script that a man and woman in a couple write for each other or accept as having been written for them, it very soon comes to be written in indelible ink rather than sketched out in pencil. Once a habit or an expectation is allowed to develop, then whether or not it is fun or fair or practical, it tends to persist.

It is easy to look at past relationships and see the scripts that you have allowed yourself to play and to wish them in some ways different. Such an insight does not necessarily make it easier for you to change, or easier for you to change him, although that will not stop you from trying.

But—and here is the magic part—with a new man, you get to begin to write a new script for your lives together. You can create habits and expectations which, although probably similar to your scripted scenarios with other men, can be slightly different in ways that are important to you.

How do you go about creating new scripts? For a start, you do not let the old and undesirable habits from old and undesirable relationships repeat themselves. Suppose, for example, that one of your perennial laments with your high school steady was that he always decided where you would go and when so that you never got a vote or participated in planning things. If you later married that high school steady, as an amazing number of heads-up women seem to do, is it surprising that twenty years later, he is still automatically taking charge even though you are now thirty-six instead of sixteen? With a twenty-year habit, he is not now going to change. Attempts to take control may make him angry or confused or amused, but it will not change him.

A new lover, however, does not know that men always make the plans. If you don't want to get into that pattern again, you must begin immediately in the relationship to show initiative. If he makes the first invitation (and changing times or not, this is usually the case), then you make the second.

If he suggests one alternative, suggest a modification. "Yes, I'd love to go to a movie, but I always go to the gym to exercise on Tuesday nights. Would Wednesday be OK?" Or "It's nice of you to offer to pick me up, but I'd rather go right from work and meet you there."

These little modifications are polite, reasonable, and trivial. They do, however, make an important point in the politics of everyday life: events are something that we plan together, not something organized and structured by only one person.

On a more important level, consider the issue of initiation in lovemaking. If you have slept for ten years with a man who always made the sexual advances and if you now begin to come on to him, if the man in question is your very own husband, then he may react with startled embarrassment. However, your new lover does not have that response set. If you want sex to be more mutual then, from the beginning, be sure that while you are sometimes responsive to his approaches, you also expect him to be responsive to yours.

Many women who think they are assertive or even aggressive in bed do not notice that they take on this role only after the man in question has said, by word or action, "Hey, how about it?"

The same principle applies in all other areas. It is difficult to change established habits, but it is not so difficult to establish new ones in a new relationship.

RECIPROCITY: THE ELIXIR

OF MUTUALITY

Watch out for men who have Mothers.
—Laura Shapiro, *Ms.*

The chauvinist is long accustomed to the idea that women will serve him and take care of him as in the personal service that used to be provided by servants. Indeed, in this expectation, he is not far from wrong.

Men routinely encounter waitresses, secretaries, clerks, chambermaids, receptionists, and others in service occupations—the majority of whom turn out to be women. Women fetch and carry, they tend and attend, and they take care of him often in much the same way that mothers take care of children. Certainly in the same way that mothers take care of favorite sons.

Emancipated women who are sensitive to chauvinism in many other areas may make exceptions for their sons. The more devoted the mother is—and the longer the son has been at home—the more pronounced the attitude becomes. Guess who later gets to play Mommy and take care of him?

The traditional attitude in marriage is that the provider brings home the bacon and the little homemaker cooks and serves it ... after she has gotten him a beer, found the TV guide, answered the phone, and quieted the children.

In traditional marriages, a man who would leap to his feet when a strange woman comes into the room is the same man who, at home, automatically takes the best chair in the room, asks his wife to bring him the paper, and does not move until dinner is served.

Providing personal services is a way of being considerate and of showing affection. No one would want to have lovers and friends give up such nice little touches as making dinners and drinks, helping someone on and off with a coat, and putting the coat in the closet, running a bath, lighting a fire in the fireplace, fetching the mail, answering the phone, changing the cell phone, plumping up the pillows, arranging a footstool, getting a sweater, finding your glasses, and a thousand and one other ways of making someone comfortable. What is important in a lover is that these touches are *reciprocal*, not one-sided. And that they are not expected or demanded.

Unless you are a commercial sex worker, you do not have to continually give more than you receive, and you should not. If you are clear from the start about your expectations of quid pro quo and consistent in their application, most men will learn quite quickly how to scratch a back back.

"YOUR PLACE OR MINE?"

Visit, that ye be not visited.

—Don Herold

A complication of chauvinism is that the conventional rules that govern dating and require the man to invite a woman on a date—making him the host, and her, his guest—also govern the interactions of host and guest relationships in general. The person who issues the invitation and is the host owes many little services to the person who is the guest; this dynamic can reinforce chauvinist ideologies. The solution to this dilemma is to alternate the roles of host and guest.

The one who issues a dinner invitation decides where to eat and picks up the tab. Sometimes, that will be him; and sometimes, it will be you. You make dinner when you invite him to dinner at your house; he makes dinner when he asks you to his house. The person who owns the car you are using is the person who drives it, puts gas in it, and decides how fast to go. The man who can never be comfortable unless he is in the driver's seat, literally and figuratively, is acting out yet another subtle form of chauvinism in everyday life. Sometimes, you both go in his car; sometimes, you drive your own.

For two single people, one habit of consequence is imbedded in the cliché question: "Your place or mine?" If you take him to your home for the all-important first time, you have the all-important "home advantage" of being on your own turf and in more control of the situation. You look around for a razor for him the next morning and hope that you did remember to buy bacon after all and that you have clean towels. And you wait for him to leave before you go to work so that you can lock the door without giving him a key.

If you take him home the second time and the third and the tenth, then you have created a habit that when the two of you make love, you "always" do so in your space. Maybe that is how you want it for one reason or another.

But if you would prefer to have a more reciprocal arrangement of the roles of host and guest, don't wait until the tradition is established, and then try to change it.

Men are very comfortable with a double standard when it comes to homes: your home belongs to both of you, but his pad is his own. Whatever he does, he does with your consent. He cannot communicate with you by e-mail if you choose not to respond. He cannot phone you at all hours unless you answer the phone and are willing to chat. He cannot drop in without notice unless you give him a key or answer the door. Early on, be sure that "Your place or mine?" remains a real question rather than a rhetorical one. Shared space should come from both of you.

Rule Six: Do Your Part to Make the Affair Successful

Women claim that they want equal rights, equal respect ... You don't
get respect because you want it; you get respect because you earn it; by
being competent, intelligent, trustworthy, flexible, and generous.
—Marion A. Asnes

Women, especially young women and especially attractive ones, are used to being courted. They have often been encouraged to sit back and be entertained, to sit back and evaluate various offers from various men, and to take their time weighting one offer against the next. They expect to bring to the relationship first of all their beauty and then, *if* the price is right emotionally or otherwise, the gift of their sexuality. They expect men to make the effort to amuse and to entertain; they expect to let themselves be won and not much more.

If women are going to move beyond a role in which sexuality is exchanged for many other things to a situation where sexuality is mutual and where they are allowed to court as well as to be courted, then they must also take responsibility for making the resulting love affair successful and satisfactory.

Throughout this book, we have been listing and describing the various things that make a man attractive. We have outlined the intrinsic attributes that he should have and have suggested many nice things which he could do. Now for the surprise: *let the woman do the same.*

If you like to hear him say your name, learn to say his as well. If you like clever, funny little love gifts, think of some to give him. If you like a man as well-groomed as possible and wearing some exotic scent, then come to him as well-groomed as possible, with an exotic scent of your own.

If you hate unilateral decisions on matters of joint interest, make sure you don't make such decisions for him. If you rage at inaccurate generalizations about women, be sure you don't make equally inaccurate generalizations about men.

If you hate the feeling of being pressured into having sex when you don't really feel like it, be sure you don't try to pressure him into it when he doesn't really feel like it. If you need someone to understand the cross-pressures inherent in trying to juggle a marriage and a career and children and a love affair, then take note of the fact that he may have the same sort of juggling act to perform.

The golden rule is not news and it is not perfect, but it's still the best guideline there is. If you treat your man the way you would like to be treated, most of the time, he will be delighted. And most of the time, it will come back to you many times over.

Rule Seven: Respect

Privileged Information

I lay it down as a fact that if all men knew what others say of them, there would not be four friends left in the world.

—Blaise Pascal, *Pensées*

One of the crucial components of the intimate relationship is the sharing of the self. With a mate or with a lover, there develops a sense of trust which means, among other things, that there is a willingness to let down your guard and reveal more of your true self, including some components that do not make you especially proud. The willingness to be psychologically naked in front of the other is an important component of love. It is also an important part of making yourself vulnerable to being loved.

The sense of knowing the other in an intimate relationship comes not only from this voluntary exposure but also from having seen that other person, backstage as it were, in a number of unflattering circumstances. If you have lived for years with someone, you *know*. That knowledge carries with it an obligation not to reveal what you know.

There is a real temptation with a lover to discuss intimate details. If you are married, you may well be tempted to reveal details about your marriage. Remember in doing this that you have a right to reveal what *you* feel, what *you* want, what *you* have experienced, and other things about yourself. You do not have a right to reveal the inner life of one man to another. If you do, he will justifiably wonder how much of his inner life you may later reveal to some other man.

The secrets of the bedroom should be seen like the secrets of the confessional or of the psychiatrist's couch. Inviolate.

The prohibition against discussing the details of one relationship in the context of another is difficult to maintain since a major motivation for having an affair may be to have someone to discuss your marriage with, meaning someone to complain to about the troubles you've seen. When you are tempted to launch a diatribe against your marriage, remember the observation offered by the American Jewish writer and publisher Harry Golden: "The ultimate betrayal is not a wandering wife, but a wandering wife who tells her lover that her husband doesn't make as much as everyone thinks."

Rule Eight:

Minimize Jealousy

Yet he was jealous, though he did not show it,
For jealousy dislikes the world to know it.
—George Noel Gordon, *Lord Byron: Don Juan*

In any relationship, whether or not the couple is married, there is the specter of jealousy. The woman may be jealous of the man's money and the power it conveys; the man may be jealous of the woman's education and cultural refinement. A husband may be jealous of his wife's right to stay home and not confront the rigors of the marketplace; his wife may be jealous of his exciting career which contrasts too sharply with her own dull domestic existence. A father may be jealous of the affection the children shower on their mother, while the mother may be jealous of her husband's ability to reap the benefits of parenthood without contributing sufficiently to its physical and emotional demands.

In other words, there may exist in a given relationship a state of barely suppressed outrage that, for one reason or another, one person is getting more than his share of joy and the other more than her share of grief (or vice versa). It's not fair! If you add to that the possibility of one person having a lover or lovers, then the potential is increased many fold.

In our culture, men, even more than women, have been socialized to think of love in terms of possession. Nearly any man will rebel at the thought of any other male being with "his" woman. The man with whom you have only a casual relationship may well be presumptuous when he regards you as "his": the husband or the long-term lover has a more valid case. The most legitimate kind of jealousy and the one the world most readily understands and takes seriously is jealousy stemming from another love relationship. Sexual jealousy, although strong, is not necessarily more or less intense than jealousy from other sources. The root of jealousy is in whatever one partner feels insecure about. Once you have assessed what that is, then you have some insight into what the sources of trouble are likely to be with a particular man.

A problem with minimizing jealousy is that many women rather like their men to be jealous. They view it as a sign of love, and the more intense the response, the more loved they feel. Sometimes, a woman will deliberately go out of her way to provoke jealousy: when her man reacts to the red flag she is waving, she feels desirable and powerful.

Creating jealousy is not only an unkind and inconsiderate act, but it is also a tactic of dubious worth in terms of providing emotional reassurance. The intensity of a man's jealous response does not necessarily tell you much about his love for you or lack of it. As de La Rochefoucauld points out in one of his many maxims, "Jealousy is always born with love, but it does not always die with it."

A man's jealousy may tell you more about his own insecurities and his possessiveness than it does about his feelings for you. Unless your intention is unkind and you wish to torment and punish, deliberately creating jealousy is playing with fire, which is always a dangerous game.

PARANOIA, PROJECTION,

PROTESTATIONS

A man does not look in the closet unless he has stood there himself.
                                                              —Leonard Levinson

The English have a saying that it is reformed rakes who make the best husbands. One wonders at its veracity, but whether or not it is true, it is certainly true that it is reformed rakes who make the most suspicious husbands.

If a man is himself a veteran of many affairs of the heart, with many ladies married and otherwise, he *knows* what duplicity can lurk in the hearts of women and how unflattering and even ridiculous the imposed role of cuckold can be. One might hope that such a man of the world would be wise enough to turn a blind eye to suspicious circumstances. If he does not choose to do so, then he will be very difficult to deal with. It goes without saying that his own behavior, past and present, does little to increase his tolerance for yours.

The best defense against jealousy in simultaneous affairs is to keep one relationship as far away as possible from the other in terms of time and of space. The point is to avoid confrontations at all costs. In the abstract, the idea of another relationship may be vaguely upsetting. In the flesh, it may be enraging. Whether the man in question is a husband or a boyfriend or something in between, he should be protected as much as possible from having to deal directly with the reality of another affair.

The double standard is not just a masculine flaw: it is part of the human condition. If you are having another affair, even if he "knows" that such might be the case and even if he "permits" it, he should never have to deal with finding the wrong brand of underwear in his underwear drawer or a package of incriminating snapshots or a carelessly displayed love letter or e-mail.

The best advice, and very important advice it is, is simple: at all times, act as your own detective.

In *Same Time, Next Year*, the hit Broadway comedy by Bernard Slade, George and Doris have an affair for twenty-four years. They meet every year in a hotel in California, he supposedly on an annual business trip, and she supposedly at a retreat. As the play unfolds from one year to the next, we see how they share their lives and how the affair is a meaningful part of them. Apart from illustrating how an affair can be incorporated into a marriage and may actually strengthen it, the play provides an ideal circumstance for a tryst. When they are together, both are away from their respective homes and routines, and they relate only to each other. The more separate one affair from the other is, in time and space, the better.

AVOID INVIDIOUS COMPARISONS

Don't say "And you know, you are the first," because he would pretend
to believe it but it would be sheer courtesy. But say: "Before I knew you,
I didn't know what it was" because that men always believe.
— George-Armand Masson

It is a cliché to affirm that each man—or woman—is unique. Why is it then that so many women who have found one lover who has pleased them implicitly spend so much time trying to find another lover who also pleases them in exactly the same way?

You are not the same person you were then; he is not the same man you had then. So why do you expect the relationship to therefore be the same? And why do you wail and fret when it is not?

The secret of love is to live in the present affair. That does not mean that you forget your first love or your former love. Nor should it. It does mean that you do not judge your present circumstance by past glories. Each affair has something unique to offer, if you are attentive and receptive to it. If you are nostalgic, keep it to yourself or tell it to your mother or a friend. To your lover, all comparisons are invidious.

One woman who had had a number of lovers over the years amused herself with what she called her Academy Awards. "Harry received the Best Dressed Award; he was always impeccably turned out. Charles was the quintessential handyman; I gave him the Mr. Fix-it Award. I knew a Herman who could always make me laugh, even when I was almost in tears: he gets the Academy Award for Humor and Distraction. And then of course, there is a young man I knew only briefly who was awarded the Five *P* Award: proud possessor of the practically perfect pecker. Unfortunately, he did not have much else to recommend him although he did have that. The most important award in my books is the Boon Companion Award. That is the Oscar that really counts."

This kind of game is amusing, and it helps to reaffirm what you should always remember: that each man is valuable in his own way. But keep it as a game of solitaire or for your memoirs when you are old.

If you want to minimize jealousy, avoid the temptation to brag about old loves and old conquests. Do not discuss one man with another, not even if the discussion focuses on his negative points. He doesn't want to hear it, he has no right to hear it, and you have no right to tell it anyway.

Rule Nine: Beware the Monster That Is Habit

The less of routine, the more of life.
—A. B. Alcott

In a love affair, or in any relationship which is valued intrinsically, one needs continually to guard against that monster that devours everything, the monster of habit.

A blonde and glamorous and much married movie star was once asked why she had divorced her latest husband. Waving a bejeweled and lacquered hand, she exclaimed, "But, darling, he made love to me on Wednesdays."

"And what is wrong with Wednesdays?" inquired the reporter.

"Nothing is wrong with Wednesdays," she exclaimed. "But, darling, he made love to me only on Wednesdays and always on Wednesdays. It was all just too predictable."

When life's great moments become just too predictable, they cease to be great moments. When people have to face great adversity, from physical handicaps to prison camps, they console themselves with the cliché that you can get used to anything.

Alas, you can also get used to anything good. If every night you have caviar, lobster, and champagne, eventually you groan, "Oh god, caviar *again!*"

The jet-setters have learned, if nothing else, that *contrast is* everything. That cold of the ski slopes is crisper if you are still tanned from lying on a beach, the luxury of a grand hotel is grander if you have just returned from safari, and wallowing in a hot Jacuzzi is more relaxing if you have just survived ten days of testing your limits with Outward Bound.

The joy of a love affair is often that it is something different from your ordinary life. The death of a love affair often begins when the difference becomes a routine part of one's daily life.

The most exciting kind of lover is one who is aware of the somnolent effects of routines. Whether he has this sensitivity or not, you should yourself make sure that the habituation effects in an affair are minimized. Make it a point to vary the experience, not just in terms of how you make love but also with regard to what you eat, what you talk about, where you go, whom you see, and where and when you see each other.

Someone once observed that young people love to take a vacation because it is a break in the routine, and old people hate to take a vacation for the same reason. In a love affair, try to maintain the youthful attitude and punctuate your routine as often as you can.

Rule Ten: Take Time
to Savor Love

Plenty of people miss their share of happiness, not because they never found it, because they didn't stop to enjoy it.

—William Feather

In general, men are more achievement oriented and career conscious than are women, although the gap has narrowed significantly. Men, especially young men, spend enormous amounts of time and energy trying to get ahead and to build a secure niche for themselves. Their priorities are often in terms of work; and often, that work is an end in itself, as well as a means to money and success.

Many women do not understand the drive that propels some people to work sixty-hour weeks. They believe there should be a balance between work and other priorities and frequently complain that their men do not spend enough time with them. They feel they are wasting their time as they languish hour after hour, waiting for the man of the moment to stop working and pay attention to them. The best kind of lover is one who takes time to savor a love affair and who considers time with you to be a high priority.

Men may be more likely to be short of time and to tend to hurry from one thing to the next than are women, but they are not the only ones who make this mistake. Women may also find their lives so full that they have little time to pause and reflect and enjoy. Career women may be workaholics, obsessed with the knowledge that, as a woman, if she is to go half as far her male counterparts, she must be twice as good. Young mothers may virtually martyr themselves to their children's real and imagined needs. Housewives may work twelve-hour days in a futile attempt to keep everything perfect all the time.

If you want a lover and if you want a love affair, then take the time to enjoy it. Think of the importance of watching a sunset versus getting a report done or ironing the towels. You don't have to stop and smell the roses, but you should. And if your lover does not yet know this, then you should teach him to slow down as well.

Journalist David Grayson expresses this sentiment well: "Many times in my life I have repeated Rodin's saying that 'slowness is beauty.' To read slowly, to feel slowly and deeply; what enrichment! In the past, I have been so often greedy. I have gobbled down books—I have gobbled down work (I have even gobbled down friends!)—and indeed had a kind of enjoyment of all of them. But rarely have I tasted the last flavor of anything, the final exquisite sense of personality of spirit that secretes itself in every work that merits attention, in every human being at all worth knowing."

Love takes time. Make time to enjoy it.

CHAPTER 13

THE SECRET AFFAIR: HOW TO RELATE TO A PARAMOUR

If you cannot have your dear husband for a comfort and delight, for a breadwinner and a crosspatch, for a sofa, chair, or hot water bottle, one can use him as a cross to be borne.

—Stevie Smith

It is one thing to reflect upon your life and to decide that you would like to have a lover in it. It is quite another thing to do that when you are already married. A woman's husband is, theoretically, supposed to eliminate the need or the desire for a lover; unfortunately, very often he does not.

The lover of a married woman is by definition an illicit lover, although he may not be a secret one. The special term for illicit lovers of either sex is "paramour." The French *par* plus *amour* means "by or through love." The role of paramour seems to have evolved simultaneously with the roles of husband and wife. In some cultures, the paramour was more blatant than others, but he has always hovered provocatively in the background.

THE EXTRAMARITAL

CONNECTION

Adultery: democracy applied to love.
—H. L. Mencken

Sexual encounters outside of marriage have such a negative connotation in our culture that it is difficult even to discuss them in neutral and objective terms.

The technical term "adultery" means sexual intercourse by a married person with someone other than a spouse. It is often illegal and is generally considered to be a sin as well by most major religious groups. In addition, the term is not very precise, for it does not include the wide range of sexual experiences other than conventional intercourse.

The verb "to adulterate" means to debase or to make impure by the addition of inferior materials. It conjures up negative images such as contaminated food. People who have extramarital involvements are said *to be unfaithful* or to *betray* their vows or *to cheat*. The common phrase "sleeping around" implies a very casual and promiscuous behavior, presumably involving more than two beds. "Playing around" has a connotation of something other than serious intent. The most neutral wording to refer to the relationship of a married woman and her paramour, or a married man and his, is simply as an "extramarital relationship," meaning one which exists in addition to a conjugal one.

Technically, you can only commit adultery if you are legally married. Moreover, if you are legally married, then any sex with anyone other than your spouse is adultery. In the spirit of the law, the relationship inherent in an "extramarital relationship" could be considered the same for any two people who cohabit as husband and wife, whether they are legally married or not. Being unfaithful to a common-law husband is a lot like being unfaithful to a legally married husband, if the couple's understanding is that they are in fact in a "husband-wife" relationship. "Married but not churched" is how my grandmother would have described it.

The situation is less clear when you have two people who are lovers but are not married or living together as husband and wife. They do not have the same obligations to each other as would formalized couples that are legally married, living common-law or are registered domestic partners, in that they have *not* promised to forsake all others forever and ever. They have almost no legal privileges involving the relationship, but they also have almost no obligations. In that context, value-laden words such as "unfaithful" are even less appropriate.

Anyone discussing the virtues and vices of contemporary marriage usually brings up the importance of *monogamy*. The term "monogamy" does not refer to relationships at all but to a certain kind of marital structure involving one husband and one wife: "mono" for one, "gamy" for marriage. An alternative to monogamy would be *bigamy*, in which one person has two husbands or two wives, and bigamy is considered illegal everywhere in the Western world. The person with an extramarital connection is not, usually, a bigamist. He or she has one spouse and one or more other relationships with the opposite sex.

Erica Jong does not exactly clarify the issue when she explains, "Bigamy is having one husband too many. Monogamy is the same."

THE SEVENTH COMMANDMENT

If wishing damns us, you and I,
Are damned to all our heart's content;
Come, then, at least we may enjoy
Some pleasure for our punishment!

—Thomas Moore

Marriage in our culture is defined traditionally by the Judeo-Christian ethic, an ethic which is quite unambiguous on the question of adultery. Moses brought down the Word carved in stone and the word was "no." It is written clearly in Exodus: "Thou shalt not commit adultery."

To underline the message even more strongly, one was not even supposed to *want* to commit adultery. The tenth commandment goes on to specify: "Thou shalt not covet . . . thy neighbor's wife."

"Covet" is an evocative word. It means to desire inordinately. Perhaps desiring ordinately is all right. (My neighbor's wife has been generally unappealing to me, but I have lived in neighborhoods where I could have been said to covet my neighbor's ass.)

But in fact, even ordinate desire is not acceptable, for the Bible then goes on to prohibit even quiet longing. It is written in Matthew: "Whosoever looketh on a woman to lust after her hath committed adultery with her already in his heart." Remember Jimmy Carter's interview in *Playboy* where he quoted that passage and admitted that he had lusted in his heart?

If you take these prohibitions literally, then this chapter is not for you. There is no provision to be made for negotiation about extenuating circumstances. If you do proceed anyway and decide you would rather commit your sins in bed than in your heart, then you can expect a certain amount of moral outrage from the more devout. Remember that in the Bible, it is also written: "Thou shalt not suffer a witch to live." Watch out for anachronistic Pilgrims!

ADULTERESS AS VILLAINESS

A hundred years ago Hester Prynne of "The Scarlet Letter" was given
an A for adultery; today she would rate no better than a C-plus.
—Peter De Vries

Throughout history, women who were caught in adultery have suffered
grievous punishments. In India, they might have been burned. In Persia, men
favored beheading adulterous women. In Turkey, the traditional punishment
was the lash, a painful prospect but one offering more hope than in traditional
China, where errant wives might be imprisoned for life.

Under Sharia law in certain Islamic countries, all it takes is two male
witnesses swearing that the woman is an adulteress, and she can be stoned
to death even if she never committed adultery.

In the literature of the Western world, women who are, as they say, "taken
in adultery" are not punished as blatantly, but they do not fare well. The
world's literature is, of course, written primarily by men and may, consequently,
reflect more the position of an outraged husband than it does the sentiments
of the outraged wife.

In Dante's *Inferno* (ca. 1300), Francesca loved not only her husband but
also his younger brother, Paolo; and when they were discovered, both were
put to death. This sad tale, repeated in other literary versions, is unusual
in that both guilty parties were punished. Usually, the double standard
results in the errant woman being the focus of concern and punishment.
In Hawthorn's classic novel *The Scarlet Letter*, Hester Prynne was forced
to wear an embroidered scarlet letter on her dress to show that she was an
adulteress and then required to stand in the pillory holding her illegitimate
child. In Tolstoy's tragic story of *Anna Karenina*, the social disapproval of
the lovers is so pervasive and extreme that Anna disintegrates and ultimately

throws herself under the wheels of a train. There are a plethora of other examples of the same ilk, conveying the message that crime does not pay and that the woman who strays from the domestic hearth will come to a tragic end.

Ribald Wit: The Humors of Adultery

"Come, come," said Tom's father, "at your time of life,
There's no longer excuse for thus playing the rake.
It is time you should think, boy, of taking a wife."
"Why, so it is, Father—whose wife shall I take?"
—Thomas Moore, "A Joke Versified"

Thomas Moore wrote these ironic lines at the beginning of the nineteenth century. They illustrate a paradoxical aspect of our views of adultery. On the one hand, it is supposedly a very serious affair, a major sin, and a cause for outrage and retribution. On the other hand, it is incorporated into the jokes and wisecracks of everyday life in such a way as to suggest that it is not really all that serious.

People laugh at the prospect of adultery in ways they do not (yet) laugh about things they regard as more beyond the pale, such as child abuse or incest. "Do you suppose," the comedian wonders, "if infants have as much fun in infancy as adults do in adultery?" "A man can sleep around, no questions asked," quips Joan Rivers, "but if a woman makes nineteen or twenty mistakes, she's a tramp!" Marty, a comic, reports a conversation with his friend Art. "Your wife is gorgeous! Tell me, is she faithful?" asks Marty. "My wife is too good to be true," replies Art. And Rodney Dangerfield jokes, "I have good-looking kids. Thank God, my wife cheats on me."

The ubiquity of humor about adultery suggests that it is quite a commonplace occurrence, in actual fact as well as in fantasy. It implies an ambivalence about it which softens the sense of prohibition.

It does not matter whether or not you happen to find jokes about cuckolds and horns funny. What is significant is that adultery is often seen as being, literally, a joking matter.

Taking Chances: Wives Who Have Affairs

The chains of marriage are so heavy that it takes two to bear them, and sometimes three.
    —Alexandre Dumas: *fils, L'Esprit d'Alexandre Dumas*

The double standard of sexuality has always been more tolerant of the husband who strays than of the wife who strays. Nevertheless, a large proportion of married woman do have extramarital sex, at least once, during the course of their marriages. Quite a large proportion take a lover and have an affair which continues over time on a number of occasions. Some have more than one affair. How large are these proportions? No one knows, but they would seem to be an increasing minority.

Back in 1948, Kinsey and his associates reported in *Sexual Behavior in the Human Female* that about 20 percent of all wives had had extramarital sex at least once. In 1972, Hunt published a survey done by *Redbook* magazine, which suggested approximately the same ratio, with rates slightly higher among young women. In her book *The Monogamy Myth*, Peggy Vaughan estimates that 40 percent of women will have an extramarital affair while married. The rate is likely to vary depending on the type of women interviewed, with the highest probably to be found among younger wives working in urban areas.

While extramarital sex is still a relatively secretive activity, it is becoming more and more of an open secret. Elaine Denholtz provides an account of women who are *Having It Both Ways*, based on a series of very intimate anonymous interviews. Mary Anne Wollison does much the same thing in her discussion of *Affairs: The Secret Lives of Women*, as does Linda Wolfe in her book *Playing Around: Women and Extramarital Affairs*.

Some people who commit adultery do incur most unfortunate results, just as the folk literature tells us. However, in real life, many women have affairs which no one knows about except the participants. Many women have affairs which are eventually discovered but which do not automatically bring destruction and ruin about their heads. Many women have many affairs and live to tell the tale and, eventually, live happily ever after.

The real message may be that it is not an extramarital connection per se that is bad for one's mental health, but the wrong extramarital connection, undertaken with the wrong person for the wrong reasons and managed in the wrong way. There is not much instruction given wives on the important subject of how to have a successful affair, with the result that there is a lot of on-the-job training. As one wife sighed, "The trouble with on-the-job training is that you can make so many mistakes."

Help may be on the way. In the early 1980s in Los Angeles, psychologist Cynthia Silverman began to offer workshops for married women who are having—or thinking of having—extramarital affairs. While such groups may offer some psychological support and may be useful in dealing with guilt, they are most noteworthy for the changing attitudes they represent.

A married woman who contemplates an affair should take into account all of the rules of safe conduct outlined in the previous chapter. In addition, however, she needs to contend with two other factors: the risk of exposure and the special problems of pregnancy.

First Caveat: Facing the Risk of Exposure

You may fool all the people some of the time; you can even fool some of the people all of the time; but you can't fool all of the people all of the time.

—Abraham Lincoln, *Lincoln's Yarns and Stories*

In relating to a paramour, the first thing a wife must decide is just how secret her affair has to be. To decide this usually means deciding whether or not she wants to maintain the viability of her marriage and, if so, for how long. If a couple who embarks upon an illicit affair takes seriously the need to remain undetected, both participants can usually avoid exposure and embarrassment. Most of the time, they get away with it, and no one is the wiser. Most of the time.

A word of warning. A serious word. If someone, a husband or a lover, decides that he does want to know what you do, where you go, and when and with whom, then he can find out. A skilled detective can know more about you in a few weeks than you care to know about yourself. A bugged telephone is not entirely a far-fetched idea if total surveillance is what someone has in mind. Such techniques are expensive, but even those of modest means may decide that the price is worth it if the stakes are high. Few husbands are this unscrupulous or this paranoid, but if there is enough at stake, it is always possible for such drastic measures to be taken.

When a married woman has an affair, she must also remember that there are more people potentially involved in the question of secrecy than herself and her husband. She may also be subject to scrutiny by her lover's wife, or girlfriend, who resents her poaching on what she considers "her" territory.

406

Your lover's wife may need to be able to prove his adultery to establish her own alimony payments, and you end up being an unwilling co-respondent in a divorce action. His girlfriend may be simply curious to know what is going on. And if he is in a position of power and authority, he is always vulnerable to the blackmail of opponents who will resort to whatever techniques they think will work.

Jealousy can be a desperate thing leading to desperate measures. Adultery may also involve serious practical issues: who gets a divorce, contested or otherwise; who gets custody of the children; who does or does not pay alimony. It is unlikely that anyone will be interested enough in your affairs to go to such drastic lengths to discover and document them, but it is possible, and that possibility is something to assess and to keep in mind.

One outraged husband, determined to avoid alimony and to keep custody of his children, led his wife to believe that he would be out of town overnight. He anticipated that she would take advantage of his absence, as she had on other occasions, to entertain her lover in their master bedroom. He quietly let himself into the house and, using equipment he had set up the previous day, secretly taped her activities, using her own video recorder. She was so appalled at the video tape he subsequently produced that she meekly signed over everything to him and retreated to a commune in New Mexico to think things out.

Schoolchildren often advise each other, "Be good. If you can't be good, be careful." Out of the mouths of babes can come some sound advice. Be careful.

SECOND CAVEAT: NO BASTARD

CHILDREN

There is no word equivalent to "cuckold" for women.
—Joseph Epstein

In medieval times, a man whose wife deceived him with another man was called a cuckold, a pejorative term which fortunately is not used much anymore. The origin of the term "cuckold" is revealing. If you are interested in ornithology, the study of birds, you may have come across accounts of the habits of the cuckoo bird. Cuckoos solve the problem of the perpetuation of their species by the simple expedient of laying eggs in other bird's nests and departing, leaving other birds of another species to raise the young cuckoos.

Once upon a time, observers might signal the approach of a man who was committing adultery with someone's wife, or who had designs in that direction, by warning the husband with a whispered "cuckoo, cuckoo." Eventually, the term got changed around to refer to the betrayed not the betrayer and became "cuckold."

Shakespeare and other authors perpetuated the literary myth that such a man was burdened with a set of horns on his head, which others could see, but of which he was blissfully unaware. It was another version of the truism that the husband, or the wife, is often the last to know. In Italy, one of the most unforgivable insults still is to make the sign of the "cornu" at someone: taking your index and pinkie and putting them on top of your head to resemble horns.

On the issue of bastard children, there are some real legal and moral differences in the situation of single women compared with married ones.

If you are single, you might decide to have a child but choose not to get married. You have a right to become a mother without becoming a wife. It is the contention of many that, as long as you expect nothing of the father, you do not need to have his consent or, indeed, do not even need to inform him. It would seem that, if such is your intent, having a child through artificial insemination would be a better alternative, but there is nothing to stop you using the old-fashioned way if this is your decision.

However, if you are married, any child you have is legally the child of your husband and is assumed to be so socially and emotionally. A husband has the right to certainty of the parenthood of "his" own children. As the lyrics from *The King and I* caution, "But blossom never ever float from bee to bee to bee." A basic assumption is that the married woman having an affair has no right to get pregnant by another man. Her body is her own, as is her sexuality; but her children are to be shared for as long as she stays married, and usually after that.

The married woman must be especially scrupulous and fastidious not to let herself get pregnant by her lover rather than by her husband.

THE PRACTICE TO DECEIVE

The one charm of marriage is that it makes a life of deception absolutely necessary for both parties.
—Oscar Wilde, *The Picture of Dorian Grey*

Most of the time, if a man and woman want to have a love affair and if they are both serious about keeping their affiliation unknown, it is possible to do so. It is much more possible in a large city than in a small town, it is much more possible without children than with them, it is much more possible if only one of the parties is married. Nevertheless, it can be done and indeed is being done all around you all the time. Linda Wolfe, in *Playing Around: Women and Extramarital Sex*, describes her surprise at discovering that her West Side Manhattan neighborhood, which appeared on the surface to be a world exclusively of mothers and children, was in reality a world shared extensively with male paramours, some of them fantasized, others quite real. Just in her small apartment building alone, four of the eight married women with small children were having affairs.

Sometimes, the cuckolded husbands and wives involved are very naive; more often, they have decided at some level of consciousness that they would rather not know. Sometimes, the participants are skilled at maintaining a suitable image so that there is no reason for suspicion. Sometimes, they are skilled at dispelling any suspicions which do arise.

And sometimes, of course, they eventually just don't care and gleefully toss cats out of their bags and let them land where they may.

COLLUSION: THE BLIND EYE

I pray that I may not be married
But if I am to be married
that I may not be cuckold
but that if I am to be a cuckold
that I may not know it
but if I know it
that I may not care.
—Anonymous Bachelor's Prayer, circa 1650

In a number of cases, the practice to deceive a husband about an ongoing or prospective affair is simplified by his implicit, and sometimes explicit, agreement not to notice anything. The wife and her husband enter into what amounts to collusion, thereby saving face on both sides. If he does not ask, she does not have to lie; if he does not know of an affair, then he does not have to do anything about it.

Such an arrangement may often occur in a marriage of convenience where there is little pretense of affection between the husband and wife. They simply agree to lead separate lives and come together only when the business of the marriage, in the form of children or property or social functions, demands it.

A parallel arrangement may also exist for couples who are quite fond of each other but have made a realistic assessment of the importance of their sexual bond. In fiction, the well-known story of Lady Chatterley and her lover involves the explicit permission of her husband to take a lover, and indeed to have a child by him, since the husband was crippled and paralyzed and could not provide an heir for himself. Righteous indignation eventually came, not because she had an affair but because she selected a gamekeeper who was too déclassé to be considered an equal.

History provides some real-life examples of husband-wife collusion. When Lord Horatio Nelson began his infamous affair with Lady Emma Hamilton, they were both living in the same house as her husband Sir William Hamilton, her senior by thirty years. Husband and lover were friends, although there is little doubt that Sir William knew the real parentage of "his" daughter, especially when Lady Emma named her Horatia. He simply announced his quiet determination that the peace of his household would not be disturbed, and apparently it was not.

Similar situations occur in the contemporary world. There is a vivacious, sensuous wife, a mother of two, who habitually goes out to play bridge or to see a movie or something equally innocuous and returns home at two or three in the morning and explains that she and the girls "just got to talking and forgot the time." She has been married for nearly twenty years and has been playing bridge far into the night for at least eighteen of them. She has learned a lot more than Goren and the Blackwood convention.

Her suburban husband watches the eleven o'clock news and then goes to bed and goes to sleep. Sometimes if he wakes up at four and she is still not back, he worries. She could have had a car accident or be in some kind of trouble. He is reassured when she comes home all right and goes back to sleep. Sometimes, since he is awake anyway, they make love first.

Eighteen years. He does not ask how the bridge game went. Various men show up at various times to take her to lunch. After lunch, they tend to stay for dinner at the house. The husband is gracious enough, plays the good host, and then retires to his study and his books.

Peering through the window into the mystery of other people's marriages, one must conclude that the husband does know what is going on but chooses not to recognize it. This is what is meant by "the blind eye."

Unless a man has decided that he wants to divorce his wife, presenting a blind eye to her affairs or to the possibility of her affairs is an excellent and wise strategy. If he officially knows, then he is required to act, and none of the available options for action is very appealing. Oliver Goldsmith considered all of this and concluded that, in the Western world, not seeing may well be the best answer. In *The Citizen of the World*, he writes, "If I were an English husband, I would take care not to be jealous, nor busily pry into the secrets my wife was pleased to keep from me . . . Whenever I went out, I'd tell my wife where I was going, lest I should unexpectedly meet her abroad in the company of some dear deceiver. Whenever I returned, I would use a particular rap at the door, and give four loud 'hems' as I walked deliberately up the staircase. I would never inquisitively peep under her bed, nor look behind the curtains. And even though I knew the Captain was there, I would calmly take a dish of my wife's cool tea and talk of the army with reverence."

There are two players in such a charade: one who deceives and one who agrees to be deceived. Vicki Baum puts the same message somewhat differently in *And Life Goes On* when she observes, "Marriage always demands the greatest understanding of the art of insincerity possible between two human beings."

Discreet Indiscretions

Be discreet in all things, and so render it unnecessary to be mysterious about any.

—Arthur Wellesley, First Duke of Wellington

If you decide to have an affair and to keep it a secret, take yourself seriously. If you want to write letters or e-mails—and that is an important part of many friendships and love affairs especially when one cannot be in daily contact—then rent a mailbox or use a private e-mail address your partner can't access.

If you want to keep letters or endearing Hallmark cards, as most people do, rent a safety deposit box. If you have a key to his apartment, put it on a separate key chain and keep it out of sight. Pretend, in other words, that you are your own detective on your own trail and try to be a difficult subject.

Your worst problem in managing an affair is the disruption of your known habits. If you always shop for groceries on Wednesday, then not getting groceries on a Wednesday is a cause for comment. The more you establish yourself as an erratic person with an erratic routine, the more freedom you have. This will mean, of course, that even when you do not have a lover, or when he is not available, your nonpredictable patterns must still prevail.

When we are concerned about protecting the chastity of young girls, one of the first measures taken is to impose a curfew. Young ladies in good schools must be home at ten o'clock on weeknights or at midnight on weekends. We assume that there is safety in numbers so that as long as one is out in a group, in the daytime, all is well. Such structuring only shows the lack of imagination of the chaperones and means that, a generation ago, college girls missed a lot of afternoon classes, which they had to make up some other time. After their "matinees," they went back to their carefully supervised official residence and were snug in their own beds, alone, by "lights-out."

Husbands and wives think much the same way. The only really serious problems of accountability occur when you have two married people, who are not married to each other, alone together, and when they are alone at a time so far into the night that there is nothing for them to be officially doing. How late is "late" depends on where you live. In many small towns, everything is closed up by 10:30 p.m.; in New York, there would still be many activities happening at 2:30 a.m. Wherever you are, four o'clock in the *A* of the *M* is too late.

The first prudent rule, therefore, is to concentrate your activity in the daylight hours. A second protective strategy is to surround yourself with other people. In Hollywood, the coming and goings of the stars are conspicuous and of considerable interest to the public. It is difficult for anyone who is even a minor celebrity to remain incognito for long. So to cope with this problem, there has evolved a custom of going out in the evening in the company of a "beard." In this context, a beard is a friend who accompanies an illicit couple out in public, thereby creating a group instead of a dyad. A beard can be a man or woman but is usually a man. If a woman is out with two men, or with three, then officially, she is not really out with any of them. She is just "out with the boys." The beard who comes along to offer his or her protection understands his or her role as third wheel but is willing to enjoy the couple's company as a favor.

It is a nice bonus that, traditionally, the beard never pays for any of the dinners or drinks and is not expected to return this hospitality. You don't have to be a movie star to find this strategy a useful distraction.

"WHERE THE HELL WERE YOU?"

An alibi is the proof that you did do what you didn't do so that others will think you didn't do what you did.

—Evan Esar

A love affair takes up time. Sooner or later, there will come to someone an awareness that all of the hours of the day do not seem to have been accounted for. First of all, it is wise never to start the habit of accounting for all of your time. If you are known to wander in art galleries, then you wander in art galleries until you are all wandered out, however long that takes.

Second, you make a point of keeping those time commitments that you do make. Ordinarily, you might come home on a working day anytime between five and seven, which as the French know are the prime times for various kinds of assignations. However, if you say you will be home at five for some reason, then on that day (and that day only), you should be.

Third, when your alibi is in doubt, you do not offer an explanation unasked, but you do offer substantiating evidence. A woman who goes shopping comes home with things she has bought. Sometimes, they were bought three days in advance, in which case she is careful with the sales slips. A woman who has seen a movie has seen a movie, but perhaps, it was on Tuesday afternoon rather than Thursday.

Golly, How the Truth Will Out

The best laid schemes o'mice and men
Gang aft a-gley.

—Robert Burns, "To a Mouse"

And women too, however they were laid.

Even with exquisite care and planning, accidental revelations do happen. A husband who is away on a three-day business trip never leaves town because of a problem with the plane's engine. A busy executive who is never home before seven comes home at three with a migraine. When you should not have been missed, you find that everyone has been frantic to reach you because your mother is ill. A water main bursts in the basement, but you don't notice because you are not there when you ordinarily should have been, and you return to find that the entire basement is completely flooded and you have no explanation for your absence.

If you are going to have an affair, you must realize that no matter how discreet you are, it is always *possible* for an unforeseen circumstance to lead to an inadvertent exposure of your activities.

Mistakes, Misfortunes, and Dead Giveaways

Beware the man with Lover's eyes.
He knows your heart; he feels your cries;
He seeks the guile in your disguise
Then strips your soul and sees your lies;
They never close, those Lover's eyes.
—Jadah Vaughn, "Lover's Eyes"

With a little thought and planning, being discreet enough to deceive most of the people most of the time is not difficult. Being discreet enough to deceive a *really* attentive man or a lover's *incessantly* suspicious wife may be almost impossible.

One consequence of being in love is a passionate interest in the other person and in all of the details about that man or woman. A man who is in love with you really looks at you, studies you, memorizes you. All of the little details about you are of consuming interest, which is all very nice but which in the end can be very difficult.

There was once a young lady who was having an affair with her boss and who, like many before her, found a long lunch hour a perfect occasion for what they called a matinee. In the same office was a smitten coworker who had amorous aspirations of his own but who had not been successful.

One day, she came back from lunch on time—cool, poised, and well-groomed—and he looked at her with a significant look and stomped out of the room in a huff. It was only much later that she uncovered how her admirer could "know" about her matinee with such certainty. This was the era before panty hose. Before lunch, a small run was to be seen in her left stocking; after lunch, the little run had mysteriously run to the right leg.

One wife who had assembled herself in haste out of a state of dishabille was chagrined to notice her husband noticing her slip—which just happened to be on inside out.

One young husband rummaged in his wife's purse for a package of matches. He found, to his mortification, a package of condoms: Trojans, to be precise. Since he had gotten a vasectomy the previous year, he was not amused. Her attempts to explain away the evidence were rather thin.

The best protection from such incriminating mistakes is the protection of time and distance. Anyone involved in an extramarital affair is in most danger when the tryst is in too close proximity to the domestic scene. It is best to set aside or leave enough time to have a shower and change clothes before resuming the daily round.

Alas, this is a luxury which may mean that you see your lover on fewer occasions.

THE NEED TO BE CAUGHT

"Thou shalt not get found out" is not one of God's commandments, and no man can be saved by trying to keep it.

—Leonard Bacon

If they really wanted to do so, most couples could figure out how to conduct an affair in secrecy. I know of several such liaisons which would never have come to light had the women not confided in me after hearing that I was working on this book. Unless lovers are so very unlucky as to be discovered together unconscious in a crashed car, or in some other circumstance over which no one has any control, they will likely go on for years in a discreet and precious alliance, their private life kept quite separate from their mates, their children, and their careers.

Other couples, however, seem to be sabotaged by their own subconscious. There seems to be a need to get caught. Without going into the psychopathology of guilt and its manifestations, consider for a moment if at some level you *do* want to be found out, or if he does.

The circumstances under which otherwise rational men and women seem to want to be caught—and practically beg to be unmasked—are endless. A man leaves in his suit coat the key to a downtown hotel. A woman forgets to take from her purse the incriminating letter or book of matches.

You buy your lover a cashmere sweater and write the check to a men's boutique in the joint checkbook and then look unconvincingly blank when your husband asks you about it.

One husband called his girlfriend in another city without thinking about the cell phone bill. When it came, and his wife processed it with the other bills, there was a record of many long calls to the same number. The wife called the number and asked for her husband by name, only to have the girlfriend explain that he was "not here yet" but would be soon, and could she take a message?

She was given a very clear message.

SABOTAGE!

It is just as foolish to destroy a compromising letter as it is to writes one.
—Evan Esar

If you are clear in your mind that you do not want to be caught and are therefore committed to keeping your relationship with your lover a secret from your husband, are you equally certain that you do not want *him* to be caught? Are there ways in which you sabotage his discretion? Conversely, a lover may be more concerned with his own image than with yours and act so as to sabotage your efforts at discretion.

It is not always clear if acts of sabotage are deliberate or unconscious. One wife of my acquaintance habitually wore perfume. On more than one occasion, when refreshing her scent, she managed to pour perfume directly on her lover's coat.

One husband who should have known better claimed to have become so carried away that he "accidentally" left a hickey love mark on the neck of his lover where her husband was quiet likely to see it. Women may do the same thing with long nails, leaving telltale traces across the back of a husband supposedly working late in the office.

A single girlfriend of a friend of mine was growing increasingly resentful of her married lover and increasingly skeptical that he was ever going to leave his wife. She left affectionate little notes in his coat pockets and in his cigarette package so that later he would have the pleasant surprise of finding them. She kept on doing it until, finally, his wife had an *un*pleasant surprise instead. The lover claimed that she meant no harm, but just coincidentally she did succeed in precipitating a marital confrontation and a crisis.

Mysterious telephone calls have similar effects although they are not as unambiguous. Either sex may blatantly disregard each other's timetables, so as to make someone unaccountably late, or cause someone to miss a critical plane or train. Some mistresses are never so loving as just before a man has to leave.

The worst saboteurs are those who have nothing to lose . . . the single person going home to an empty house to eat a TV dinner while you must run to have time to change before your charity banquet. Keeping you late is an understandable way of expressing his resentment at the lack of balance in your lives.

Another kind of sabotage is the collecting of the evidence that may, at some point in time, be used against you. The dedicated photographer will take pictures of the lover or the mistress, "just for us," of course; but meanwhile, the telltale pictures, negatives, and digital photos on his cell phone exist and can be found, or left to be found, or even to be shown.

I am not suggesting the kind of premeditated blackmail that can well go on with some version or another of the old "badger game" that has been around since at least the early nineteenth century and is often perpetrated on married men. Typically, this con game involves an attractive woman who approaches a man, preferably lonely, married, of some financial means, and from out of town. The woman entices the man to a private place with the intent of maneuvering him into a compromising position that usually involves a sexual act. Afterward, an accomplice presents the victim with photos, video, or similar evidence and threatens to expose him unless blackmail money is paid.

Rather, these mistakes by people of good intent suggest a subterranean need to be caught, which does not require psychoanalysis to figure out.

When you see it happening, in yourself or your partner, the next question to ponder is why.

Sometimes, you or your partner have a kind of death wish, or at least, a death wish for a particular marriage. If you need to get out of a situation and do not know how, then letting yourself be caught in an unforgivable situation is one way out, albeit a dangerous way. The depressed person who does not have the courage to slash her wrists, but is found driving intoxicated at ninety-five miles an hour, may very likely deny she was trying to kill herself if asked. However, you don't have to be a psychologist to suspect that at some level that is what she had in mind.

The depressed wife, who takes her lover nude on the living room rug, because she "knows" her husband never comes home until 5:30 p.m. and it is only 4:45 p.m., is behaving much the same way. As with people who make half-hearted suicide attempts to reap attention from someone other than the Grim Reaper, she is likely to stay on this path of destruction, making the timing closer and closer and the risk higher and higher until she finally gets her wish and is caught.

Resisting Sabotage

Not even a spider likes a tangled web.
—Jayson VanVerten

One factor to consider in the conduct of an affair, and in being exposed to sabotage, is the phenomenon of what amounts to psychological masochism. Some men and women thrive on crisis and confrontation. They are, at their best, in the throes of intense conversations and dialogues; and if none are occurring spontaneously, they manage time and again to conjure them up. The tears and the anguish, the all-night truth session and promises are all valid enough. But you should be suspicious of anyone who finds the whole process too interesting. People like that are creating a dramatic script in which they are the star, and often, they don't much care if they are the victim or the villain as long as they get a starring role.

Worse yet, such people often have a desperate need to confide in someone. Under the guise of seeking advice for their terrible problem, they will guarantee that the number of people privy to your affair will far exceed the two of you or your betrayed mates. The wider the audience and the more dramatic the gestures, the better.

The psychological masochists who seek out confrontations do have a point. The conversations are exciting. The passions of the moment do sometimes bring out truths and feelings that would otherwise remain hidden. The excess of emotion which is generated can spill over into quite intense and exceptional lovemaking.

However, if you do wish to keep your marriage intact and unshaken, do not let yourself be drawn into someone else's fantasy. The risks involved are too great, not only for yourself but for your family.

DEALING WITH JEALOUSY

As we all know from witnessing the consuming jealousy of husbands who are never faithful, people do not confine themselves to the emotions to which they are entitled.

—Quentin Crisp, *The Naked Civil Servant*

The husband whose wife is having an affair has a right to be jealous. He believes he has that right, whether or not he too is having extramarital sex. He believes he has that right whether or not he still loves his wife, and whether or not he cares if he keeps her. If the efforts to protect him from confronting this knowledge have not been successful, then some level of indignation is almost certain to result. The jealousy goes back, in part, to the chattel concept of marriage. "Not with my wife you don't!" is a common battle cry.

When the anthropologist Robert Ardrey talked about *The Territorial Imperative,* he was referring to the characteristic of some animals to define a territory as their own and to defend it against other members of the same species. His examples drew heavily from the primates but also included birds and wolves and even some fishes and reptiles. In marriage, a husband's outrage against an adulterous wife may not be so much a matter of ordinary jealousy as a sense of having had his territory invaded.

It was not that long ago when at a ball or social function, a man might turn to a husband and ask him, "May I dance with your wife?" The husband would either grant or deny permission without his wife having a say in the matter. Such a husband is quite preoccupied with the traditional idea of woman as chattel. He genuinely believes that having married you, he now owns you. *My* woman, *my* wife, *mine, all mine.* His sense of outrage at an affair is not that different from what he'd feel if a stranger drove off in his car without permission.

One husband who caught his wife in a compromising situation sputtered, "He came into *my* house, he drank *my* liquor, he sat by *my* fireplace, then he seduced *my* wife." I had the bad judgment to point out to him that it was also *her* house, *her* liquor, and *her* fireplace, and to inquire if he would have felt better if they had gone to a hotel. The point was lost on him. It is especially difficult to deal with this attitude when the marriage itself is a hollow shell and the husband in question is not himself loving. The fact that he has not touched his wife in six months does not necessarily mellow his indignation if someone else does.

BEING NICE AT HOME

An ideal wife is one who remains faithful to you but tries to be just as charming as if she weren't.

—Sacha Guitry

Jewelers and florists have always known that their prime customers are men who are having an affair and so have been behaving badly at home or are feeling guilty, or both. They seek to appease their consciences with small pearl earrings or a bouquet of roses, and women may become justifiably suspicious. They wonder, "What is he up to this time? Why is he being so nice?" If you are the one having an affair and you want to remain undetected, it is wise to continue to behave exactly as you always have. Wise perhaps, but difficult.

When someone new loves you, when you love someone new, there is a tendency to become even more critical of your long-suffering husband. By concentrating on his shortcomings, you can begin to justify your affair in your own mind; so the more shortcomings he has, the more justified you are. Consequently, just when you are behaving at your worst, in the sense of being preoccupied elsewhere, you may also be behaving badly and critically in other little ways. Such inconsideration may foment a rebellion in the most permissive and understanding of husbands.

When you are having an affair, it is doubly important to be nice to the man you live with and to reassure him of his continued importance in your life. The faithful wife often feels that because she is virtuous that is all that should be required of her: she does not also have to be gracious. If you are not faithful, you must at least be nice if you want to keep your marriage intact.

Avis Rent A Car once claimed that they tried harder because they were number 2, after Hertz Rent A Car. If your husband is the number 2 man in your life, then you—not he—must try harder at your relationship.

Some Men Are More

Threatening Than Others

All the world loves a lover—except the husband.
—Evan Esar

Sometimes, a husband is not as much concerned with the fact of his wife having an affair as he is appalled by the man she chooses to be involved with. Some potential lovers are less psychologically threatening to the husband than others and would be tolerated when other lovers would arouse great resentment and anger.

Any husband is most jealous of men who compete with him in areas in which he considers himself vulnerable. However, some will tolerate other men around if they seem to him to be comparatively inadequate. For example, one dimension of masculinity in our culture is what has been called paycheck manhood. This means that men sometimes assess themselves, and each other, in terms of how much money they make. One man says of another scornfully, "I could buy and sell him any day." The less wealthy man can be dismissed and disregarded as a lesser man who does not have to be taken into account.

If your husband has internalized the concept of the "paycheck manhood," then you can predict that he will be most jealous of a man who makes as much as he does or—God forbid—more. Such a man could theoretically "outbid" him for your favors and attentions. Whether or not you use this standard, he very well might. A husband with this worldview will be quite sanguine about a beachboy or a poor artist or a starving student but incensed at the prospect of another executive.

Similarly, a man who views himself as cultured and educated—as someone aware of the finer things in life such as art, music, theater, and generally what he thinks of as gracious living—will not be perturbed by someone he can dismiss as an uncultured thug. He will, however, sit up and scowl at a prospective lover who offers you a season's pass to the opera.

A beautiful man, secure in his image of himself as attractive, will accept with a somewhat patronizing air the prospective lover who is short or fat or gray or old or just all-purpose ugly. He will bristle at another man who is also tall and handsome, especially if it is possible that his rival is actually taller and more handsome.

If you want to carry on a love affair which your husband knows about, or at least suspects, it behooves you to minimize the implicit threat posed by his potential rivals. You might be able to select the kind of man you know he will not consider very threatening. If that is not possible, you should at least be a skillful enough player of the game to assuage his feelings wherever possible. Feel free to point out your lover's shortcomings, but be very sparing indeed in singing his praises. And never, but never, make any comparisons, implicit or otherwise, which put your lover in a more favorable light than your husband, however tempting this might be in the heat of an argument.

Some Scenes Are More Threatening Than Others

There are only about 20 murders a year in London and not all are serious—some are just husbands killing their wives.
—G. H. Hatherill, British policeman

A husband who knows that his wife is having an affair, or has had one, may be upset and saddened. However, as long as that knowledge is abstract and imprecise, conveyed in generalities with few of the incriminating details, it may remain possible for him to come to terms with it, to understand it, and eventually, even to accept it.

The husband who knows that his wife is having an affair, because he was there and watched, has quite a different kind of knowledge. If he has found her and her lover *in flagrante delicto*, the images of those bodies entwined together will be burned onto his retina forever. In many Southern states, indeed in many parts of the world, the murder of the offending spouse and the cuckolding man is considered a "crime of passion." It is considered understandable, if not entirely justified, and is treated differently from other murders.

From this: a rule, an absolute rule. Never, but never, but absolutely never go to bed where you could be caught in the act. If that means that you miss some possible opportunities which would probably be safe, consider that "probably safe" is like being "a little bit pregnant." Probably safe is not really safe, and really safe is what you are after.

People may suspect many things, they may believe many things, but they never actually know until they see for themselves. And then it is too late.

THE JEALOUS PARAMOUR

Your husband locks the door, the night divides us,
and I, night's outcast, weep my futile tears.
Of course, the brute will take you in his arms
And kiss you, more than kiss you . . .
Until he has his husbandly reward.
—Ovid, *The Dinner Party*

The married woman with a lover knows her husband may be jealous and has a right to be, and she tries as best she can to forestall that response. Sometimes, it is only later that she realizes she must also deal with a jealous paramour.

The paramour is in a difficult position in that he must willingly and knowingly relinquish you back to the arms of your legal husband. As he becomes fonder of you, or as he falls in love with you, this has the potential for more and more anguish on his part. This problem is essentially unsolvable, but it can be minimized. At least two strategies help, at least in minor ways.

First, it is important not to discuss in detail your conjugal sex life. Whether you say that sex with your husband is great or sex with your husband is terrible, you raise the specter of comparisons, which are by definition invidious. The best accounting, of course, is to claim that although you are still living with your husband, you are not sleeping with him. Well, maybe "sleeping with" because there is only one bed and one bedroom, but nothing other than sleeping.

This is what errant husbands have been telling their mistresses for centuries, and I suppose sometimes it is even true or as true as "my wife doesn't understand me." (It does become rather awkward, of course, when the supposedly celibate wife becomes pregnant again.) Even if you do still have sex with your husband, sometimes, this may be an acceptable falsehood in that it is a face-saving one.

The second strategy which helps to minimize sexual jealousy and possessiveness is to try to contrive some period of time between the tryst with your lover and your return home. There will be times when people in this complex situation literally get out of one bed, get dressed, drive home, get undressed, and get back into another bed.

From the point of view of the abandoned lover, it does not bear thinking about. The fact and circumstances of the marriage bed should be kept as remote and as abstract as possible.

A word of warning: a paramour—who is reasonably sanguine about your having sex with your husband, because he knows you don't like it and are only doing your duty—can become wildly jealous at the possibility of another lover. He may foam at the mouth and rant and rave and become quite paranoid.

If you should want to have two lovers, remember that jealousy of the first for the second may far exceed any problems you might have with your husband.

CHAPTER 14

PAYING THE PIPER

There are two tragedies in life. One is to lose your heart's desire. The other is to gain it.
—George Bernard Shaw, *Man and Superman*

If you think about what you would want in the kind of man you would like for a lover, you probably can come up with an image that fires your imagination and speeds up your heartbeat. If you decide to have a love affair, you can probably find, if not the prefect lover, then one who is perfect enough.

Oscar Wilde promises that "when you really want love, you will find it waiting for you." And that is probably true.

When you stop to think about the advice and implicit recommendations you have been reading in the last few hundred pages, you might notice that there are a lot of admonitions about being brave. There are a lot of sentences that convey the need to take risks and which note some variant of "nothing ventured, nothing gained." There is a lot of talk about courage.

That should give you pause. Why do you need courage? Will something bad happen? Are the risks dangerous risks? Well, they can be. So we start with the admonition *pecca fortiter*: sin bravely.

The role of a woman with a lover, freely chosen because he is a loving, lovable man and for no other reason, is a new role. It is not yet bound by recognized rules of what is or is not likely to get you what you want.

Worse, having a lover is not yet recognized as a legitimate alternative to the traditional roles allocated to women, which tend to alternate between the virgin and the whore, between good girls—who are wives, mothers, and daughters—and bad girls who are mistresses, tramps, and hookers.

433

Everyone knows that he who pays the piper calls the tune. It is equally clear, if not as well-known, that she who calls the tune must pay the piper.

Taking a lover can be a grand adventure. It can also be a costly one.

Taking a lover has several real risks. You may seriously fall in love, with all of the pain that can entail. You have to learn new roles for new relationships, and some of those are harder than the traditional roles. And then, of course, you will meet with disapproval.

Pecca fortiter. The piper must be paid, but you will dance.

The Hard Master

When first we met we did not guess
That Love would prove so hard a master;
Of more than common friendliness
When first we met we did not guess
Who could foretell this sore distress,
This irretrievable disaster,
When first we met! We could not guess
That Love would prove so hard a master.

—Robert Bridges

What can happen in a love affair? Some couples, alas, are unhappy from the start. As we have noted, Romeo and Juliet were the original star-crossed lovers. As Shakespeare wrote their classic story, their stars—that is, their astrological signs—were at cross-purposes; and from the beginning, they were doomed to a short and unhappy life together. You don't have to believe in astrology to notice that some couples do seem to be star-crossed in that their troubles seem legendary and perpetual.

What can happen in a love affair? Well, sometimes the affair can be *too* successful. You may begin by seeking entertainment or distraction or amusement and end by accidentally finding a great passion. You can start with clear intentions of remaining emotionally aloof or of preserving you marriage or of tolerating someone else's marriage and find that you have changed your mind.

If you really fall in love and he loves you back and you are both free to hold hands and drift off into the sunset together to live happily ever after, then all is well. If, however, you really fall in love and it doesn't work out that way, then you find yourself in real trouble.

Perhaps he does not love you back or does not love you back enough or in the right way. Perhaps you are not free to leave your present relationship and must pine from a distance. Perhaps you are free or are willing to get yourself free, only to find that he is not ready or willing to leave his marriage.

The pain of love unrequited is hard to exaggerate. The despair of hopeless love is true despair. If you have lived through the breaking and ending of an important love affair, you know that, most of the time, you survive and go on to love again. Most of the time. At the time you are enduring it, survival may seem of dubious value.

You can decide whether or not you will take a lover and have a love affair; you cannot decide in the same rational way whether or not you will fall in love, and, if so, how deeply and with whom. And once you have fallen in love, you cannot decide to stop feeling it. Love may leave, but you cannot make it leave. It can be dangerous game.

Piet Hein, the Danish author and poet, puts it well, "Our choicest plans have fallen through, our airiest castles tumble over, because of lines we neatly drew, and later neatly stumbled over."

THE PRINCIPLE OF

LEAST INTEREST

*In every relationship, there's a Gardener
and a Flower.*

—Anonymous

In an ideal love affair, the woman's interest in the relationship is exactly met and matched by the man's interest in it. In reality, as de La Rochefoucauld pointed out long ago, "Between two lovers, there is always one who loves, and one who consents to be loved."

One person is more involved, more enthusiastic, more committed than the other. It might be the man, or it might be the woman. Or it might be first one and then the other as the passions rise and fall, and they take turns.

When you think about power in an affair, you must take into account "the principle of least interest": *other things being equal, the person with the least interest in maintaining the affair has the most power in it.*

If he is more in love with you than vice versa, then that power rests with you. However, if you are more in love with him than he is with you, then he has power over you that has nothing to do with male and female roles or with masculine chauvinism.

There are real hazards, emotional and psychological, in the complex web of erotic affairs. When you love someone, you give up some of your independence. You invest some of your happiness into the keeping of another, who may or may not treat you kindly. No wonder, lovers often try to hide the depth of their emotions and approach the feeling of love with trepidation as well as with awe.

SURVIVING THE LOSS OF LOVE

All you need to know, all we know that's true:
Sometimes you leave them, sometimes they leave you.
—Jadah Vaughn

What happens in a love affair? Well, sometimes the affair can be successful and make you feel wonderful, and then something happens. Passions cool, or a rival comes along and woos your man away, or your lover simply grows tired of you.

If you both gradually drift apart, it is not terribly painful. But if one of you loves longer than the other, you have to deal with not only a loss of power but also a loss of hope. The death throes at the end of an affair can be devastating. Worse, the humdrum of everyday life seems all that much more dreadful when compared to the exaggerated happiness of the affair.

You do survive the loss of love, but often only after a period of grieving. The cliché answer is, "It is better to have loved and lost than never to have loved at all."

Not everyone would agree. In any case, you cannot tell ahead of time how you might feel at the end of an affair. All you can do is take the chance and hope that if it all falls apart, it will still have been worth it.

New Hazards in New Relationships

Women do not find it difficult nowadays to behave like men, but they often find it extremely difficult to behave like gentlemen.
—Compton Mackenzie

What we have called the new courtship has many benefits and allows for a higher potential for fulfillment than did traditional roles. New privileges, however, also mean new responsibilities. Two areas in which women have to learn to deal with what used to be mostly male problems are those involving coping with rejection and those involving money.

There are, in fact, two levels of tasks to be learned: first, learning to do what is required; and second, learning to do it graciously.

In her book *From Front Porch to Back Seat*, author Beth Bailey describes how, as the twentieth century dawned across North America, parlor-based courtship began to shift "from the watchful eyes of family and local community to the anonymity of the public sphere." A new style of courtship—dating—began to supplant the traditional courtship practices of the nineteenth century. The family parlor and front porch and watchful eyes of parents were replaced with dinner and Coke dates, movies and "parking."

Under the old courtship rules, it was never acceptable for a man to call on a woman without first being "invited"; to do so was considered poor etiquette. Under the new dating rules, a girl was warned never to invite a boy home or anywhere because it was off-putting to boys.

While calling on a young woman at home was free, dating-based courtship involved money—men's money. Access to entertainment or even a place to sit and talk, away from the prying eyes of parents, cost money;

and the man, having invited the woman on a date, was expected to provide door-to-door transportation, which included the cost of gas. In general, he alone was expected to open his wallet. As Bailey points out, this led men to view "dating as a system of exchange best understood . . . as an economic system." In a sense, according to Bailey, the woman was "selling her company to him." And in the man's eyes, "dating didn't even involve exchange; it was a direct purchase."

Dating-based courtship altered the host-guest relationship. Men, not women, were now the "host." As the host, a man invited a woman on a date; and she, as the guest, accepted or rejected the man's invitation. Because women were not permitted to extend a dating invitation, they never risked direct rejection, as did a man, who had to learn to accept a woman's rejection gracefully and without personal affront to his ego. While most men learn the graceful art of rejection at a relatively young age, those who don't are viewed with a jaundiced eye by both women and men alike.

Coping with Rejection:

The Gracious Lover

A woman will sometimes forgive the man who tries to seduce her, but never the man who misses an opportunity when offered.
—Charles Maurice de Talleyrand-Périgord (attributed)

In traditional dating-based courtship, as we have been discussing it, men took most of the initiative, but they also took most of the psychological risks. One reason there was such a negative image of the reaction of a woman scorned is that she was almost never in a position to *be* scorned. When she did make herself vulnerable that way, she was very vulnerable, indeed, and so responded to the wrong answer very vehemently.

It was not exactly that men did not mind being scorned; they had been trained to anticipate it and to accept it as part of the game. The man was the one who had to do the asking, and there were a variety of reactions that he could expect. The woman in question might not remember who he was. She might laugh. She might laugh and then tell all her friends. She might be angry. She might refuse to take it seriously. It was a risky business, as any man reflecting on his teenage years well remembers.

In the new courtship, with the asking and the initiative going both ways, there exists the possibility that if you choose to pursue a man, you may actually be turned down. As a woman, especially a young woman, you are used to being pursued and may feel that all you really should be expected to do, to initiate a relationship, is to run more slowly or maybe stop running at all. When you initiate a move, however, you must expect that the man might say no and you must learn to accept rejection gracefully while protecting your ego.

Selecting a lover and then being rejected by him is not an enjoyable experience, but sometimes, it can be a learning experience. Maybe you approached a prospective lover in a gauche way or, at least, in a way that seemed gauche to him. Maybe he is so committed to a traditional role that any approach seems inappropriate. Maybe he was too busy or too preoccupied with another woman. There are many reasons, including the possibility that he only likes tall redheads and you are a short brunette. Maybe he only likes Earth Mothers, and you are a high-heels-and-stockings kind of gal. One woman shrugged philosophically: "My breasts are like raisins on two cookies. He was after jugs. I never had a chance." Maybe he likes boys.

It may be that he is "just not that into you" as Miranda, of *Sex and the City*, discovered. Having been rejected by several men she'd proactively pursued, Miranda's self-esteem was in shambles. She took the rejection personally and was hurt and baffled by the rejection. After all, she was an attractive, intelligent, professional, and financially independent woman. What possible reason could a man have for rejecting her? As she expressed her despair to her best friend Carrie and Carrie's boyfriend Berger, who responded very matter-of-factly, "They probably were just not that into you, so what's the big deal?" Berger, like all men, had learned long ago to accept rejection without taking it personal. The 2009 hit movie *He's Just Not That Into You*, based on the popular self-improvement book of the same name, explores this theme in great detail.

The point is that if you assert the right to initiate a relationship or a sexual encounter, you risk rejection. That risk is part of the psychological cost of paying the piper. As long as you treat men with tact and understanding and as long as your approach is subtle and sensitive, that rejection should never be too devastating or too overt for either of you.

BRASS TACKS AND GOLD CARDS:
ON SHARING EXPENSES

I'm tired of love, I'm still more tired of rhyme,
But money gives me pleasures all the time.
—Hilaire Belloc

Traditional sex roles were not all bad for everyone, or they would never have lasted the minimum of two thousand years of recorded history. Throughout most of that time span, men in the Western world have been more or less in control of women's destinies and have had a disproportionate amount of power.

With that power went, at least for most of them, a certain sense of *noblesse oblige*. In other words, superior or senior status, like nobility once had, also carried certain obligations—one being to provide for dependent persons. Wives had to at least promise to obey their husbands. In return for that obedience, wives had a right to expect bed and board and to expect their children to be recognized and supported as well.

The result was a complex set of explicit sex roles in which men were socialized to be relatively compliant and friendly bill-paying animals. Traditional men expected to pay for their pleasures when they interacted with women. With good women, they expected to pay with social status and a home; with not-so-good women, they expected to pay with favors or presents or hard cold cash.

It all starts in grade six when a boy asks a girl to go to the movies with him. He has to save his allowance to pay her way, which included buying her popcorn and a soda. It continues to the point where he asks his wife for a divorce and has to save his money to pay her alimony and child support.

Traditionally, men did not have to be nice. They did not have to obey or act loving or be compliant or form meaningful relationships. They did, however, have to have the wherewithal to provide bed, board, and baubles for the women they were involved with.

Under the terms and conditions of the new courtship, many of these basic premises have changed. In the first place, it is assumed that women have access to resources that free them from having to depend on a man for money. In the second place, it is assumed that the male-female relationship is arranged on the basis of mutual attraction rather than on the exchange of sexuality for nonsexual benefits. This does not mean that we eliminate the economic factor from erotic love relationships. But it does not mean that its possibilities are extended.

A willingness to share expenses is the "nitty" part of the nitty-gritty reciprocity involved in a relationship of equals.

Avoiding Obligations

There is no such thing as a free lunch.
—American folk saying

What is involved in the verb "to court"? Even penguins know that it means to present gifts. The poor old male penguin scuffles around to find a stone which he then rolls over to the lady penguin in the hopeful anticipation that she will find it a good stone with which to build a nest. If she does, he plunges into the sea to find a fish to give to her as well. And if she likes that, then the male penguin is "in like Flynn" and they make many little penguins.

People who are courting potential partners, who proposition, who propose, add to their proposition some enticement beside themselves. "To court" means, in part, to give gifts in an effort to persuade. It is a subtle, or sometimes not so subtle, kind of bribe. To accept a gift is to create, at some level or another, a kind of obligation.

There's a well-known saying, "Beware of Greeks bearing gifts," which dates back to the battle between the ancient Greeks and Trojans. Troops of Greek soldiers hid in a huge wooden horse which was presented to the city of Troy as a "gift." Once the horse was allowed through the city gates, the Greeks hidden in the bowels of the "horse" disembarked in the middle of the night to slaughter the Trojans in their own beds. Men who are serious about courting you come bearing gifts, and you should beware of them whether they are Greeks or not.

A gift is supposedly something which is free and which bears no price tag. In fact, a gift does create a sense of obligation. Even if the gift is something as casual as a compliment, the appropriate response is supposed to be "thank you." If you let a man spend money on you, you implicitly create an obligation. You can debate how much of an obligation you are creating, and how you are going to repay it, but the fact of the obligation is there all the same.

445

The solution to this is quite simple: do not accept the gift in the first place. Girls of a generation ago were taught that they should not accept important gifts such as jewelry of real value or intimate gifts, such as lingerie from a man; but in other circumstances, they expected a man to pay. In the new morality, it is safer to assume that one should hesitate to accept even minor gifts. The asymmetry that is involved leaves an assumption that the imbalance will be evened out in some other way. For many men, that other way is often an implicit expectation of sexual favors.

According to an American Medical Association survey, conducted a few years ago, more than half of the boys surveyed (ages eleven to fourteen) thought that forced sex is acceptable if a man had spent "a lot of money" on his date. In Margaret Mitchell's *Gone with the Wind*, Rhett Butler offers to give Scarlett O'Hara a Parisian bonnet as a gift. She desperately wants to accept, but she knows that if she accepts it, she will be obliged to give him something in return. Rhett—perfectly aware of her dilemma—warns Scarlett, "I am tempting you with bonnets and bangles and leading you into a pit. Always remember I never do anything without a reason, and I never give anything without expecting something in return. I always get paid." If the American Medical Association survey is correct, today's men expect to "get paid" as well.

Going out on a date and then demanding that the bill be split down the middle for coffee or for dinner is not a friendly gesture. It would be off-putting between two same-gender acquaintances, and it is even more off-putting across gender lines. It violates the ordinary expectations of a guest toward a host and implies that you do not trust the other person enough to be under even the slightest obligation to him.

Alternatively, it implies that you do not trust the guest eventually to pull his or her own weight. Whether the man insists that he divide the bill or the woman does, the mood of the evening will be somewhat clouded. Consider the plight of Charlie and Suzie as reported in a women's magazine a few years ago. Both Charlie and Suzie agreed that Charlie had asked Suzie out, and they had a wonderful time. However, "When the dinner check came, I took it," explained thirty-two-year-old Charlie. "But Suzie reached for her wallet. 'Can I help pay?' she asked. My heart sank. I was sure she didn't like me. I figured if a woman wants to split the check she's telling you that she wants to be friends. After that, the evening ended kind of awkwardly, I didn't know if I should kiss her or anything, so I kind of hastily said good night."

Suzie, twenty-eight, on the other hand, saw the date quite differently. "I offered to split the check because I didn't want him to feel obliged to pay for me. I figured if he had really liked me, in a girlfriend/boyfriend way, he wouldn't have taken my money—not on the first date anyway. And I guess I was right: he didn't try to kiss me or say anything about another date."

How then do you avoid the creation of obligations without creating resentment and without sabotaging the relationship?

You do it by avoiding serious obligations, and by polite insistence on taking turns for not-so-serious ones. On the first date, the woman may offer to pay, but if you are on a date and he asked you out, it is his right and role as a host to pay the bill. Your role as guest is to be gracious about it. If there is never going to be a next time, you can try harder to pay your half of the bill or just write it off.

If there is the possibility of a next time, you say, "That was very nice of you. Next time you must let me take you out."

And you follow it up with a reciprocal invitation.

If your lover has more money than you do, and certainly if he has a lot more money, your invitation need not be as lavish as his. One charming secretary laughingly explained, "Of course, Mike and I take turns. He buys me lobster for dinner, I buy him sandwiches for lunch. Fair is fair!"

Well, perhaps not exactly fair, but close enough.

Paying the piper for an egalitarian relationship has its drawbacks. If you are not a working girl, then you will not have a fat-but-rich sugar daddy to remind you "diamonds are a girl's best friend." In an egalitarian relationship, you don't have to sleep with him or even laugh at his jokes; but on the other hand, you don't get any diamonds. You have to either give up diamonds or earn enough to buy your own.

You will not be as bejeweled, but you will be free enough to call your soul your own. And your body.

ON PICKING UP TABS

Love is the grandest thing on God's earth, but fortunate the lover who has plenty of money.
—Russell H. Conwell, *What You Can Do with Your Will Power*

The person who does the courting is the one who initiates the interaction. That person has the first and strongest desire to establish a relationship, and it is that person who must bring gifts and pay expenses or, at least, pay the lion's share.

The same principle holds if the object of desire is an employee to be enticed away from an employer, a lesbian to be enticed away from her current lover, or a woman to be enticed into a love affair. If you follow this line of reasoning to its logical conclusion, it is clear that if women wish to court men, they must also be prepared to give gifts. It is not enough to be willing to pay half: women who are *really* equal must sometimes be willing to pay more than half.

In the new man-woman relationship, which has many of the same ambiguities found in gay relationships or same-gender friendships, there is a new rule. If both partners do not contribute equally to the expenses of the liaison, then *the person with the greatest desire for the relationship pays more* than his or her share of the bills.

Men who want to court women are resigned to picking up tabs, especially in the early stages of the courtship. They are not necessarily threatened and insecure when they realize that, having bought a girl an expensive dinner, she listens to them with an apparent interest in the conversation and a very real interest in the lobster. The man expects to be loved, or at least he hopes to be loved, for himself alone, but not necessarily immediately. Women need to learn the same patience in courtship and to bet on the possibility of attracting the right man in the long run.

It is unfortunately true that you cannot expect to have it both ways. If a man invites you out to dinner, you have a right to expect him to pay. But if you invite a man to dinner, if the initiative for the possible seduction is yours, you pay. You may make it more oblique by having the dinner at your own home rather than in a restaurant, but the fact remains that if you ask, you offer at least the entertainment for the evening. And being a lady, as he is supposed to be a gentleman, you do not assume that such an offer entitles you to more than a polite hearing of your implicit or explicit offer.

In the short run, women may encounter some hungry men who eat and run. Women have been eating and running, as fast as possible, for decades. Men of the world shrug and play the odds. Women of the world who presume to want a lover must learn to do likewise.

Women do not do very well when it comes to shelling out. Partly, they tend to feel underpaid compared with men. At any income level, they feel themselves relatively poor.

It's partly that they have not had enough practice. They did not start paying in the sixth grade, and no one told them that that was what "real women" should do.

They think that real women should be more like Cleopatra and hold out for all of Egypt. They understand that they should be beautiful or try to be beautiful. But they don't understand that sometimes they must supplement their appeal with material advantages as well.

Sometimes, if they are really "liberated," they might get all the way up to check sharing or even check splitting.

However, they tend to resist check grabbing.

Sexually Transmitted

Diseases

Despite a lifetime of service to the cause of sexual liberation, I have never caught a venereal disease, which makes me feel rather like an Arctic explorer who had never had frostbite.

—Germaine Greer

As if it were not bad enough that taking a lover might lead to the agony of unrequited love or cost you a lot of money or make you feel rejected, there is yet another serious hazard to take into account: the risk of getting a sexually transmitted disease (STD).

Suppose that you are a virgin until you get married, and then suppose that you marry another virgin, and then suppose that both of you are absolutely sexually faithful to each other for all the rest of your days. Under these conditions, where the two of you remain hermetically sealed, so to speak, you do not risk ever getting an STD. However, if even one of the above assumptions is ever violated, then you are at risk.

My purpose is not to rehash the dangers of sexually transmitted diseases in the graphic and lurid ways once used as a teaching tool in army training films. But being sexually active is potentially hazardous to one's health, and safe sex must be a priority when entering into any sexual liaison for whatever reason.

Until the early 1980s, the worst consequence of sexual intercourse was contracting a non-life-threatening sexually transmitted infection or becoming pregnant. STDs were relatively rare in the overall heterosexual population and were for the most part treatable. While getting an STD, becoming pregnant out of wedlock or becoming pregnant through an adulterous affair carried considerable social stigma, they were seldom life-threatening. However, since the advent of the acquired immunodeficiency syndrome (AIDS) epidemic, sex can kill. It may no longer kill immediately perhaps, but nearly everyone infected with human immunodeficiency virus (HIV) will sooner or later develop AIDS and die.

We can no longer assume that "nice" people are immune to such consequences. For that to be so, you would have to be willing to vouch, not only for the purity of all of the men you sleep with, but also for the purity of any of the women they have ever slept with and also the purity of any of the men that those women had ever slept with and so on. It requires very few steps to conclude that someone might have slept with someone who slept with someone who had an STD.

Consider that you might well be sexually active for more than fifty years—from perhaps the age of sixteen to long after your sixty-sixth birthday. Such a time span does entail some risk of exposure to sexually transmitted diseases, and the awkward necessity of then having to seek treatment and to offer even more awkward explanations to the other persons intimately involved.

HIV/AIDS was initially observed among gay men and soon after among intravenous drug users. However, with the maturation of the AIDS epidemic, the percentage of people who contract AIDS from heterosexual transmission has risen slowly and steadily. In fact, in some parts of the United States, such as New York City, the incidence of HIV/AIDS is now greater among heterosexual men and women than among homosexual men.

To date, efforts to develop a vaccine to prevent HIV infections have not been successful and refraining from risky behaviors, such as sharing contaminated needles and unprotected sex, remains the only effective way of fully preventing infection. Treatment regimens to slow the progression of HIV disease, on the other hand, have met with much more success. But there is still no cure, and it does not appear likely that there will be one in the near future.

Given the drastic consequences that may result from becoming infected with an STD, particularly HIV, it is imperative that you practice safe sex with all your lovers each and every time you have sex with them—independent of whether you have known them for a long time or short time or have committed to a long-term affair with them.

Having acknowledged that contracting a STD is possible and that the consequences are serious, you should also try to minimize your risk by considering the type of lover you pick. Obviously, your chances of such an unfortunate outcome are greater if you pick up a swinger in a singles bar than if you have a series of discreet encounters with your local minister. Likewise, a bisexual male or intravenous drug user will present greater potential risks than a married man in a small town who has had few opportunities to stray from hearth and home. There are, however, no guarantees. It is never possible to know everything about a person, but you will know much more if you take the time to ask some questions.

There are risks in everything we do. Getting up in the morning and getting in the car to drive to work has its risks. We do our best to limit those risks by observing the rules of the road: wearing our seat belts, not driving when intoxicated or under the influence of drugs or when sleep deprived. If, for some reason, you are willing to risk having unsafe sex, which is not advised, then interviewing prospective lovers before you have sex can go a long way toward minimizing your potential risk of being exposed to an STD.

What types of people are they sexually attracted to, and whom do they include in their social circles? Do they have or have they ever had an STD? How many lifetime sex partners have they had? When were they last tested for HIV and other STDs? Have they ever had sex with another man or an intravenous drug user? Are they by nature high- or low-risk takers? Do they always drive faster than the speed limit? Do they like to live on the edge?

And remember that looks can be deceiving, so don't assume you know the answer to any of these questions based on someone's appearance. If any doubts should arise about the purity of your potential lover, then you both should get screened for all possible STDs before deciding to enter into a sexual liaison. This may be a good idea no matter what, considering the possible ruinous consequences that could occur should you contract an STD. An ounce of prevention is indeed worth a pound of cure.

There is a kind of gallows humor about such things, born perhaps of desperation and a sense of fate, as evidenced by a beat-up Volkswagen Beetle I recently saw with the name Herpes and the subtitle the Love Bug painted on its hood.

THE BUBBLE REPUTATION

Until you've lost your reputation, you never realize
what a burden it was or what freedom really is.
—Margaret Mitchell, *Gone with the Wind*

Shakespeare observed that soldiers "seek the bubble reputation even in the cannon's mouth." It appears to be a fine thing for a man to have a reputation, however fleeting. It is something else for a woman.

A reputation for a woman is indeed a curious thing. When she is out getting a reputation, she is at the same time losing it. Having gotten it, which is to say having lost it, she is supposed to be distressed. Fear of the bubble reputation is a major factor in controlling women, especially in controlling their sexuality.

Conversely, the irretrievable loss of her reputation or indifference to it is a significant step toward sexual freedom.

One meaning of reputation is that conveyed by the phrase, "a woman of ill repute," meaning prostitute. Other words that come up in such conversations include "whore," "slut," "hooker," "tramp," and so on: all words that convey the idea of selling sex.

In the context in which we are discussing the lover-mistress relationship, one does not sell one's reputation for a song or for anything else. One gives it away. The relationship is not one of a working girl, and so the pejoratives with a connotation of sex for sale are not appropriate.

Nevertheless, having a lover or being a mistress seems—to many people to be behaviors which are—well, which are not quite *nice*.

If, in the folk wisdom, good girls are asexual and unawakened as opposed to bad girls who are erotically aware, then the rather paradoxical question has to be asked, "So what's so bad about being bad?"

If you have a lover, people will talk. Perhaps they will talk anyway. The poet Ogden Nash reflects on this problem and offers good advice, "If you want to get the most out of life, why the thing to do is be a gossiper by day and a gossipee by night."

The Power of Pejoratives

She's a broad, she's a dame,
She's a slut with no name,
She's a babe, she's a witch,
She's a vamp, she's a bitch:
She's every other kind of vice
But worst of all—she's not nice!
—Jadah Vaughn, "Be a Lady"

Right after little girls are dressed in pink and just before they are taught to keep their knees together and their skirts pulled down, they are told in no uncertain terms, "Be nice!"

Unfortunately, the commandment to be nice encompasses everything from not eating with your knife to not speaking too loudly or using bad language. The insidious part of niceness is its vagueness. Polite versus rude is perhaps a matter of judgment, but at least, it refers to definite behavior. So does careful/reckless, submissive/pushy, or obedient/disobedient.

Niceness, however, is not only vague but can be a justification for making someone do something she might not want to do or *not* do something she *does* want to do. "Don't do that!" "Why not?" "Because it's not nice."

Finally, one figures out obliquely that what is really not nice is sex. Nice girls don't flirt, don't kiss, don't neck, don't pet, don't make love, don't stay out all night, and definitely, do not get pregnant from any of the above.

Being admonished to be nice (that is to be asexual), at twelve, is one thing. Still being nice at twenty-two is not so great and still being nice at thirty-one is verging on the absurd.

For a boy, it is nice to be a "nice little boy." You can grow up into a nice guy, and you don't necessarily finish last. A nice boy is still nice at fifteen. A nice boy at twenty-five is doubtless still a joy to his mother. A nice boy at forty

455

is something else. So why is it that grown women, who are self-sufficient and responsible adults, are still concerned with trying to remain nice girls?

A girl or a woman who is not nice is likely, sooner or later, to be called promiscuous. This is an easy, but somewhat meaningless, appellation—at least—as it is unusually used. In the literal sense, to be promiscuous is to engage in indiscriminate, casual, or irregular sexual union. The usage of the term, however, is something else.

The noted sexologist Albert Ellis makes this point very well, "Take, illustratively, a handsome, intelligent woman who is literally besieged with propositions by male aspirants for her favors. Suppose she finally selects one out of a hundred of such males and takes him as her paramour. Suppose she has sex relations with him for a year or so and then, for one reason or another, replaces him with another lover, whom she again selects with much serious contemplation from several highly scored applicants. Suppose, finally, that every year or two she repeats this process . . . will this woman, under such circumstances, be having sex relations in an indiscriminate, casual, or irregular manner? Of course not. But will she, by most of the members of our society, be labeled as a promiscuous woman? Of course. Suppose that the woman takes only three or four inamoratos in her entire lifetime . . . but suppose, also, that she has all these sexual partners simultaneously, perhaps for a long period of years . . . But will she be labeled as promiscuous? Naturally. In other words, the mores of our day seems to be so opposed to sexual promiscuity that virtually any kind of (successive or simultaneous) plural sex union, no matter how discriminately or selectively it may be indulged, is viewed as being a promiscuous one."

Ellis was writing in 1960, but I do not think that the views of many people have changed that much since then as the practical definition of promiscuous continues to be, for many people: "Someone who has had more love affairs than I have."

Once you have come to terms with your own standards and internalized them, you will come to recognize pejoratives as more of the stuff, which makes grass grow and respond to them accordingly.

There are some dogs that have been sent to obedience school until they have learned their manners, and they come home very sensitive to the disapproval of their masters. You point your finger at such a dog and say sternly, "Bad dog!" and he visibly wilts before your eyes. He turns over and cringes, looking thoroughly miserable. He looks like a whipped dog although no physical force has been used. Being out of favor is in itself a punishment.

When you try the same trick with a cat, it doesn't work so well. There are no obedience schools for cats. Say sternly, "Bad cat!" and she will serenely wash her paws, flicking out one claw at a time for inspection. Cats will also love you back, and they certainly love warm fireplaces and warm cream, but they are in charge of their own dignity. You can negotiate with them, but you can't very readily bully them.

At the risk of stretching a metaphor, I would suggest that many women react to the whispered "bad girl" in a canine rather than a feline way.

The great film star Tallulah Bankhead had a less repentant attitude when she blithely proclaimed, "I am as pure as the driven slush," as did Mae West when she exclaimed, "Good girls go to heaven. Bad girls go everywhere."

Marriageability

A woman with a past has no future!

—Anonymous

In assessing the morality of eroticism, many people, and especially many men, have a new variation on the double standard. It is not one set of rules for men and another for women, but one set of rules for women and another set for wives.

If you want to marry, then you want some man to think of you as *his* wife, with the accent on the possessive case. It is a small step from there to the proclamation, "Not with *my* wife you don't!"

Some men do not care about such things, as witnessed by the success of former prostitutes in getting married. Others, however, care very much.

Men today may not insist upon virginity at marriage. However, a woman who is known to have had many lovers may in fact find herself less marriageable. How many is "many" depends on the woman's age. For a woman of eighteen, "many" may be two or more lovers. For a woman of thirty-five, it may be five to ten lovers. Whatever the number, she should not have had so many as to have established a reputation as a promiscuous floozy.

If what you want to do is to marry—and especially if what you want to do is to marry well—then it is important to minimize the extent of your past in order to maximize your future.

It is only the woman who is no longer trying to sell herself on the marriage market who is entirely free to exercise her sexuality as the spirit moves her.

MORAL INDIGNATION:

JEALOUSY WITH A HALO

Perhaps no phenomenon contains so much
destructive feeling as "moral indignation,"
which permits envy or hate to be acted out
under the guise of virtue.

—Erich Fromm

Pejorative terms may hurt your feelings, but they do not really do much harm unless you let them. Not all of the consequences of your reputation are so harmless however. There are some people who are not directly involved with you or with your lover who will nevertheless go out of their way to make trouble for both of you. They take it upon themselves to be the community's moral watchdogs, just like the nosy neighbor on the 60s TV series *Bewitched* who watched all of Samantha's comings and goings from behind her living room curtain.

The journalist and orator Wendell Phillips was correct in his observation that "the Puritan's idea of hell is a place where everyone had to mind his own business." The Puritans among us—and they include many people besides those who happen to endorse that particular kind of Protestantism—are perhaps as full of envy as they are of indignation. Be that as it may, if you take a lover and thereby flaunt the moralistic expectations of the community, you may find yourself confronted with indignant moralists who can make life very, very unpleasant.

One consideration to take into account in sexual decision making is this: How vulnerable are you to a negative public image? Can you afford bad publicity?

459

In some occupations, as for example some people in show business, an exotic erotic reputation actually seems to be an asset. Mae West did not make much of an effort to be discreet, nor did Anna Nicole Smith, whose public indiscretions made her infamous as a woman of questionable repute. However, if you are a primary schoolteacher in a private school in a Catholic community, your behavior can have drastic consequences for your career. You might well wish to reflect on the aphorism "Discretion is the better part of valor" and exercise a great amount of discretion and a small amount of valor.

Early on, it is important to choose between a pragmatic course, which minimizes trouble, or the desire to be political and to change the way things are defined. We need crusaders in the vanguard of sexual liberation. Be warned, however, that crusaders are often incipient martyrs.

It is not too difficult to get used to the disapproval of parson's wives, who look as if they had been weaned on a very sour pickle. It is quite another thing to get used to it if you work at the parsonage.

Epilogue: Waiting For The Third Wave

Plus ça change, plus c'est la meme chose.
The more things change, the more they stay the same
—French maxim

The first wave of feminism washed over North America at the end of the Roaring Twenties. It brought with it the vote and the temperance movement; it brought bobbed hair and the Charleston; it brought cigarettes and blue stockings.

The idea of birth control began to be accepted, although it was far from available to all, and women were being allowed to consider the option of getting married *or* of having a career.

The second wave of feminism began with the challenging of *The Feminine Mystique*. It brought with it the all-important Pill, which made possible a great leap forward in the sexual revolution. It brought long hair and no-hands dancing and new and interesting cigarettes. It brought the choice of childlessness for those who did not want children and daycare centers for those who did.

Women were allowed to consider the option of getting married *and* having a career. They were even allowed to have the option of not getting married at all.

At the turn of the twentieth century, Susan B. Anthony voiced the critical issue, "The only question left to be settled now is, are women persons?" The answer, in subsequent decades, seems finally to have been that they *are*.

As persons, you are finally beginning to act for yourselves rather than merely to react to the actions of men. As persons, you are taking responsibility

461

for yourselves and for your lives. As persons, you now have a range of options and opportunities that far outstrip the possibilities of your grandmothers or even your mothers.

The veil of the third wave of feminism is now starting to lift as the ideas and the opportunities—until recently the province of only an elite few—begin to filter down to become part of the day-to-day reality of many women. While it is true that many of the sexist assumptions and restrictions still remain, it is also true that real changes have taken place. And it is true that more changes, more drastic ones, are in the wind. Women have been waiting for two millennia for the third wave of feminism to wash across their shores. They will not have to wait much longer.

Somerset Maugham reflects, "It's a funny thing about life—if you refuse to accept anything but the best you very often get it."

Within this context, we have explored throughout the pages of this book a rather revolutionary idea—that you, as a woman, should be free to pick a lover—if you so choose, for no reason other than your own emotional and erotic fulfillment. What's more, we have offered a road map to help you navigate this unfamiliar territory, taking into account the considerable challenges you are likely to encounter should you decide to journey down this road. My ultimate goal here has been a simple one: to provide you with some insight and guidance on how to pick the most perfect man available for the most perfect love affair possible, whether you are single, married, or already have a lover.

To accomplish this goal, we covered a broad range of topics. We began by looking at the notion of men as sex objects rather than providers and protectors while focusing on attributes that contribute to a man's masculine appeal as a lover. We also discussed in detail specific traits and characteristics you need to consider when picking a lover along with those you should avoid. We examined the traditional role of women in North American society and how it has evolved over the past several generations. Special attention was given to the heightened sexual feelings that women now have and their consequential desire for more sexually and emotionally fulfilling lives. We also looked at the evolution of dating-based courtship and how it has changed the way men and women engage one another when seeking a relationship, along with factors that motivate women to want a lover. General guidelines for increasing your likelihood of a successful and worthwhile affair of the heart were also outlined, with some that were specific to married women.

So now, it is time for you to stop buying how-to books. It is time to boldly go where few women have gone before—just go out and do it!

REFERENCES

Austin, Elizabeth. 2003. "In Contempt of Courtship: Why we love to watch others date, but hate to do it ourselves," *Washington Monthly*. June. *www. washingtonmonthly.com*

Bartlett, John. 1955. *Familiar Quotations. (Thirteenth revision)*. Boston: Little Brown. (Also some from eleventh edition, 1938).

—1982. *Familiar Quotations (Fifteenth revision)*. Boston: Little Brown.

Battista, O. A. 1977. *Quotations: A Speaker's Dictionary*. New York: Pedigree.

Bermant, Gordon. 1976. Sexual Behavior: hard times with the Coolidge effect, Pg. 76-103 in Michael H. Siegel and H. Philip Seigler, *Psychological Research: The Inside Story*. Harper and Row, New York,

Cawein, Madison, ed. 1911. The Book of Love. New York, Freeport: Books for Libraries Press. Reprinted 1970.

Cohen, J. M., and M. J. Cohen, ed. 1971. *A Dictionary of Modern Quotations*. Middlesex, England: Penguin.

Colombo, John Robert. *Colombo's Concise Canadian Quotations*. Edmonton, Alberta: Hurtig Enterprises. 1976.

Colombo, John Robert, ed. 1979. *Colombo's Hollywood: Wit and Wisdom of the Moviemakers*. Toronto: William Collins Sons and Co.

Comfort, Alex. 2002. *Joy of Sex: Revised and Updated for the 21st Century.* Simon and Schuster, New York: Pocket Books.

Conant, Kim. 2007. *Sex Secrets of an American Geisha.* Publisher Group, Berkeley, CA.

Dowd, Maureen. 2005. What's a Modern Girl to Do? *The New York Times.* October. *www.nytimes.com*

Edwards, Tyron. 1973. *The Dictionary of Thoughts.* New York: Standard Book Co.

Ellis, Albert. 1960. *The Folklore of Sex.* New York: Random House.

Esar, Evan. 1968. *20,000 Quips and Quotes.* Garden City, New York: Doubleday.

Evans, Bergen. 1968. *Dictionary of Quotations.* New York: Delacorte Press.

Fitzhenry, Robert. 1981. *The Fitzhenry and Whiteside Book of Quotations.* Toronto: Fitzhenry and Whiteside.

Flesch, Rudolf. 1957. *The Book of Unusual Quotations.* New York: Harper and Bros.

Frank, Leonard Roy. 2001. *Quotationary.* New York: Random House.

Geoffrey, William, ed.1940. *The Complete Lover.* London: Michael Joseph Ltd.

Green, Jonathon.1982. *A Dictionary of Contemporary Quotations.* London: Pan Original Books.

Gross, John. 1983. *The Oxford Book of Aphorisms:* New York: Oxford University Press.

Hamilton, Robert M. 1952. *Canadian Quotations and Phrases.* Toronto: McClelland and Steward.

Hamilton, Robert M., and Dorothy Shields. 1979. *The Dictionary of Canadian Quotations and Phrases.* Toronto: McClelland and Stewart.

Harris, Betty A. 1991. Female Courtship Strategies as a Function of Sexuality Standards" Data Guru. *www.dataguru.org*

Hein, Piet. 1967. Grooks. The MIT Press, Cambridge Mass.

Henry, Lewis C. 1945. *Five Thousand Quotations for All Occasions*. New York: Doubleday.

Holden, Greg. 2005. *Absolute Beginners Guide to Online Dating*. 800 East 96th Street, Indianapolis.

Hubbard, Elbert. 1923. *Scrap Book*. New York: William H. Wise.

Hyde, Janet Shibley. 1982. *Understanding Human Sexuality*. New York: McGraw Hill.

Keesling, Barbara. 2001. *The Good Girl's Guide to Bad Girl Sex*. New York: M Evans and Company, Inc.

Levinson, Leonard Louis. 1967. *Webster's Unafraid Dictionary*. New York: Collier.

Lewis, Alec. 1980. *The Quotable Quotations Book*. New York: Cornerstone Library.

McPhee, Carol, and Ann FitzGerald. 1979 *Feminist Quotations: Voices of Rebels, Reformers and Visionaries*. New York: Thomas Y. Cromwell.

Millay, Edna St. Vincent. 1959. *Collected Lyrics*. New York:Washington Square Press.

Morse, Anne. 2000. The Dating Game: The dangers of cash-based courtship. Boundless. *www.boundless.org*

Murphy, Edward F. 1978. *The Crown Treasury of Relevant Quotations*. New York: Crown Publishers.

Narayan, Seth. 2005. *The Complete Idiot's Guide to Long Distance Relationships*. New York: Alpha Books.

Needham, Richard. 1982. *You and All the Rest: The Wit and Wisdom of Richard Needham*. Toronto: M. Sutkiewicz Publishing.

Okun, Milton ed. *Great Songs of the 70s*. New York: New York Times Books.(Paul Simon, "50 Ways to Leave Your Lover.)

Oxford University Press. 1980. *The Oxford Dictionary of Quotations: Third Edition*. New York: Oxford University Press.

Partnow, Elaine, ed. 1975. *The Quotable Woman: An Encyclopedia of Useful Quotations 1800-1975*. Los Angeles: Corwin Books.

Peter, Lawrence, J. 1977. *Peter's Quotations: Ideas for our Time*. New York: William Morrow.

Ray, Robin. 1975. *Times for Lovers: A Personal Anthology*. London: Weidenfeld and Nicolson.

Reader's Digest. 1975. *The Reader's Digest Treasury of Modern Quotations*. New York: Reader's Digest Press.

Rowes, Barbara. 1979. *The Book of Quotes*. New York: Ballantine Books.

Safian, Louis A. 1965. *Two Thousand Insults for All Occasions*. Secaucus, New Jersey: Citadel Press.

Safire, William, and Leonard Safire. 1982. *Good Advice*. New York: New York Times Books.

Schwartz, Pepper. 2006. *Finding Your Perfect Match*. New York: Berkeley Publishing Group.

Seldes, George, ed. 1967. *The Great Quotations*. New York: Kangaroo Books.

Sessions Stepp, Laura. 2003 Modern Flirting: Girls find old ways did have their charms. *Washington Post*. October. *www.washingtonpost.com.*

Stallworthy, Jon, ed.1973. *The Penguin Book of Love Poetry*. Penguin Books.

Uris, Dorothy. 1979. *Say It Again*. New York: E. P. Dutton.

Van de Velde, Theodoor Hendrik. 1965. *Ideal Marriage: Its Physiology and Technique*. New York: Random House.

Van Verten, Jayson. 1980. *The Maverick Eye: Cogent Observations on Our Times*. New York: Hollanger, Hobson and Sons.

Vaughn, Jadah. 1969. *The Consort At Arms: An Anthology of Women Poets*. London: Empire Enterprises.

Wallace, Irving, et al. 1981. *The Intimate Sex Lives of Famous People*. New York: Dell.

Warren, Neil Clark. 1992. *Finding the Love of Your Life: Ten principles for choosing the right marriage partner*. New York: Pocket Books.

William, Oscar, ed.1952. *A Little Treasury of Modern Poetry*. New York: Charles Scribner.

Wolf, Linda. 2000. *Playing Around: Women and extramarital sex*. Lincoln, NE, iUniverse.com, Inc.

INDEX

Y

Breinigsville, PA USA
17 January 2010
230879BV00005B/24/P